TRAVELER'S GUIDE TO

CAMPING MEXICO'S BAJA

Explore Baja and Puerto Peñasco With Your RV Or Tent

Sixth Edition

Mike and Terri
Church

ROLLING HOMES PRESS

Published by
Rolling Homes Press
161 Rainbow Dr., #6157
Livingston, TX 77399-1061
www.rollinghomes.com

Printed in the United States of America
First Printing 2017

Publisher's Cataloging in Publication

Church, Mike.
Traveler's guide to camping Mexico's Baja : explore Baja
    and Puerto Peñasco with your RV or tent / Mike and Terri Church–Sixth
    Edition
    p.cm.
    Includes index.
    Library of Congress Control Number: 2017954245
    ISBN 978-0982310175

    1. Baja California (Mexico : State)–Guidebooks. 2. Recreational vehicles–Mexico–Baja California (State)–Guidebooks. 3. Camp sites, facilities, etc.–Mexico–Baja California (State)–Guidebooks. 4. Recreation areas–Mexico–Baja California (State)–Guidebooks. I. Church, Terri. II. Title.

F1246.2.C48 2017   2017 954245
917.2'204836–dc21

*This book is dedicated
to our good friends*

**Sophie, Giovanni, and Sarah
Aoki-Fordham**

Other Books by Mike and Terri Church
and
Rolling Homes Press

Traveler's Guide To
Mexican Camping

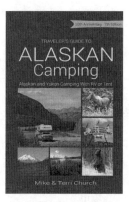

Traveler's Guide To
Alaskan Camping

Pacific Northwest
Camping Destinations

Traveler's Guide To
European Camping

RV and Car Camping
Vacations in Europe

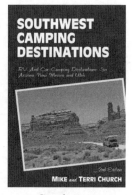

Southwest
Camping Destinations

A brief summary of the above books is provided on pages 270 and 271

When traveling by RV the most complete and up-to-date information on RV parks is always important. To provide our readers with the most current and accurate information available we maintain a website which lists all known updates and changes to information listed in our books. Just go to our website at www.rollinghomes.com and click on the *Online Updates* pull-down menu to review the most current information.

Warning, Disclosure, and Communication With The Authors and Publishers

Half the fun of travel is the unexpected, and self-guided camping travel can produce much in the way of unexpected pleasures, and also complications and problems. This book is designed to increase the pleasures of Baja camping and reduce the number of unexpected problems you may encounter. You can help ensure a smooth trip by doing additional advance research, planning ahead, and exercising caution when appropriate. There can be no guarantee that your trip will be trouble free.

Although the authors and publisher have done their best to ensure that the information presented in this book was correct at the time of publication they do not assume and hereby disclaim any liability to any party for any loss or damage caused by errors, omissions, or any other cause.

In a book like this it is inevitable that there will be omissions or mistakes, especially as things do change over time. If you find inaccuracies we would like to hear about them so that they can be corrected in future editions. We would also like to hear about your enjoyable experiences. If you come upon an outstanding campground or destination please let us know, those kinds of things may find their way to future versions of the guide or to our internet site. You can reach us by mail at:

Rolling Homes Press
161 Rainbow Dr., #6157
Livingston, TX 77399-1061

You can also communicate with us by sending an email through our website at:

www.rollinghomes.com

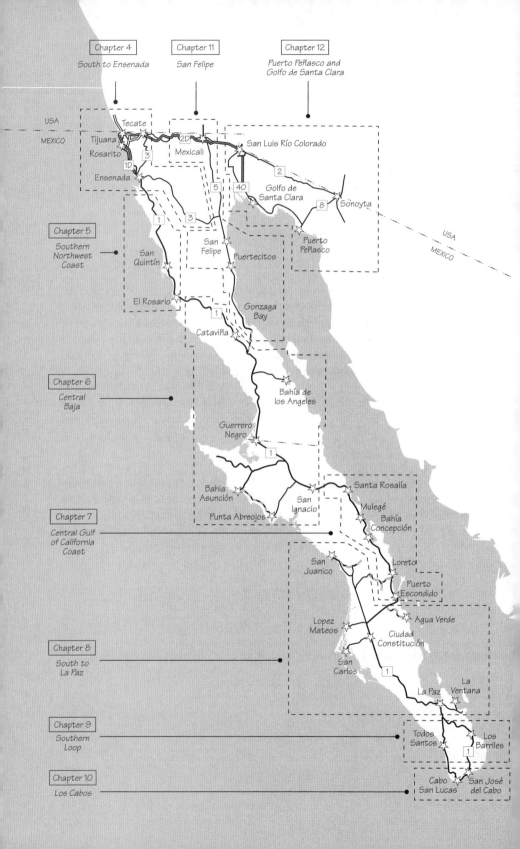

Chapter 4
South to Ensenada

Chapter 11
San Felipe

Chapter 12
Puerto Peñasco and
Golfo de Santa Clara

USA
MEXICO

Tecate

Tijuana
Rosarito

Ensenada

2D

Mexicali

San Luis Río Colorado

Golfo de
Santa Clara

Sonoyta

USA
MEXICO

Chapter 5
Southern
Northwest
Coast

San
Quintín

San
Felipe

Puertecitos

Puerto
Peñasco

El Rosario

Cataviña

Gonzaga
Bay

Chapter 6
Central
Baja

Bahía de
los Angeles

Guerrero
Negro

Chapter 7
Central Gulf
of California
Coast

Bahía
Asunción

Punta Abreojos

San
Ignacio

Santa Rosalía

Mulegé

Bahía
Concepción

San
Juanico

Loreto

Puerto
Escondido

Chapter 8
South to
La Paz

Lopez
Mateos

San
Carlos

Ciudad
Constitución

Agua Verde

La Paz

La
Ventana

Chapter 9
Southern
Loop

Todos
Santos

Los
Barriles

Chapter 10
Los Cabos

Cabo
San Lucas

San José
del Cabo

TABLE OF CONTENTS

Introduction

Traveler's Guide to Camping Mexico's Baja is one of seven guidebooks we write for campers. The titles of the others are *Traveler's Guide to European Camping, Traveler's Guide to Alaskan Camping, Traveler's Guide to Mexican Camping, Pacific Northwest Camping Destinations, Southwest Camping Destinations,* and *RV and Car Camping Vacations in Europe.*

Like all of our books this one is a guidebook written specifically for camping travelers. As a camper you don't need the same information that a fly-in visitor does. You don't care much about hotels, restaurants, and airline schedules, but you need to know what campgrounds are near, how to drive right to them without making wrong turns, and where to buy supplies. We want our book to be the one that you keep up front where it's handy, the one you refer to over and over because it contains what you need to know in a convenient format.

This is the sixth edition of *Traveler's Guide to Camping Mexico's Baja.* It's been four years since we completed the last edition. We love to travel the Baja and doing the research to update this book is a great excuse to do it. You'll find several new campgrounds here, and if you're familiar with the Baja you'll find that a few have disappeared, particularly in the Los Cabos area.

In fact, of the two big changes in this edition the decline of campgrounds in the Los Cabos area is the first. There are few options left in Los Cabos, most RVers in the very south now stay in Los Barriles.

The other big news is the upcoming opening of a new route south through San Felipe. There's much more about that in Chapter 11 - San Felipe.

This book also includes information about two destinations in northwest Sonora. The reason we've included this information is that these two locations offer many of the same attractions to RVers that the Baja does. They're just to the east of the Baja, close to the border, have great weather, and offer lots of outdoor attractions. If you haven't yet traveled to Mexico as a camper we recommend that you give Puerto Peñasco or Golfo de Santa Clara a try. Once you get your feet wet you might opt for a trip down the Baja or even one to mainland Mexico.

Updating the information and expanding the book has been a lot of fun. The Baja is one of our favorite camping destinations, we enjoy it more each time we visit. The peninsula is a Mexican jewel that is easily enjoyed by anyone with an RV or a tent and a sense of adventure. We hope to see you there!

B A J A

Pictures - Clockwise From Top Left

Camper in Cataviña Desert
Mangrove Warbler at Estero El Coyote
Sunrise on Bahía Concepción
Petting the Whales at Lopez Mateo
Mission Church San Ignacio
Lands End Cabo San Lucas

Chapter 1
Why Camp The Baja Peninsula?

The border between the U.S. and Mexico's Baja Peninsula is like no other border on earth. It divides two countries with huge contrasts in culture, language, wealth, lifestyle, political systems, topography, and climate. Mexico is a fascinating place to visit and we think that driving your own rig and staying in campgrounds is the best way to do it. We hope that with this book in hand you will think so too.

People from north of the border have been exploring the Baja for years. The trip became much easier in 1973 when the paved Transpeninsular highway was built. Today this paved two-lane road leads to unparalleled camping opportunities.

Probably the largest number of folks who visit the Baja do so as fly-in tourists bound for the Los Cabos area at the end of the peninsula. There they find huge hotels, beaches, golf, fishing, and a bit of Mexican culture. That may be the easiest way to visit, it certainly is the most expensive. You can visit Los Cabos too, but as a camping traveler you'll also see the rest of the peninsula as you drive south, and you'll probably find many areas you enjoy as much or more than Los Cabos.

While not really on the road to Los Cabos, Puerto Peñasco and San Felipe offer an easy introduction to Mexico. Both have easy to use border stations and good roads leading to seaside resorts that cater to the RV crowd. These are small, friendly towns that are easy to get around. There is a tradeoff, of course. Neither has great fishing and the new golf courses are just getting started. They do have great winter weather, decent prices, campsites along the beach, miles of back roads to explore with your four-wheeler, grocery stores, restaurants, and crafts markets. If you have any doubts about heading into Mexico these two towns can help you get your feet wet.

While San Felipe is not usually thought of as a stop on the way to Los Cabos and the southern Baja Peninsula this is about to change. Within just a few years there will be an excellent paved route through San Felipe and south to meet with Hwy 1, the current main highway down the peninsula. The route is now passable but rough and not good. There is more about this in Chapter 11.

The west coast of the Baja near the California border, from Rosarito Beach south to Ensenada, is more of a weekend destination for folks from California than a long-term RVing destination. That's a simplification, many people have permanently-located RVs in this area. Others bring their rigs south for a month or two. The attractions here are bigger Mexican cities; lots of top-quality shopping, restaurants, and entertainment; golf; and decent fishing. You should be aware that unlike the rest of the Baja, this area is more popular as a summer destination than a winter one because winter weather is cool.

For those interested in desert flora and fauna the Baja between El Rosario and Santa Rosalía is a fascinating place. For over 300 miles (480 km) the road winds its way through a variety of desert terrain with a wealth of cactus species and rock gardens perfect for photography. There's even a sight offered nowhere else on earth - desert whales! During January through March you can visit the California gray whale nursery lagoons and actually closely approach the whales with government-supervised small boat tour operators. Another unusual attraction of the area is the cave paintings left by ancient Baja inhabitants.

If your real dream is to boondock in your RV on a quiet beach next to tropical waters there are many places you can go on the Baja. Many great camping beaches are located along the Gulf of California between Santa Rosalía and Puerto Escondido. Lots of people go no farther south, they're perfectly satisfied to stay on one beautiful beach for the entire season.

Fishermen love the Baja. Both coasts offer great fishing. Some places require heavy open-water boats so you either have to bring a big boat from north of the border or charter. In other places a small car-top aluminum boat or an inflatable will give you access to plenty of fish. Fishing right off the beach is also an option. There are many places to go if you want to find excellent fishing, some favorites are the East Cape near Los Barriles, the Loreto area, and Los Cabos.

Are you looking for a winter destination offering a comfortable full-hookup campground with the services of a larger city, lots to do, and great weather? Consider La Paz. It has a population of about 220,000, large supermarkets, airline service, and two campgrounds with full hookups. Los Cabos is only a day trip from La Paz. For an increasingly popular smaller town also within day-trip distance of Los Cabos try Los Barriles. It offers excellent fishing as well as a growing number of good RV parks, good restaurants, and interesting nearby destinations.

A Possible Itinerary

Probably the best way to actually show you what Baja has to offer is to outline a tour down the peninsula. This is a seventeen day tour, that's the bare minimum, better would be a month, or three months.

The 1,060 mile (1,731 km) long Mex 1 stretches the entire length of the Baja Peninsula, from Tijuana in the north to Cabo San Lucas at the far southern cape. The two-lane highway gives access to some of the most remote and interesting country in the world including lots of desert and miles and miles of deserted beaches.

This proposed itinerary takes 17 days and allows you to see the entire length of the peninsula. There are layover days at Guerrero Negro, Bahía Concepción, La Paz, and Los Barriles. Many travel days require only a morning of driving leaving lots of time to relax and explore.

The most tempting modification to this itinerary will be to spend more time at each stop. There are also many additional stopover points along this route, just take a look through this book. Finally, it is possible to take a ferry from either La Paz or Santa Rosalía to the Mexican west coast where you can turn north for home or head south for more fun. If you plan to do that don't forget to take our other Mexico book, *Traveler's Guide to Mexican Camping,* along.

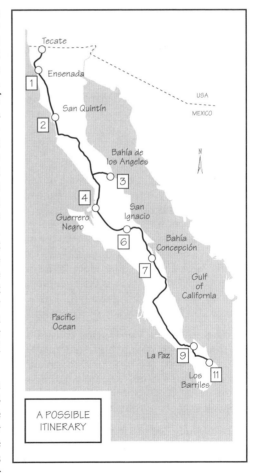

A POSSIBLE ITINERARY

⛺ Day 1 – Tecate to Ensenada, 67 miles (108 km), 1.5 hours driving time – This first day you cross the border at Tecate. It's a nice quiet crossing. You'll have to stop at the border to pick up a tourist card unless you've already taken care of this important bit of paperwork. A recently improved two-lane highway makes it an easy drive through the northern hills and the Guadalupe Valley wine country. You reached Ensenada before noon so there's plenty of time to look around town and pick up some groceries at one of the large modern supermarkets. Instead of spending the night at the campground in town or to the north you might decide to stay at the beautiful Estero Beach Hotel/Resort campground beside the ocean a few miles south of Ensenada. You can celebrate your arrival in Mexico by having dinner at the excellent hotel restaurant after a dip in the pool.

⛺ Day 2 – Ensenada to San Quintín, 122 miles (197 km), 4 hours driving time – This will be another short day so there's really no hurry to get started. Once on the road you pass through rolling hills with the countryside getting dryer as you progress south. At San Quintín you have a choice of campgrounds, try the

Posada don Diego in Vicente Guerrero if you want full hookups and a restaurant or maybe Fidel's El Pabellón Palapas Alvinos to sample a simple campground with miles of windswept beach out front.

Day 3 – San Quintín to Bahía de los Angeles, 219 miles (353 km), 6.25 hours driving time – This is a longer day's drive so get a fairly early start. You'll want to stop and explore the cactus and rock fields in the Cataviña area before leaving Mex 1 and driving east on a beautifully paved highway to Bahía de los Angeles for your first glimpse of the Gulf of California. There's not a lot to the town itself so perhaps the best option is to head north of town to a no-hookup campground along the water. If you have a small boat you might give the fishing a try. This is also great kayaking water.

Day 4 – Bahía de los Angeles to Guerrero Negro, 121 miles (195 km), 3.75 hours driving time – Today's destination is back on the other side of the peninsula, the salt-producing company town of Guerrero Negro. You'll spend two nights here because you want to visit the California gray whale nursery lagoon (Scammon's Lagoon) south of town. Spend the first night at the Malarrimo RV Park and visit their well-known restaurant. The second day you can either take a tour to see the whales from the Malarrimo or spend the night at the primitive camping area right next to the lagoon after a day on the water with the whales.

Day 6 – Guerrero Negro to San Ignacio, 89 miles (144 km), 2.25 hours driving time – San Ignacio is a true date-palm oasis in the middle of desert country. There's a good hookup campground here, the Rice and Beans Oasis. It has a popular restaurant. Don't forget to visit the plaza at the center of town to visit the cave art museum and the old mission church.

Day 7 – San Ignacio to Bahía Concepción, 95 miles (153 km), 2.5 hours driving time – Today, once again, you return to the Gulf of California side of the peninsula. You'll pass two interesting towns en route, Santa Rosalía and Mulegé. Neither has much room for big rigs so don't leave the main highway when driving through. At Santa Rosalía you might leave your rig along the highway and take a stroll to see the Eiffel-designed metal-framed church. You'll probably have a chance to explore Mulegé later since it is quite close to the evening's destination at Bahía Concepción. Many people decide to end their journey at this point and go no further since the ocean-side camping along beautiful Bahía Concepción is a camping paradise. We'll assume you'll be strong and only stay for two nights.

Day 9 – Bahía Concepción to La Paz, 291 miles (469 km), 8.25 hours driving time – Since you are all rested up after that time along the bahía you decide to get an early start and blast on through all the way to La Paz. Don't forget to drive into Loreto for a quick look around, this was the first permanent Spanish settlement on the peninsula. You'll have to ignore the golf course too, even though you'll see people teeing off as you pass.

You will find your progress along the coast to be quite scenic but slow, especially as you climb up and over the Sierra de la Giganta, but later for a long stretch on the plains to the west the roads are flat and straight allowing you to make good time. A late arrival in La Paz shouldn't be a problem because there's a hookup campground at the entrance to town, but it's certainly best to arrive before dark. You can take it easy the next day and explore the city.

Day 11 – La Paz to Los Barriles, 63 miles (102 km), 1.5 hours driving time – The drive today takes you south to what has become the center of RVing on the very southern part of the Baja Peninsula. Los Barriles has a selection of campgrounds with full hookups and offers fishing, beaches, kiteboarding, off-road exploring, and decent restaurants. It makes a good base for exploring the remainder of the 134 mile (216 km) southern Baja loop including San Jose del Cabo, Cabo San Lucas, and Todos Santos. This is an excellent place to spend several weeks to relax and gather yourself for the trip north.

Day 14 through 17 – Los Barriles to Tecate, 976 miles (1,574 km), 26 hours driving time – You really have two choices for the return to the border. Many folks catch a ferry from La Paz to Topolobampo near Los Mochis and then drive north on four-lane Mex 15 to cross the border at Nogales near Tucson, Arizona. Others simply drive back the way they've come. By putting in decently long days of driving you could make the trip in four days with overnight stops at Ciudad Constitución (194 miles or 313 km), San Ignacio (255 miles or 411 km), and El Rosario (305 miles or 492 km). The final day to the border in Tecate is 220 miles (355 km).

How This Book Is Arranged

Chapter 2 - Details, Details, Details is filled with essential background information. It tells you how to prepare your rig, how to cross the border, and how to deal with unfamiliar things while you are in Mexico.

Chapter 3 - How to Use the Destination Chapters gives a brief guide to using the information making up the bulk of the book.

Chapters 4 through 12 - These are the meat of the book. They describe the route down the Baja and also San Felipe and Puerto Peñasco. Along the way we provide a location map and description of virtually every formal campground on the Baja. You'll also find information about places to explore and things to do along the way.

Have Fun!

Backroad Driving

It is hard to think of any other location in North America with such a wealth of backroad driving opportunities. While this is not a guidebook to Baja's backroad destinations we have tried to give readers some idea of what is available.

It seems that every guide to the Baja uses some system to rate the quality of the back roads. This is necessary, since they vary from wide graded roads to rocky tracks really only suitable for a burro. We've tried to skip the burro routes, but you should bear in mind that all back roads in this part of Mexico are very changeable. A winter storm can make even the best of them impassable for months and it's hard to predict when someone will run a grader along a road improving it in a major way. When you drive the back roads you must be prepared for the unexpected. Check road conditions with the locals, travel in groups of at least two rigs, and bring along equipment for getting out of trouble as well as for enduring several days in the hot dry desert. Some of the roads are very remote, you may have to save yourself if you have a problem.

We grade the roads into three types, the classifications are based upon the type of rig that is suitable:

Type 1 - An unpaved road usually suitable for motorhomes to 35 feet, and trailers that are not large or heavily loaded. Logic rules out big bus-type motorhomes, large fifth- wheels, and large trailers for travel off the pavement. These roads are occasionally graded but may have miles of washboard surfaces forcing you to creep along at very low speeds.

Type 2 - An unpaved road suitable for smaller RVs but not trailers. Our definition of smaller RVs requires good ground clearance, a maximum length of about 22 feet with no long or low rear overhangs, the ability to make steep climbs, and sturdy construction. The most common vehicles of this type are pickups with small slide-in campers but many vans also qualify.

Type 3 - Requires four-wheel drive, lightly loaded, lots of clearance, and drivers with rugged constitutions and off-road experience.

We've rated roads based upon their normal condition but the roads do change and the ratings may become outdated. Check with someone who has recently driven the backroad route you are considering to see if conditions have changed.

Campgrounds

Mexican campgrounds vary immensely, especially on the Baja. They range from full-service campgrounds near the border comparable to anything in the U.S. to places that are boondocking sites where nothing is provided except perhaps an outhouse.

Bathroom facilities in Mexican campgrounds are often not up to the standards of Canadian and U.S. private campgrounds. Cleanliness and condition vary widely, each of our campground descriptions tries to cover this important subject. Campers in larger RVs probably won't care since they carry their own bathrooms along with them. Other campers might keep in mind that many of the campgrounds they fre-

THE BAJA HAS A WEALTH OF BACKROAD DRIVING OPPORTUNITIES

quent in the U.S. and Canada, especially in national, state, or provincial parks, have pit toilets and no shower facilities just like many of the places on the Baja.

In rural Mexico it is usually not acceptable to put used toilet tissue in the toilet bowl, a waste-paper basket is provided. Toilet tissue creates problems for marginal plumbing and septic systems, it plugs them up. Travelers who have visited other third-world countries have probably run into this custom before.

Many Baja campgrounds have hookups for electricity, water, and sewer. The condition of the outlets, faucets, and sewer connections may not be of the same quality that you are accustomed to in the U.S. or Canada. We find that in many campgrounds the hardware wasn't great when installed, and maintenance doesn't get done unless absolutely necessary. It is often a good idea to take a look at the connections on a parking pad before pulling in, you may want to move to another one.

Mexico uses the same 110-volt service that we use in the U.S. and Canada so your RV won't have to be modified for Mexico. Many campgrounds only have 15-amp household-type sockets so be sure that you have an adapter that lets you use these smaller sockets. Many sockets do not have a ground, either because the plug is the two-slot variety without the ground slot, or because the ground slot is not wired. It is a good idea to make yourself an adapter with a wire and alligator clip so you can provide your own ground.

When we identify a hook-up as 15 amp it usually just means that there is a normal two prong household-style outlet. Often it is impossible to determine the actual breaker capacity, sometimes one breaker serves many sites, and it is even possible that there is no breaker. On the other hand, often there is a 30-amp breaker even when the outlet isn't adequate. You'll see many burnt-out or blackened sockets in Mexico because much more than the designed load has been pulled through the outlet.

It is a good idea to test the electricity at your site before hooking up. You can buy a tester at your camping supply store before heading south that will quickly indicate the voltage and any faults of the outlet. This is cheap insurance.

Air conditioner use is something of a problem in Mexico. Heavy air conditioner use can cause voltage drops because most campgrounds do not have adequately sized transformers and wiring. Our understanding is that service of less than 105 volts can damage your air conditioner, so keep an eye on voltage.

Water connections are common, but you may not want to trust the quality of the water even if the campground manager assures you that it is good. See the *Drinking Water* section of this chapter for details on how to cope with this.

Sewer connections in Mexican campgrounds are often located at the rear of the site. You should make sure that you have enough sewer hose to reach several feet past the rear of your RV before you come south. You will find it difficult or even impossible to buy sewer hose south of the border.

There are two references you may see in our campground write-ups that need a little explanation. We sometimes make reference to "government campgrounds". When the Transpeninsular was built the government put in many campgrounds for travelers. These soon deteriorated, generators stopped working and most were abandoned, at least for a time. Now many are in operation again as virtual boondocking sites run by individuals or ejidos.

You will also see references to ejidos or ejido campgrounds. Ejidos are a unique Mexican social enterprise. Space does not allow explanation of the whole idea here, but among gringos on the Baja the phrase ejido generally refers to a farming village while an ejido campground is one owned or operated by a Mexican village or family.

Caravans

An excellent way to get your introduction to Mexico is to take an escorted caravan tour. Many companies offer these tours, you'll see lots of caravans on the Baja. These range from luxury tours costing over $100 per day to months-long escort-only arrangements that are much less expensive.

A typical caravan tour on the Baja is composed of as many as 20 RVs. The price paid includes a knowledgeable caravan leader in his own RV, a tail-gunner or caboose RV with an experienced mechanic, campground fees, many meals and tours at stops along the way, and lots of camaraderie. Many people love RV tours because someone else does all the planning, there is security in numbers, and a good caravan can be a very memorable experience. Others hate caravans, and do so for just about the same reasons.

Remember that there will be a lot of costs in addition to those covered by the fee paid to the caravan company including fuel, insurance, maintenance, tolls, and gro-

A COUPLE OF CARAVANS SHARE THE BEACH AT PLAYA SANTISPAC

ceries. We hear lots of good things about caravans, but also many complaints. Common problems include caravans that do not spend enough time at interesting places, delays due to mechanical problems with other rigs in the caravan, and poor caravan leaders who do not really know the territory or speak the language. A badly run caravan can be a disaster.

We've given the names, addresses and phone numbers below of some of the leading caravan companies. Give them a call or check their websites to get information about the tours they will be offering for the coming year. Once you have received the information do not hesitate to call back and ask questions. Ask for the names and phone numbers of people who have recently taken tours with the same caravan leader who will be in charge of the tour you are considering. Call these references and find out what they liked and what they didn't like. They are likely to have some strong feelings about these things.

Adventure Caravans, 125 Promise Lane, Livingston, TX 77351 (800 872-7897 or 844 872-7897, www.adventurecaravans.com).

Baja Amigos, (866 999-BAJA, www.bajaamigos.net).

Baja Winters Travel Club, 364 2nd St., Suite 1, Encenitas, CA 92024 (760 402-2806, www.bajawinters.com).

Fantasy RV Tours, 2650 Lake Sahara Dr. #190, Las Vegas, NV 89117 (800 952-8496, www.fantasyrvtours.com).

Vagabundos del Mar Boat and Travel Club, Adventure Tours, 190 Main St., Rio Vista, CA 94571 (800 474-2252 or 707 374-5511, www.vagabundos.com).

Cash and Credit Cards

Mexico, of course, has its own currency, called the peso. As we go to press the exchange rate is about 17.7 pesos per U.S. dollar. The currency has been weak lately, as low as 21.95 pesos to the dollar, but it's headed up now as the dollar devalues against most currencies. Some visitors to Mexico, particularly on the Baja Peninsula, never seem to have any pesos and use dollars for most purchases. They pay for the privilege, prices in dollars are often higher than if you pay in pesos.

Cash machines are now widespread in Mexico and represent the best way to obtain cash. If you don't already have a bank card you should take the trouble to get one before heading south, make sure it has a four-digit international PIN number. Don't be surprised if a machine inexplicably refuses your card, bank operations and phone lines are both subject to unexpected interruptions. If you can't get the card to work try a machine belonging to another bank or just go directly to a teller inside the bank. You should consider bringing a back-up card in case the electronic strip stops working on the one you normally use or in case the machine eats your card. This last is infrequent but does happen. Most cards have a maximum daily withdrawal limit, usually about $400 U.S. In Mexico the limit is sometimes lower than in the U.S. or Canada.

There are cash machines in Tijuana, Rosarito, Ensenada, Tecate, San Quintín, Guer-

CASH MACHINES (ATM) ARE THE BEST WAY TO GET PESOS IN MEXICO

rero Negro, Vizcaíno, Santa Rosalía, Mulegé, Loreto, Ciudad Constitución, La Paz, Los Barriles, Todos Santos, Cabo San Lucas, San José del Cabo, Mexicali, San Felipe, and Puerto Peñasco.

Traveler's checks are a decent way to carry money for emergencies. You never know when your debit card will inexplicably stop working. You'll probably be required to produce a passport for identification.

Visa and MasterCard credit cards are useful on the Baja. Restaurants and shops, particularly in tourist areas, accept them. Outside metropolitan and tourist areas their acceptance is limited. Pemex stations increasingly accept cards and large supermarkets in Ensenada, Ciudad Constitución, La Paz, Cabo San Lucas, San José del Cabo, Mexicali and Puerto Peñasco usually accept them. It is also possible to get cash advances against these credit cards in Mexican banks but the fees tend to be high.

Crossing the Border
(Insurance, Tourist Cards, Vehicle Permits, Fishing Licenses, Crossings)

One of the reasons campers choose the Baja over mainland Mexico is that it is easier to cross the border because less paperwork is required. Unlike the mainland, Baja does not require Temporary Import Permits (TIPs) except for boats.

You must have a passport or a passport card to travel to Mexico. You'll be required to show it to get your FMM going into Mexico, when you return the FMM at the

Mexican border when leaving Mexico, and then at the U.S. border crossing back into the U.S.

You must have a **tourist card** (officially a Forma Migración Multiple or FMM) if you are going to travel on the Baja except for short trips in the tourist corridors to Puerto Peñasco, or Golfo de Santa Clara. These are obtained at the Migración office at the border or from agents in the U.S., notably Discover Baja or Vagabundos del Mar (see insurance broker list below). To get your card you must present identification in the form of a passport or passport card. The FMM is issued for up to 180 days. Make sure to get a card giving you enough time even for unexpected extensions. There is a fee of about $25 per person for the card. If you purchase one from an agent in the U.S. there may be an additional fee. If you are buying your card from an agent in the U.S. you pay when you get it, but you still must get the card stamped when you cross the border at the Migración office there.

Note that if you are in Mexico for less than 7 days you do not have to pay for the tourist card, but you will still need to have the card and get it stamped.

A word of warning is in order. The border crossings are very crowded and it can be difficult to find a place to park while you go inside to get your tourist cards. Many people find it easier to spend the night near the border the day before going into Mexico. They walk across the border from the U.S., get their cards, and then come back into the U.S. That way they can just drive on across the next day with no stop.

You are required to turn in your FMM when you cross the border heading north. Failure to do this may result in a fine and difficulty entering Mexico at a later date. There's an important twist to this. Watch carefully when picking up your card because sometimes the border officials stamp your passport with an entry date. If so, you must get another stamp when you leave – in addition to turning in your tourist card. Some travelers have been charged with healthy fines for having an entry stamp but no exit stamp in their passport.

The towns of **Puerto Peñasco and Golfo de Santa Clara** fall within a free tourist corridor. The FMM and vehicle permits (other than boat permits, see below) are not required to travel to these locations.

If you plan to take a ferry from Santa Rosalía or La Paz to the mainland you will have to get your **Temporary Import Permits (TIPs)** before you will be allowed onto the ferry. It is possible to do this in La Paz. They are issued at the ferry ticket office at the port. To get a vehicle permit you will need a driver's license for each motorized passenger vehicle (however, one driver can bring an RV and also a passenger vehicle); a Visa or MasterCard in the name of the vehicle driver; and your registration and title. If the vehicle is not registered in your name you need a notarized letter from the owner stating that you can take it into Mexico. A fee of $60 to $80 will be charged on the card for each vehicle, you will be given a packet of paperwork, and a sticker will be placed on the inside of your front window in the upper middle. When you return to the U.S. you must stop at the Mexican border station and have them remove the sticker. They must do it, not you. There is also a deposit required. It varies from $200 to $400 per vehicle depending upon age, and is returned when the vehicle returns to the U.S. The deposit can be in cash or charged to your credit card.

A quick note. At the time of publication three-quarter ton and one-ton pickups were not being allowed onto the mainland. This, we hope, is temporary. Check our website, rollinghomes.com, for updates related to this.

See below for special information about temporary import permits for boats.

When coming to the Baja from the mainland you can no longer give up your stickers or get your deposit back at the ferry terminals. Instead, you must do this at a border crossing that is equipped to receive them. The San Ysidro and Mexicali West ports are not prepared to do this.

Your **automobile insurance** from home will not cover you in Mexico. Insurance is required in Mexico. If you have an accident and have no insurance it is possible that you might be detained (in jail) for a considerable time. You can make do with only Mexican liability insurance but that's a bit risky since your U.S. comprehensive coverage probably won't cover you in Mexico. Check this, and if it doesn't you should seriously consider getting Mexican comprehensive coverage.

Don't believe the old saw that all Mexican insurance costs the same, this is not true. Get several quotes and compare coverage. People who go into Mexico for just a short time usually buy daily coverage. This is extremely expensive, if you are planning to be in Mexico for over three weeks a six-month or one-year policy makes more sense. Some people get short-term coverage for the week or so it takes to get to their favorite campground. Once there they park the vehicle and don't use it until they buy more short term coverage for the drive home.

Longer term coverage, for six months or a year, is much cheaper. It is comparable with the cost of insurance in the U.S. Here are names and phone numbers for a few of the companies that offer Mexican insurance:

ADA Vis Global Enterprises, Inc., PO Box 744, Temecula, CA 92593; (800) 909-4457; Website: www.adavisglobal.com.

Caravan Insurance Services, 125 Promise Lane, Livingston, TX 77351; (844) 872-7897; Website: www.caravaninsuranceservices.net.

Discover Baja Travel Club, 3264 Governor Drive, San Diego, CA 92122; (800) 727-2252 or (619) 275-4225; Website: www.discoverbaja.com.

Lewis and Lewis Insurance Agency, 11900 West Olympic Blvd. #475, Los Angeles, CA 90064; (800) 966-6830 or (310) 207-7700; Website: www. mexicanautoinsurance.com.

Point South Insurance, 340 Rosewood Ave., Suite P, Camarillo, CA 93010; (800) 421-1394 or (805) 445-9943; Website: www.mexican-insurance.com.

Sanborn's Mexico Auto Insurance, 2009 S. 10th Street, McAllen, TX 78503; (800) 222-0158; Website: www.sanbornsinsurance.com.

Vagabundos del Mar Boat and Travel Club, Adventure Tours, 190 Main St., Rio Vista, CA 94571; (800) 474-2252 or (707) 374-5511; Website: www. vagabundos.com.

Some of these are travel clubs requiring that you join, others are not. Additionally, most caravan companies (listed under *Caravans* in this chapter) also offer Mexican insurance, even to people not taking one of their caravans.

We recommend that you use the phone to compare costs and coverage long before you hit the road toward the Baja.

Fishing licenses are required for fishing from a boat in Mexico. They are available from Mexican travel clubs like Discover Baja Travel Club (800 727-BAJA) and Vagabundos del Mar (800 474-BAJA). You can also directly contact Conapesca, the Mexican department of fisheries in San Diego, by calling (619) 233-6956. They will fax or mail you an application for fishing licenses so that you can do everything by mail. Their address is 2550 5th Ave., Suite 101, San Diego, CA 92103. You can also get the form on their website: www.sportfishinginMexico.com.

An important note about fishing licenses. You do not need a license to fish from shore but you do need one if you are going to fish from a boat. If there is any fishing equipment in your boat at all, even a hook, you are required to have licenses for everyone on board. Additionally, even if you are only fishing from shore it is a good idea to have a fishing license since not all local police understand the rules. It's easier to have the license than to argue about a ticket.

It is necessary to have a Temporary Import Permit (TIP) to bring a boat over 15 feet into Mexico. This does not include kayaks and canoes. This is true even though other vehicles are exempt on the Baja. These can be obtained at the crossings into Mexico except San Ysidro, Mexicali West, Algodones, or the crossing to Puerto Peñasco (Lukeville/Sonoyta). For the last crossing ask at the border, they may direct you to a station a few miles east of Sonoyta on Mex 2. To get a boat TIP you will need a passport or passport card, your FMM, the boat registration or title, the motor serial number, and if there is a lienholder, a letter of permission from them for taking it in to Mexico. You pay with a Visa or MasterCard in the name of the applicant. Temporary Import Permits for boats are available from Discover Baja Travel Club (800 727-BAJA) or by contacting Banjercito directly. The website is *https://www.banjercito. com.mx/registroVehiculos/*. The permits cost about 950 pesos and are good for ten years.

Now, what can you bring in to Mexico? Campers tend to bring more things along with them when they visit Mexico than most people. When you cross the border you may be stopped and your things quickly checked. You are actually allowed to bring only certain specified items into Mexico duty free and most RVers probably have more things along with them than they should. Fortunately Mexican border authorities seldom are hard-nosed, in fact they usually don't do much looking around at all. Lately we have heard that people bringing large quantities of food sometimes have problems getting it across the border. Now that Mexico has such good supermarkets there is really little need to bring in food.

What can't you bring in to Mexico? Guns, ammunition, and illegal drugs. Any of these things will certainly get you in big trouble. If you travel much on Mexican highways you'll eventually be stopped and searched by either police or the Mexican military. Guns and drugs are exactly what they will be looking for. It is illegal for any non-Mexican to have a firearm of any type without a special Mexican permit. These are for hunters and must be obtained through licensed Mexican hunting guides.

There are a limited number of **border crossings** for visiting the Baja and northwest Sonora. Here are the details.

Tijuana has two crossings: San Ysidro and Otay Mesa. Of the two we prefer San Ysidro even though it is closer to the center of town. When you are heading south the route to the toll road is straightforward and not difficult, we have included a driving log in the section *Tijuana to Rosarito* of Chapter 4 detailing the route. Heading north there can be terrible waits at both crossings, we prefer Tecate. Both crossings are open 24 hours a day.

The **Tecate** crossing is small and usually not crowded, especially going south. The disadvantage of the crossing is that it is a little out of the way on both sides of the border. Crossing northwards Tecate usually has much shorter waits than either San Ysidro or Otay Mesa. This crossing is open from 5 a.m. to 11 p.m.

Mexicali has an in-town crossing (Mexicali West) and one about 7 miles east of town (Mexicali East). We prefer the one east of town as it allows you to avoid driving through the center of this large city. The in-town crossing is open 24 hours, the east-of-town crossing is open from 3 a.m. to 12 a.m. We have included a driving log to reach the highway south from the crossing east of town in the *Mexicali to San Felipe* section of Chapter 11.

Algodones is a crossing just west of Yuma, Arizona. We do not recommend crossing here as it's really best for foot traffic and connection to the road system is not as good as in nearby San Luis Río Colorado. Northbound there are long waits and the line is difficult to access in a large vehicle. The crossing is open 6 a.m. to 10 p.m.

The **San Luis Río Colorado** crossing is about 26 miles (42 km) south of Yuma, Arizona. It is usually not extremely busy, crosses into a small easy-to-navigate Mexican town, and is open 24-hours a day.

Finally, the **Sonoyta** (Lukeville) crossing north of Puerto Peñasco is just outside a small town in the middle of nowhere. People crossing here are almost all headed for Puerto Peñasco. The crossing can be very busy on weekends and holidays, but otherwise is pretty quiet. It is open from 6 a.m. to 12 a.m. seven days a week.

Coming back into the U.S. you will need to be concerned about what you can bring back without duty. You are allowed $800 in purchases, 50 pounds of food, 200 cigarettes or 100 cigars, and 1 liter of alcohol per person.

As far as food items are concerned, rules about these things are complicated and do change over time. Check the U.S. government website at: *https://help.cbp.gov/ app/answers/detail/a_id/1276/~/food--bring-personal-use-food-into-the-u.s.-from-mexico* for current information.

The following paragraph is an old set of rules given to us at the border one time, we've carried it with us for many years. It's much more complete than what you are likely to find elsewhere and it still seems to work pretty well.

All fruits are prohibited except bananas, blackberries, cactus fruits, dates, dewberries, grapes, lemons, limes (sour, the little ones), lychees, melons, papayas, pineapples, and strawberries. Avocados are prohibited but are allowed if you remove the seed, but not into California. All vegetables are allowed except potatoes, (Irish, sweet, and yams) and sometimes okra. Cooked potatoes, however, are allowed. Nuts are prohibited except acorns, almonds, cocoa beans, chestnuts, coconuts (without husks or milk), peanuts, pecans, piñon seeds (pine nuts), tamarind beans, walnuts, and waternuts. Eggs are prohibited if not cooked. Pork, raw, cooked, or processed is prohibited except some shelf-stable canned pork and hard cooked pork skins (cracklings). Poultry is prohibited if it is raw, thoroughly cooked poultry is allowed. Beef is sometimes not allowed under the mad cow rules.

Don't try to sneak anything in. You are required to report all food items when requested at the border. Let them decide.

Distances

As you plan your Baja trip and as you drive the highways you'll find the nearby *Distance Table* to be very helpful. Give yourself plenty of time. On long days start early so you can keep the speed down. Driving fast on Baja's roads is a good way to have an accident.

Drinking Water and Vegetables

Don't take a chance when it comes to drinking Mexican tap water. Even water considered potable by the locals is likely to cause problems for you. It is no fun to be sick, especially when you are far from the border in an unfamiliar environment. There are several strategies for handling the water question. Many people drink nothing but bottled water. Others filter or purify it in various ways.

We use a simple system. We purify all of the water that goes into our RV's storage tank with common bleach. Then we use a filter to remove the bleach taste, the microorganisms in the water have already been killed by the bleach. This means that we never hook up permanently to the local water supply, we always use the stored water in our rig. The advantage of this system is that you do not need to keep a separate supply of drinking water underfoot. The proof is in the results. We are almost never sick, and if we are it is usually possible to trace the problem to something we ate or drank while away from the RV. The filter we use is commonly offered as standard equipment on many RVs, it is manufactured by Everpure. Other charcoal filters probably work equally well to remove the taste of bleach.

The system we use is called superclorination. Add 1/6 ounce (1 teaspoon) of bleach (sodium hypochlorite) per each 10 gallons of water. The easiest way to do this is to measure it into the same end of your fill hose that will attach to or into your RV. That way you purify the hose too. Check the bleach bottle to make sure it has no additives, Clorox and Purex sold in Mexico are usually OK. You can tell because they have instructions for water purification right on the label.

If you don't want to bleach your water the best alternative is to drink bottled water. Everywhere in Mexico you can buy large 19 liter (approximately five-gallon) bottles of water. They are available at supermarkets, purified water shops, or from vendors who visit campgrounds. These are very inexpensive, you can either keep one of the large bottles by paying a small deposit or actually empty them into your own water tank.

Occasionally, even if you bleach your water and use a filter, you will pick up a load

DISTANCE TABLE

Miles

Kilometers

Diagonal city labels (top-left to bottom-right):

Bahía Concepción · Bahía de los Ángeles · Cabo San Lucas · Cataviña · Ciudad Constitución · El Rosario · Ensenada · Golfo de Santa Clara · Guerrero Negro · La Paz · La Ventura · Loreto · Los Barriles · Mexicali · Mulegé · Puerto Escondido · Puerto Peñasco · Rosarito · San Carlos · San Felipe · San Ignacio · San José del Cabo · San Quintín · San Rio Colorado · Santa Rosalía · Tecate · Tijuana · Todos Santos of water that doesn't taste too good. This is usually because it contains salt and other minerals. This is a common problem on the Baja. A filter won't take this out. You can avoid the problem by asking other RVers at the campground about water quality before filling up.

Another source of potential stomach problems is fruit and vegetables. It is essential that you peel all fruit and vegetables or soak them in a purification solution before eating them. Bleach can also be used for this, the directions are right on the label of most bleach sold in Mexico. You can also purchase special drops to add to water for this purpose, the drops are stocked in the fruit and vegetable department of most supermarkets in Mexico.

Drugs, Guns, and Roadblocks

Visitors to Mexico are not allowed to possess either non-prescription narcotics or guns (except those properly imported for hunting). Do not take either in to Mexico, they can result in big problems and probably time spent in a Mexican jail.

Roadblocks and vehicle checks are common in Mexico. Often the roadblocks are staffed by military personnel. These stops can be a little intimidating, the soldiers carry automatic weapons and bring them right in to your RV when doing an inspection. English, other than a few words, is usually not spoken at the checkpoints but not much communication is really necessary, we have never had a problem. In general you will probably be asked where you came from (today), where are you going, do you have drugs or guns, and perhaps why you are in Mexico. It seems like every third RV or so gets inspected so don't get paranoid if yours is chosen. Accompany the person inspecting the rig as they walk through to answer any questions they might have, sometimes they have trouble figuring out how to open unfamiliar cabinets and storage areas. We generally discourage offering a beverage or anything else to officials at checkpoints, this might be considered a suspicious bribe, or might get the inspecting soldier in trouble with his superiors. It can also create expectations by the guards that later RVers will have to deal with.

Ferries

There are now two companies servicing La Paz and another servicing Santa Rosalía.

In La Paz there are two choices, both serving both Topolobampo and Mazatlán. Note that these companies are likely to change their schedules and offerings frequently and on short notice. Also note that you should make reservations in advance with these companies. Many people make a reservation when they arrive in La Paz on the way south and then come back to take the ferry in a week or two.

Baja Ferries offers almost daily service to Topolobampo and three times a week to Mazatlán. The Topolobampo run takes about six hours while the Mazatlán run takes 16 to 20 hours. Their office is out at the Pichilingue terminal. The telephone number is (800) 337-7437 or (612) 123-6397 and their website is www.bajaferries.com.

The second company making runs to Mazatlán and Topolobampo is Transportación Maritima de California. We've heard that they will let you stay in your RV on the Mazatlán route. You may have to request a special boat or parking location for this so be sure to check. This company also has an office at the Pichilingue terminal. Their telephone number is (800) 744-5050 and their website is www.ferrytmc.com.

From Santa Rosalía to Guaymas the company is Ferry Santa Rosalía. They have a very small ship but it will transport RVs. They run three times a week. Their telephone number is (800) 505-5018 and their website is www.ferrysantarosalia.com.

To take a vehicle to the mainland from the Baja Peninsula you must have a Temporary Import Permit (TIP). These are available at the ferry terminal in Pichilingue and perhaps at the terminal in Santa Rosalía, but check this early if you are planning to use that ferry. You may have to go to La Paz to get your permit, or you may need to pick it up at the border before heading south. See the *Crossing the Border* section above for details.

Fishing

Fishing is one of the most popular activities on the Baja. Today there are not as many fish as during the glory years of the 40s and 50s, but the fishing is still good. You can fish from shore, kayaks and canoes, car-top aluminum boats, trailer boats, or charter pangas or cruisers. They all can give you access to excellent fishing in the appropriate places and at the appropriate times.

Like fishing anywhere it helps to know the ins and outs of fishing on the Baja. Charter operators provide this as part of the package but if you are a do-it-yourselfer we suggest some research before you head south. See the *Internet* and *Travel Library* sections of this chapter.

Be sure to have the proper paperwork if you are going to fish or are on a boat with anyone fishing. You also need a Temporary Import Permit to bring a boat over 15 feet (not kayaks or canoes) from the U.S. See the *Crossing the Border* section above for details.

Fuel and Gas Stations

Until recently deciding which brand of gas you were going to buy was easy in Mexico. All of the gas stations were Pemex stations. Pemex is the national oil company, it is responsible for everything from exploring for oil to pumping it into your car. Gas is sold for cash, increasingly (but not always) credit cards are also accepted. There are often two grades of Pemex gasoline. Magna Sin in green pumps has an octane rating of about 87. A higher octane unleaded called Premium is in the red pumps. Diesel is carried at many but not all stations.

Recently a new law allows other brands of fuel to open stations in Mexico. So far we've seen very few of these. The new law lets stations (including Pemex stations) sell fuel for prices not regulated by the government so right now they vary slightly but not much. We'll see what happens.

Users of diesel fuel have a serious consideration when planning a Mexico trip. Diesel powered vehicles sold in the U.S. and Canada beginning in 2007 require the use of ULSD (Ultra Low Sulfur Diesel), diesel with a sulfur content of no more than 15 ppm (parts per million). This fuel has not been widely available in Mexico. Use of non-ULSD may have both mechanical and warranty repercussions, particularly for 2011 and later model years that use diesel exhaust fluid (DEF). To repeat, you might break down and you might void your warranty.

It is extremely difficult to determine whether the diesel you purchase is ULSD or not. You may see that they have LSD, that's Low Sulfur Diesel but that is 500 ppm, not 15 ppm. Some stations on the mainland have signage saying they have ULSD (the signs say they have DUBA, which stands for Diesel Ultra Baja Azufre or Diesel Ultra Low Sulfur), but we haven't seen that on the Baja. Gas station attendants either don't know or might tell you whatever you want to hear. Experienced Baja travelers tell us that from experience they believe all diesel in Baja Norte down to and including Jesus Maria is ULSD while that south of Jesus Maria is Mexican LSD. This information seems to be confirmed in Pemex documentation. The Mexican government has committed to requiring sale only of ULSD after December 31, 2018 but it's hard to tell if that is really going to happen.

There's a lot online about this. For more discussion about this just type ULSD in Mexico into your Internet search engine. You might also try searching for Ted White and ULSD in Mexico, he's generally considered the expert and can provide vehicle specific information. You'll be reading for hours.

If you do decide to take your diesel south, and if it requires Diesel Exhaust Fluid (DEF), make sure to take a lot with you. It's hard to come by in Mexico, and it's expensive. You'll probably use at least twice as much in Mexico as you use in the north.

Fuel prices in Mexico now tend to be higher than in the US. Sample fuel prices in Mexico in August of 2017 (converted to U.S. dollars and gallons) were: Magna Sin $3.48, Premium $3.81, diesel $3.67. Remember, prices now vary between stations. They now will also vary depending on exchange rates, competition, and location.

Gas stations are not as common in Mexico as they are in the U.S. and Canada. On the Baja you should always be aware of how much fuel you have. One particularly bad spot is the "Baja gas gap" between El Rosario and Guerrero Negro. See Chapter 6 for more information about this.

Almost everyone you meet in Mexico has stories about how a gas station attendant cheated them. These stories are true. The attendants don't make much money and tourists are easy prey. You can avoid problems if you know what to expect.

The reason that the attendants are able to cheat people is that there are no cash registers or central cashiers in most of these stations. Each attendant carries a big wad of cash and collects what is displayed on the pump. Don't expect a receipt unless you ask. Until the stations install a control system with a separate cashier there will continue to be lots of opportunities for attendants to make money off unwary customers.

The favorite ploy is to start pumping gas without zeroing the pump. This way you have to pay for the gas that the previous customer received in addition to your own. The attendant pockets the double payment. The practice is so widespread that at many stations attendants will point to the zeroed pump before they start pumping. Signs at most stations tell you to check this yourself.

There are several things you can do to avoid this problem. First, get a locking gas cap. That way the attendant can't start pumping until you get out of the RV and unlock the cap. Second, check the zeroed meter carefully. Do not get distracted. If several people try to talk to you they are probably trying to distract you. They'll ask questions about the rig or point out some imaginary problem. Meanwhile the pump doesn't get zeroed properly.

While the gas is being pumped stand right there and pay attention. Another trick is to "accidentally" zero the pump and then try to collect for an inflated reading. If you watch carefully you will know the true reading and won't fall for this. Sometimes the pump gets zeroed before the tank is full, so don't just assume that you can chat because you have a big tank.

The process of making change presents big opportunities to confuse you. If you are paying in dollars, which is common on the Baja, have your own calculator handy and make sure you know the exchange rate before the gas is pumped. When paying do not just give the attendant your money. He'll fold it onto his big wad of bills and then you'll never be able to prove how much you gave him. We've also seen attendants quickly turn their backs and stuff bills in a pocket. Hold out the money or lay it out on the pump, don't let him have it until you can see your change and know that it is the correct amount.

All attendants will not try to cheat you of course. You'll probably feel bad about watching like a hawk every time you fill up with gas. The problem is that when you let down your guard someone will eventually take advantage of you, probably soon and not later. It is also customary to tip attendants a few pesos, particularly if they don't try to rip you off.

Green Angels

The Mexican government maintains a large fleet of green and white pickups that patrol all major highways searching for motorists with mechanical problems. The drivers have radios to call for help, a few supplies, and quite a bit of mechanical aptitude. Most of them speak at least limited English. In Baja they only patrol the main highway and along most of Mex 1 pass by two times a day, once in the morning going out from their base and once in the afternoon coming back. The service is free except for a charge for the cost of supplies used. If they help you it is normal practice to give them a tip.

Groceries

Don't load your RV with groceries when you head south across the border. There is no longer any point in doing so. Some Mexican border stations are checking RVs to see that they don't bring in more than a reasonable amount of food. Also, at the border crossing between Baja California and Baja California Sur near Guerrero Negro officials are sometimes not allowing passage of citrus fruits, apples, potatoes, or avocados. Bananas and small limes are OK. Modern supermarkets in all of the large and medium-sized Mexican cities have almost anything you are looking for, often in familiar brand names. You can supplement your purchases in the supermarkets with shopping in markets and in small stores called *abarrotes, panaderías, tortillarías,* and *carnecerías* (canned goods stores, bakeries, tortilla shops, and butcher shops). There are now big supermarkets in the following towns: Tijuana, Rosarito, Ensenada, Ciudad Constitución, La Paz, Cabo San Lucas, San José del Cabo, Mexicali, San Felipe, and Puerto Peñasco.

Internet Travel Research

The internet is a wonderful tool for research. There are a great number of web sites with information about Mexico. Rather than trying to list them all here we have set up our own web site: **www.rollinghomes.com.** On it you will find current links to other web sites with good information about Mexico.

We have another use for our web site. As a small publisher we can only afford to update our travel guides on a two to four year cycle. In order to keep the books more current we publish updated information on the web. Our site has pages for each of our books with updates referenced by page number. We gather information for these updates ourselves and also depend upon information sent in by our readers. You can contact us through our web site or by mail with update information. This update information is only posted until we begin researching a new edition (generally about 6 months before publication), after that we only post updates for the new book.

Pets

You can take your dog or cat into Mexico. Virtually all Mexican RV parks allow dogs and cats although most do require that they be kept on a leash. Birds and other pets are subject to additional border restrictions, taking them to Mexico is not practical. We've not heard of anyone taking a pet into Mexico who has run into problems going south, a certificate of health issued by a veterinarian within 72 hours of entering Mexico is officially required but seldom checked. The rules you need to be concerned about are the ones for bringing the animal back into the U.S. The U.S.

YOU CAN TAKE YOUR PETS TO THE BAJA

Department of Health and Human Services web site says that dogs coming back into the U.S. require a rabies vaccination certificate that is at least 30 days old with an expiration date that is not expired. Your vet should have the proper form to certify this. Your dog or cat may also be examined at the border to see if it seems to be sick, if there is a question you may be required to have it examined by a vet before it will be admitted to the U.S.

Propane

Either propane or butane is available near most larger town or cities. The LP gas storage yards are usually outside the central area of town. Ask at your campground for the best way to get a fill-up, in many locations trucks will deliver to the campground. We've even seen people stop a truck on the street and get a fill-up.

We're accustomed to seeing only propane in much of the U.S. and Canada because butane won't work at low temperatures, it freezes. In parts of the southern U.S. and the warmer areas in Mexico butane is common and propane not available. This probably won't be a problem, most propane appliances in RVs will also run on butane. Make sure you use all the butane before you take your RV back into the cold country, however.

The fact is that you may never need to fill up with propane or butane at all. We find that if we fill up before crossing the border we have no problem getting our gas to last two months because we only use it for cooking. Some people run their refrigerators only on gas because the modern electronic control boards can be damaged by the fluctuating electrical voltage common to Mexican campgrounds, particularly if the batteries in the circuit are not in good charged-up condition.

Roads and Driving in Mexico

If there were only one thing that could be impressed upon the traveler heading south to drive in Mexico for the first time it would be "drive slowly and carefully". The last thing you want in Mexico is an accident or a breakdown, driving slowly and carefully is the best way to avoid both of these undesirable experiences.

Baja's roads are getting better. Most of Mex 1 is usually in excellent condition. Conditions do change, however, and you can't count on great roads. Cautious driving will mean fewer flat tires and broken springs.

One concern many travelers have about the Transpeninsular is that much of it is only nineteen feet wide (9.5 foot lanes) with no shoulders. That is indeed narrow, wide-body RVs are eight and a half feet wide not counting the mirrors. During the last few years some sections have been widened and shoulders expanded, but caution is still advised. RVer usually adjust their left-side rear-view mirror to be as close to the side of the RV as possible while still being usable. Marking the front face of the left outside mirror with high-visibility tape also helps. The best strategy to follow is to drive slowly and carefully. When you see traffic approaching; especially if it is a truck, bus, or RV; slow even more so that you have complete control of your rig, and get over as far as you safely can. The good news is that there is very little traffic on most of the Transpeninsular.

Do not drive at night. There are several reasons for this. Animals are common on roads in Mexico, even in daylight hours you'll find cows, horses, burros, goats, pigs and sheep on the road. At night there are even more of them, they're attracted by the warm road surface and they don't have reflectors. Truckers like to travel at night because they can make good time in the light traffic. Some of these guys are maniacs, in the morning you'll often see a fleet of tow trucks lined up along the edge of a highway trying to retrieve one from a gully. Truckers also often leave rocks on the road at night, this is done to keep someone from hitting them when they break down, or to block the wheels when stopped on a hill. Often these rocks aren't removed, they're very difficult to see in time at night. Finally, driving at night means that if you have a breakdown you're going to be in an unsafe position. Mexican roads are good places to avoid after dark.

No discussion of driving in Mexico is complete without a discussion of traffic cops and bribes. Traffic cops (and many other government functionaries) are underpaid, they make up for it by collecting from those who break the law. This is not condoned by the government, but it is a fact of life. Norteamericanos usually feel uncomfortable with this custom and as a result they are difficult targets for cops with a *mordida* habit. Unfortunately some cops do not yet know this.

The best way to avoid the *mordida* trap is to scrupulously follow all traffic laws. Even if everyone around you is breaking the law you should follow it. If only one person in a line of cars gets arrested for not stopping at the stop sign at a railroad crossing you can be sure that it will be the gringo in the fancy RV (we know this from personal experience). Obey all speed limits, especially easy to miss are those at schools and small towns along a highway. Stop at the stop sign at railroad crossings even though no one else will. Wear your seat belt too, this is the law in Mexico and probably the largest source of tickets.

In the event that you do get stopped we recommend against offering a bribe. It is possible that you might get yourself in even worse trouble than you are already in. If you can't talk your way out of a fine the normal practice is to accompany the officer back to his headquarters (bringing your vehicle) to pay the fine. Most fines are quite reasonable by Norteamericano standards and if you've really done something wrong it's best to go ahead and pay.

Occasionally a police officer will suggest that such a trip can be avoided by paying a reasonable fee to him on the spot, let your conscience be your guide. There are no hard and fast rules or sure-fire ways to deal with the police. We find that the best strategy is to be very polite, appear to be relaxed, speak little or no Spanish, and be prepared to follow the officer to the police station if it becomes necessary. A dishonest officer doesn't really want to spend a lot of time and effort conspicuously dealing with a gringo in a huge and hard to miss vehicle. If you haven't really done anything wrong you'll usually end up being told to "go with god".

We sometimes hear reports of RVers stopped by police who have paid large bribes. The unfamiliar situation and fear of foreign laws is no doubt the reason. Don't do this – it makes it harder on everyone who follows behind.

Everyone's least favorite thing is to get involved in an accident. In Mexico there are special rules. First and most important is that you had better have Mexican insurance. Your insurance carrier will give you written instructions about the procedure to follow if you get into an accident. Take a look at it before you cross the border to make sure you understand exactly how to handle an accident before it happens. Usually you must report an accident of any kind before leaving Mexico to receive reimbursement. See the *Crossing the Border* section above for the names of some Mexican insurance brokers.

Road signs in Mexico are usually not hard to understand. International-style signs are used for stops, parking, one way roads, and may other things. However, we often meet folks with questions about one or another sign they have been seeing during their travels. In the appendix at the back of this book you'll find pictures of signs you're likely to see along the road along with their meaning in English.

Safety and Security

Mexico would be full of camping visitors from the U.S. and Canada if there was no security issue. Fear is the factor that crowds RVers into campgrounds just north of the border but leaves those a hundred miles south pleasantly uncrowded. People in those border campgrounds will warn you not to cross into Mexico because there are banditos, dishonest cops, terrible roads, and language and water problems.

In fact, first-time camping visitors are usually amazed at how trouble-free Mexican camping is. Few ever meet a bandito or get sick from the water. The general feeling is that Mexico is as safe as much of the U.S., especially U.S. urban areas. After you've been in Mexico a few years you will hear about the occasional problem, just as you do north of the border. Most problems could have been easily avoided if the person involved had just observed a few common-sense safety precautions. Here are the ones we follow and feel comfortable with.

Never drive at night. Night driving is dangerous because Mexican roads are completely different at night. There are unexpected and hard-to-avoid road hazards, there are aggressive truck drivers, and there is little in the way of formal security patrols. If there are really any banditos in the area they are most likely to be active after dark.

Don't boondock alone except in a place you are very sure of. Individual free campers are uniquely vulnerable. Many folks don't follow this rule and have no problems, it is up to you.

Don't open the door to a knock after dark. First crack a window to find out who is knocking. Why take chances?

Don't leave your rig unguarded on the street if you can avoid it. Any petty crook knows your RV is full of good stuff, it is a great target. We like to leave ours in the campground while we explore. Use public transportation, it's lots of fun.

There are a couple of security precautions that you can take before leaving home, you probably have already taken them if you do much traveling in your RV. Add a deadbolt to your entrance door, some insurance policies in the States actually require this. If possible install an alarm in your vehicle, it can take a load off your mind when you must leave it on the street.

Spanish Language

You certainly don't need to be able to speak Spanish to get along just fine in Mexico.

All of the people working in campgrounds, gas stations and stores are accustomed to dealing with non-Spanish speakers. Even if you can't really talk to them you'll be able to transact business.

Telephones

Telephone service is rapidly improving in Mexico. The Baja is remote country and between towns cell service is often poor. One of the big surprises, however, is that cell service (in the towns) is pretty good. It's worthwhile to question your U.S. service provide about Mexican coverage. Recently it seems that all of the major carriers offer this option. Often you will find you can use your phone with little additional charge.

Mexican phone numbers now have a three digit area code and then seven digits, just like in the U.S. and Canada. You'll see all sorts of way of writing the numbers, but in this book we've just used the same format that we use up north.

To call into Mexico from the U.S. or Canada you must first dial a 011 for international access, then the Mexico country code which is 52, then the Mexican area code and number. Often businesses will advertise in the U.S. with a number which includes some or all of these prefixes. Now that you know what they are you should have no problems dialing a Mexican number.

Many Mexican towns still have phones in kiosks or booths, usually labeled Ladatel or Telmex, along the streets. To use them you buy a phone card, usually at pharmacies. These are computerized smart cards charged with 10, 20, 30, 50, or 100 pesos. When you insert them into the phone the amount of money left on the card appears on a readout on the phone. As you talk the time left counts down on the readout.

To dial an international call to the U.S. or Canada you dial 00 + 1 + area code + the local number.

To place a collect call you dial 09 + 1 + area code + local number.

To dial a Mexican long distance number you dial 01 + area code + the local number.

To dial a local number you generally just dial the local number without the area code.

Travel Library

Don't go to Mexico without a general tourist guide with information about the places you'll visit. Even if you're on the Baja for the sun and fun you'll have questions that no one seems to be able to answer. Recently updated, and really outstanding, our favorite is *Moon Baja: Tijuana to Los Cabos* by Jennifer Kramer (Avalon Travel, Berkeley, CA, 2017, ISBN 978-1631214066). It's also available as an ebook.

A map is handy on the Baja, particularly if you are traveling back roads. We like those by National Geographic. There are two: National Geographic Adventure Maps: Baja North (ISBN 978-1566952433) and Baja South (ISBN 978-1566952441).

There are a wealth of books available about the Baja. Some of the following are out of print but if they are you can probably find them used on Amazon.com or E-Bay. Don't read Walt Peterson's *The Baja Adventure Book* (Wilderness Press, Berkeley,

CA, 1999, ISBN 0-89997-231-4) if you're not sure you really want to visit the Baja because after reading it you won't be able to stay away. *The Magnificent Peninsula: The Comprehensive Guidebook to Mexico's Baja California* by Jack Williams (H.J. Williams Publications, Redding, CA, 1998, ISBN 1-89127-500-3) is just what the title says. It has lots of information about camping spots on the peninsula, and lots of other things too. A book using satellite maps of the peninsula is *The Baja Book IV: The Guide to Today's Baja California* by Ginger Potter (Baja Source, Inc., El Cajon, CA, 1996, ISBN 0-9644066-0-8). To get some good background try reading *Into a Desert Place: A 3000-Mile Walk Around the Coast of Baja California* by Graham Machintosh (W.W. Norton & Co., New York, NY, 1990, ISBN 0-393-31289-5). Fishermen will find *The Baja Catch* by Neil Kelly and Gene Kira (Apples and Oranges, Inc., Valley Center, CA, 1997, ISBN 0-929637-04-6) to be absolutely essential. Later fishing books include *The Angler's Guide to Trailer-Boating Baja* by Zack Thomas (Transpeninsular Publications, Carson City, NV, 2008, ISBN 978-0615188461) and *Hooked on Baja* by Tom Gatch (The Countryman Press, Woodstock, VT, 2007, 978-0881507263). Surfers may find **The Surfer's Guide to Baja** by Mike Parise (SurfPress Publishing, California, 2012, ISBN 978-0967910055) to be worth parting with the change. Kayakers will love *Adventure Kayaking Baja* by Andromeda Romano-Lax (Wilderness Press, Berkeley, California, 2001, ISBN 0-89997-247-0). Newer, and a beautiful book, is *The Guide to Baja Sea Kayaking* by Dave Eckardt (Paddle Publishing, 2008, ISBN 978-0964539914). For information about the landforms and plants along the highway bring along *Roadside Geology and Biology of Baja California* by John, Edwin, and Jason Minch (John Minch and Associates, Inc., Mission Viejo, CA, 1998, ISBN 0-9631090-1-4). If you are curious about the plants there's the *Baja California Plant Field Guide* by Jon P. Rebman and Norman C. Roberts (Sunbelt Publications, El Cajon, CA, 2012, ISBN 978-0916251185). For hikers there's *50 Hikes in the Cape Region Baja Sur* by Carl Dreisbach (A Big Raven Book, Seattle, WA, 2007, ISBN 978-0942153026). Closer to the border you might explore *Wines of Baja California: Touring and Tasting Mexico's Undiscovered Treasures* by Ralph Amey, The Wine Appreciation Guild, San Francisco, CA, 2003, ISBN 1-89126-765-5). Also lots of fun if you can find them are some old books about exploring the Baja back country by Perry Mason detective novel author Erle Stanley Gardner: *Mexico's Magic Square, Off the Beaten Track in Baja, The Hidden Heart of Baja, Hovering over Baja*, and *Hunting the Desert Whale*. Try libraries and used book stores for these classics.

A visit to Mexico is a great way to study Spanish. Make sure to bring along a good Spanish-English dictionary. Also handy is a Spanish textbook of some kind and perhaps some recordings for studying the language as you drive.

Most of these books can be purchased at Amazon.com. You can follow links from our web site: www.rollinghomes.com.

Units of Measurement

Mexico is on the metric system. Most of the world has already learned to deal with this. For the rest of us it takes just a short time of working with the metric system, and there is no way to avoid it, to start to feel at home. Conversion tables and factors are available in most guidebooks but you will probably want to memorize a few critical conversion numbers as we have.

For converting miles to kilometer, divide the number of miles by .62. For converting kilometers to miles, multiply the kilometers by .62. Since kilometers are shorter than miles the number of kilometers after the conversion will always be more than the number of miles, if they aren't you divided when you should have multiplied.

For liquid measurement it is usually enough to know that a liter is about the same as a quart. When you need more accuracy, like when you are trying to make some sense out of your miles per gallon calculations, there are 3.79 liters in a U.S. gallon.

Weight measurement is important when you're trying to decide how much cheese or hamburger you need to make a meal. Since a kilogram is about 2.2 pounds we just round to two pounds. This makes a half pound equal to about 250 grams and a pound equal to 500 grams. It's not exact, but it certainly works in the grocery store, and we get a little more than we expected for dinner.

Temperature is our biggest conversion problem. The easiest method is to just carry around a conversion chart of some kind. If you don't have it with you just remember a few key temperatures and interpolate. Freezing, of course is 32° F and 0° C. Water boils at 212° F and 100° C. A nice 70° F day is 21° C. A cooler 50° F day is 10° C. A hot 90° F day is 32° C.

Here are a few useful conversion factors:

1 km = .62 mile	1 mile = 1.61 km
1 meter = 3.28 feet	1 foot = .30 meters
1 liter = .26 U.S. gallon	1 U.S. gallon = 3.79 liters
1 kilogram = 2.21 pounds	1 pound = .45 kilograms

Convert from °C to °F by multiplying by 1.8 and adding 32
Convert from °F to °C by subtracting 32 and dividing by 1.8

Vehicle Preparation and Breakdowns

One of the favorite subjects whenever a group of Mexican campers gets together over cocktails is war stories about breakdowns and miraculous repairs performed by Mexican mechanics with almost no tools. Before visiting Mexico many people fear a breakdown above all else. Our experience and that of the people we talk to is that on the main roads help is generally readily available. Lots of other RVers are traveling the same route and they will stop to help.

While it is usually possible to find someone to work on the vehicle, it is often very hard to get parts. Ford, General Motors, Chrysler, Volkswagen and Nissan all manufacture cars and trucks in Mexico and have large, good dealers throughout the country. These dealers are good places to go if you need emergency or maintenance work done on your vehicle. However, many of the models sold in the U.S. and Canada are not manufactured in Mexico and the dealers may not have parts for your particular vehicle. They can order them but often this takes several weeks.

Often the quickest way to get a part is to go get it yourself. One of our acquaintances recently broke an axle in Villahermosa. His vehicle is common in Mexico, but the type of axle he needed was not used in the Mexican models. Rather than wait an indeterminate length of time for a new axle he went and picked one up himself. He climbed on a bus, traveled to Matamoros, walked across the border, caught a cab to a dealer, picked up a new axle and threw it over his shoulder, walked back across the border, caught another bus, and was back in Villahermosa within 48 hours. This works on the Baja too, there is a steady stream of busses traveling the Transpeninsular to and from Tijuana.

Avoid problems by making sure your vehicle is in good condition before entering Mexico. Get an oil change, a lube job, and a tune-up. Make sure that hoses, belts, filters, brake pads, shocks and tires are all good. Consider replacing them before you leave. Driving conditions in Mexico tend to be extreme. Your vehicle will be operating on rough roads, in very hot weather, with lots of climbs and descents.

Bring along a reasonable amount of spares. We like to carry replacement belts, hoses, and filters (and any special tools necessary to change them). Make sure you have a good spare tire.

RV drivers need to be prepared to make the required hookups in Mexican RV parks. RV supplies are difficult to find in Mexico so make sure that you have any RV supplies you need before crossing the border.

Electricity is often suspect at campgrounds in Mexico. It is a good idea to carry a tester that will tell you when voltages are incorrect, polarities reversed, and grounds lacking. Always carry adapters allowing you to use small 110V, two-pronged outlets. The best setup is one that lets you turn the plug over (to reverse polarity) and to connect a ground wire with a clip to a convenient pipe, conduit, or metal stake.

If you spend several weeks hooked up to high voltage Mexican electricity it is likely that your batteries will boil off a lot of water. It is absolutely essential to check your batteries much more frequently in Mexico than you do at home. Once a week is best. We're convinced that poorly serviced batteries are a major contributor to the problem of damage to refrigerator circuit boards. Charged batteries may provide a cushion effect against voltage spikes, dead ones do not.

Sewer hookups in many Mexican campgrounds are located at the rear of the site. Make sure you have a long sewer hose, one that will reach all the way to the rear of your RV and then another couple of feet. You'll be glad you have it.

Water purity considerations (see the *Drinking Water* title in this chapter), mean that you may need a few items that you may not already have in your RV. Consider adding a charcoal water filter for tap water if you do not already have one installed. You should also have a simple filter for filtering water before it even enters your RV, this avoids sediment build-up in your fresh water tank. Of course you'll also need a hose, we have found a 20-foot length to be adequate in most cases.

It is extremely hard to find parts or knowledgeable mechanics to do systems-related work on camping vehicles. Before crossing the border make sure your propane system, all appliances, toilet, holding tanks, and water system are working well because you'll want them to last until you get home. Marginal or jury-rigged systems should be repaired. Consider bringing a spare fresh water pump, or at least a diaphragm set if yours isn't quite new. Make sure your refrigerator is working well, you'll need it and replacement parts are impossible to find. There is one repair center for refrigerators and some other RV systems in San José del Cabo. See that section in this book for more information.

Make sure you have all the tools necessary to change a tire on your rig, and a spare tire. Many large motorhomes no longer come with jacks, tire-changing tools, or even spares. The theory must be that it is too dangerous for an individual to change a tire on one of these huge heavy RVs. This may be true but you need to have the proper tools available so that you can find help and get the job done if you have a flat in a remote location. Mexican roads are rough and flat tires common. Even if you don't normally carry a spare you should have at least an unmounted tire that can be mounted if you destroy one on your RV, it can be difficult to find the right size tire for big RVs on the Baja.

If you do have a breakdown along the road what should you do? It is not a good idea to abandon your RV while you go to get parts or help. RVs are a tempting target, one abandoned along the road invites a break-in. This is one good reason not to travel at night. Daytime drivers can usually find a way to get their broken-down RV off the road before night falls. If you are traveling with another rig you can send someone for help. If you are traveling by yourself you will probably find it easy to flag down a car or another RV. Ask the other driver to send a mechanic or *grúa* (tow truck) from the next town. Large tow trucks are common since there is heavy truck traffic on the Transpeninsular.

Weather and When To Go

The winter dry season is when most travelers visit the Baja. In a fortunate conjunction of factors the extremely pleasant warm dry season on the Baja occurs exactly when most northerners are more than ready to leave snow and cold temperatures behind. Comfortable temperatures occur beginning in November and last through May. The shoulder months of October and June may be uncomfortably warm for some people.

Be aware that August through October is the hurricane season on the Baja. Each year several hurricanes strike the southern end of the peninsula, some do a considerable amount of damage. When this happens flash floods are common and often cause loss of life, stay out of the washes during storms.

On the other hand, unlike the rest of Mexico the Baja is a popular summer RV destination too. The northern west coast of the peninsula is really a summer destination, winters can be pretty cool. Also, many people come to the Baja for the fishing, and the hot season is the best one for that.

Chapter 3
How To Use The
Destination Chapters

The focus of this book is on campgrounds, of course. A question we often hear is "Which campground on the Baja is your favorite?" Usually the person asking the question has a personal favorite in mind. Our answer is always the same – we like them all. No one campground is the best because everyone likes different things. Also, the personality of a campground depends upon the people staying there when you visit. People traveling on their own in an environment they are not accustomed to tend to be very friendly, this is one of the best things about Mexican camping. We can't tell you exactly who will be staying in each of the campgrounds in this book when you decide to visit, but we will try to give you a good feel for what to expect in the way of campground features and amenities.

Chapter 4 through 12 contain information about the many camping destinations you may visit on the Baja and in northwest Sonora. The chapters are arranged somewhat arbitrarily into regions that fall naturally together for a discussion of their camping possibilities.

Introductory Map

Each of the campground chapters (chapters 4-12) begins with a road map. The map shows a lot of information that will allow you to use it as an index to find campgrounds as you travel. The map shows the route covered in the chapter and also the most important towns. Dotted lines on the map and page numbers direct you to the section of the chapter covering the area within the dotted lines, including detailed maps showing the actual locations of the campgrounds.

Introductory Text

Each chapter starts with an introduction giving information about the region covered in the chapter. Most of this information is important to a camping traveler and much of it is not necessarily included or easy to find in normal tourist guides. On the other hand, much information that is readily available in normal tourist guides will not be found in this book. Other books do a good job of covering things like currency information, hotels, restaurants, language, and tour details. This book is designed to be a supplement to normal tourist guides, not to replace them. You'll find that it provides a framework. Other guides, or your own travels, must be used to fill it the details.

For Baja travelers the roads and fuel availability are especially important so there is a section in each chapter describing the major roads and giving the location of the gas stations. When appropriate we also include sections summarizing the details of sightseeing, golf, beaches and water sports, and fishing in the area. It is handy to have some idea what to expect.

We've also included a section titled *Backroad Adventures*. Paved roads other than the Transpeninsular are scarce, in remote areas of the peninsula you'll probably find yourself on some back roads. They are the only way to reach many of the best destinations on the Baja. You must be aware, however, that these roads are not appropriate for all vehicles, especially not for all RVs. Be sure to review the section titled *Backroad Driving* in the *Details, Details, Details* chapter. Very few of the formal campgrounds on the Baja are away from the paved highway system so don't be concerned if you don't have a rig that is appropriate for backroad driving.

Route and Town Descriptions

Following the introductory material in each chapter is *The Routes, Towns, and Campgrounds* section. You'll find campground overview maps showing the major roads and campground locations and text describing each route or town. There are descriptions of the driving routes and of the towns and recreational areas.

We have given population numbers for each major town. These are our estimates. Population figures are notoriously unreliable in Mexico, and the number of residents in an area can change rapidly since the Baja is a developing area.

We've also included many mileage figures and have used kilometer markers extensively. Almost all of the major roads on the Baja Peninsula are marked with kilometer posts. Be prepared for many missing ones, but overall they are a useful way to fix locations.

The users of this book are probably going to be folks from both the U.S. and Canada. As everyone knows the U.S. uses miles and Canada uses kilometers. We've tried to give both numbers when we mention distances. Canadians will no doubt notice our bias - the mileage figures come first. Our excuse is that most Canadians are familiar with both systems while most of us from the states aren't quite comfortable yet with kilometers.

Campground Overview Maps

Each important city or town and each region between the towns has its own campground overview maps. These maps are designed to do two things: they quickly show you the lay of the land and the campgrounds that are available, and if you examine them more carefully they will help you drive right to the campground you have decided to use.

There are two different types of campground overview maps. The first is a city map. Each city map is associated with a written description of the city and a listing of the campgrounds in that city. The second type is an area map. These usually show the road between two cities and each is associated with a description of that road and also a listing of the campgrounds on that road.

In an effort to make our maps and descriptions more useful we have included Pemex stations, the types of fuel they stock, and their numbers. Each Pemex has a unique identification number which is almost always boldly stated on the sign out front. This number seldom changes, it seems like Pemexes are the most reliable reference point on Baja roads and they're often conveniently located near crucial intersections. Since gas stations that are not Pemexes are beginning to appear, and since Pemexes are beginning to convert to other brands, we may not be able to use this system much longer. Don't be surprised if a Pemex station shown on one of our maps has become another brand – Mexico is changing.

While the maps are for the most part self-explanatory here is a key.

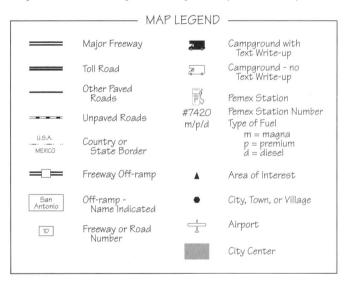

Campground Descriptions

Each campground description begins with address and telephone number, if available. While it is not generally necessary to obtain campground reservations in Mexico you may want to do so for some very popular campgrounds. If we think that reservations are necessary we say so in the campground description.

One thing you will not find in our campground descriptions is a rating with some kind of system of stars, checks, or tree icons. Hopefully we've included enough in-

TYPICAL PEMEX
SIGN

Green - Unleaded Gas (m)

Red - Premium Unleaded Gas (p)

Black - Diesel (d)

Station Number

American Express Accepted (For a Fee)

Note: Fuel types shown on maps as m/p/d

formation in our campground descriptions to let you make your own analysis.

We've included limited information about campground prices. Generally you can expect that tent campers will pay the least. RV charges sometimes depend on the size of the rig but more often are based upon the number of people with an extra charge for over two people. If hookups are available and you are in an RV you should expect to pay for them, campground owners usually do not distinguish between those who hook up and those who don't. On the other hand, it doesn't hurt to ask if there is a no-hookup rate. Some oceanside campgrounds have higher rates for spaces close to the water.

We've grouped the campground fees into the following categories in our campground descriptions:

FREE	Free	$$ $$$	Over $20 and up to $25
$	Up To $5	$$$ $$$	Over $25 and up to $30
$$	Over $5 and up to $10	$$$ $$$$	Over $30 and up to $35
$$$	Over $10 and up to $15	$$$$ $$$$	Over $35 and up to $40
$ $$$	Over $15 and up to $20	OVER $40	Over $40

All of these prices are winter prices for an RV with 2 people using full hookups if available. The prices given are for normal sites, sometimes premium site like those along the water are more expensive. Some campgrounds, particularly near Ensenada and San Felipe, actually have higher rates in the summer, but in most of the Baja you can expect to pay a little less in the summer, unless you use air conditioning.

In this book we've also included a monthly rate estimate for some campgrounds: where people frequently stay long-term.

 Up To $100   Over $500 and up to $600

Over $100 and up to $200   Over $600 and up to $700

Over $200 and up to $300   Over $700 and up to $800

Over $300 and up to $400   Over $800

Over $400 and up to $500

Campground icons can be useful for a quick overview of campground facilities or if you are quickly looking for a particular feature.

 Most of the campgrounds in this book accept RVs but not all accept tent campers. We've included the tent symbol for all campgrounds that do accept tents. If access or available room precludes RV use we say so in the text description.

Many campgrounds offer rental rooms, rental trailers, or rental casitas of some kind. If they do we give them an icon for it. This is very handy if you are expecting a family visit.

 You'll note that there are individual icons for 15 or 20-amp, 30-amp, or 50-amp outlets. This may refer to the physical outlet type only. Sometimes it is impossible to determine the actual breaker capacity, at other times there may be no breaker at all. It seems that the 30-amp outlet type we are accustomed to using north of the border must be expensive or difficult to come by in Mexico because often they are not used even when quite a bit of amperage is available. If you see a normal 30-amp outlet it's a sign that the electrical system might be more sophisticated than normal, or it might just mean that a previous occupant of your site brought his own outlet south one winter.

 The water symbol means that water is available. It may not be piped to the sites. There is usually more information about this in the write-up.

 If we show a dump icon it means that there are either drains at the sites, a dump station, or both. There is usually more information about this in the write-up.

 Showers in Mexican campgrounds often have no provision for hot water so we give separate shower symbols for hot and cold water. If there is provision for hot water but it was cold when we visited in winter we list it as providing cold water only. You may be luckier when you visit. During the hot summer months many Baja campgrounds don't run their water heaters at all because the slightly cool water is appreciated by most users.

An on-site restaurant can provide a welcome change from home-cooked meals and a good way to meet people. In Mexico almost all restaurants also serve alcohol of some kind. Often campground restaurants are only open during certain periods during the year, sometimes only during the very busy Christmas and Semana Santa (Easter) holidays. Even if there is no restaurant at the campground we have found that in Mexico there is usually one not far away.

If we've given the campground a grocery cart icon then it has some groceries. This is usually just a few items in the reception area. Check the write-up for more information.

If we include a washing machine icon it means that there is a self-service washing machine.

A swimming icon means that the campground has swimming either on-site or nearby. This may be a pool or the beach at the ocean. Swimming pools at Mexican campgrounds are seldom heated.

The telephone icon means that there is a telephone either in the campground or on the street nearby.

The cell phone icon means that we had a usable signal at the campground on our Telmex phone.

The internet icon indicates that internet service is available in the campground. In Mexico this usually means that they provide a machine for your use, data ports are unusual.

The Wi-Fi icons mean that wireless internet is available. One shows service where there is an extra charge, the other indicates that the cost of the service is included in the campground price. Sometimes service is only available near the office, but other places it is broadcast throughout the campground. The campground description usually tells more about this. We are finding more and more Wi-Fi service in Mexican campgrounds, often very good service.

The television symbol means that some kind of cable or satellite system is provided for some sites.

We've included a no pet symbol for the few Mexican campgrounds where dogs are not allowed. Predicting how welcome you and your dog are is problematic in Mexico. Many Mexican dogs are either guard dogs or strays. Well cared-for pets are becoming more common but are still a little unusual. If you have a small lap dog you're unlikely to be told that you can't use a campground. However, if you have a large dog, or if you have several dogs, expect that some campgrounds will not let you stay. Often there is a guard dog around that would not get along with your dogs, it may even attack small dogs. Our pet symbols are meant for those with small RV-type dogs. Those with large dogs or several dogs may find them unreliable. Even if we do not include a no pet symbol you should be extremely cautious with your pet. Mexico can be a dangerous place for them.

The English spoken icon means that there is usually someone in the campground office who can speak English.

 A very few Mexican campgrounds, mostly hotels with campsites, accept credit cards. Usually this would be Visa or MasterCard.

Our big RV symbol means that there is room for coaches to 40 feet to enter the campground, maneuver, and park. Usually this means we've seen them do it. The driver we saw may have been better than most, exercise caution. If you drive a fifth wheel you'll have to use your own judgment of how your rig handles compared to a coach. If you drive an even larger 45-footer you can at least use our symbol as a starting point in making your campground decisions. There's often more in the write-up itself about this.

You'll find that this book has a much larger campground description than most guidebooks. We've tried to include detailed information about the campground itself so you know what to expect when you arrive. While most campgrounds described in this book have a map we've also included a paragraph giving even more details about finding the campground.

GPS (Global Positioning System) Coordinates

You will note that we have provided a GPS Location for each campground. GPS is a modern navigation tool that uses signals from satellites. For less than $150 you can now buy a dash-mounted receiver that will show your location on a map. You can also enter the coordinates we have given for the campgrounds in this book into the receiver and it will attempt to lead you to the location.

Not all GPS units include maps of Mexico so check before buying. Most manufacturers do have a way to load Mexican maps purchased separately if Mexico is not included in the maps originally installed. Also, most smart phones can run apps that can substitute for a dedicated GPS unit, but make sure the app you choose downloads the maps you will use and does not require cell phone Internet access while you are using it.

Even with a decent map in the unit it is important not to trust the GPS too much in Mexico. Directions given by the units are often wrong since information about addresses and traffic direction is often not available. In fact, most GPS units will not accept addresses as destinations in Mexico so you'll have to enter the coordinates given in our campground descriptions yourself. You may find that the GPS is most useful in traveling from town to town. Once you've arrived in a town you're better off using the maps in the book to find the campground.

If you don't have a GPS receiver already you certainly don't need to go out and buy one to use this book. On the other hand, if you do have one bring it along. More and more drivers are using GPS mapping systems for navigation.

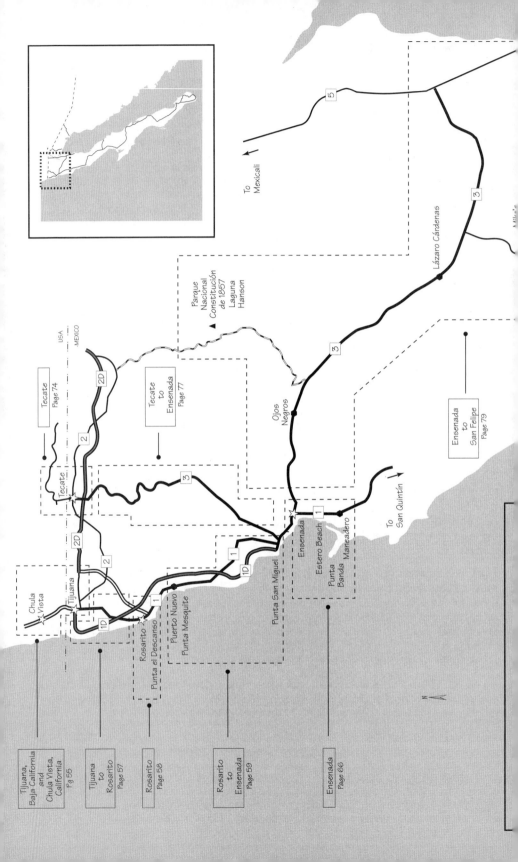

To Mexicali

5

Lázaro Cárdenas

3

Parque
Nacional
Constitución
de 1857
▲ Laguna
Hanson

Tecate to Ensenada
Page 77

3

Ojos
Negros

Ensenada
to
San Felipe
Page 79

USA
MEXICO

Tecate
Page 74

2D

2

3

Tecate

2D

2

1

1D

Punta San Miguel

Ensenada

Estero Beach
1
Punta
Banda
Maneadero

To
San Quintín

Chula
Vista

Tijuana

2

1

Puerto Nuevo
Punta Mesquite

Punta el Descanso

1D

Rosarito

N

Tijuana,
Baja California
and
Chula Vista,
California
Pg 55

Tijuana
to
Rosarito
Page 57

Rosarito
Page 58

Rosarito
to
Ensenada
Page 59

Ensenada
Page 66

Chapter 4
South to Ensenada

INTRODUCTION

The Pacific Coast south to Ensenada is a popular summer camping destination. So many people visit this area from California that it sometimes seems almost an extension of that state. In this chapter we cover the campgrounds along the coast as well as those along the inland corridor from Tecate to Ensenada and also the corridor from Ensenada to San Felipe.

Highlights

Ensenada is a fun town to visit with lots to keep you occupied. There are many day trips to places like **La Bufadora**, **Puerto Nuevo**, the **Guadalupe Valley**, and **Laguna Hanson**. And don't forget a fishing trip on one of the many charter boats based in Ensenada.

Roads and Fuel Availability

Mex 1 begins in Tijuana. From Tijuana to Ensenada there are actually two different highways. One is the free road, Mex 1 Libre. The other is a toll road, Mex 1D. The toll road is by far the best road, it is four lanes wide and for most of its length a limited-access highway. Much of the road is extremely scenic with great views of cliffs and ocean. There are three toll booths along the 65-mile (105 km) road, an automobile or van was being charged about $6 U.S. for the entire distance during the spring of 2017 and about double that for larger RVs. Both dollars and pesos are accepted as payment at the three toll booths on this highway. This is the only section of toll road you'll see on Mex 1 until you reach San José del Cabo.

The free road, Mex 1 Libre, is much less direct than the toll road. It leaves Tijuana to the south and heads directly to Rosarito. After passing through the bustling streets of this beach town it parallels the toll road on the ocean side for 20 miles (33 kilometers) to the vicinity of La Misión. There it turns inland and climbs into the hills where after 20 miles (32 km) it rejoins Mex 1D just south of the southernmost toll booth and 5 miles (8 km) north of Ensenada. The road through the mountains is scenic and fine for carefully driven big RVs but only two lanes wide, few people drive it because it takes much longer than the toll road.

There is a good alternate to Mex 1 as far south as Ensenada. This is Mex 3 which runs from Tecate on the border to Ensenada. It has recently been widened and is now a good two-lane road, even for large RVs. This is a very useful highway if you are headed north since the Tecate border crossing has much shorter waiting lines to cross into the U.S. than the Tijuana crossings. Using Mex 3 the distance from Tecate to El Sauzal and then on to Ensenada on the free portion of Mex 1 is 65 miles (105 km).

A relatively new road in this section of the Baja is an extension of Mex 2 which runs west from Tecate, passes south of Tijuana, and meets the Mex 1 Libre road south of Rosarito. People crossing at Tecate could drive west to Mex 1 and then south to Ensenada but few choose to drive those extra miles. See the Tijuana to Rosarito Map which shows the routing of this highway.

Mex 3 also continues eastward from Ensenada to meet with Mex 5 about 31 miles (51 km) north of San Felipe on the Gulf of California. This 123 mile (201 km) two-lane paved highway offers an alternative to Mex 5 south from Mexicali for San Felipe-bound travelers.

Fuel, both gas and diesel, is readily available at Pemex stations at population centers throughout this section. .

Sightseeing

This section of the Baja Peninsula offers a wealth of sightseeing opportunities. This is at least partly because there is such a large population within easy driving distance. Remember, Tijuana is Mexico's sixth largest metropolitan area and southern Californians can easily visit the entire region on day trips.

Tijuana gets most of the visitors, of course. The best way to visit is to walk across the border. Many sights are within walking distance of the San Ysidro crossing. To travel farther just use a taxi, or if you are more adventurous, catch a bus. See the *Tijuana* section below for specific destinations.

The town of **Rosarito** is best known for its beach. See *Rosarito* below for more details.

The small town of **Puerto Nuevo**, 9 miles (15 km) south of Rosarito, is famous for its restaurants. They specialize in lobster dinners. There are many of them, just pick one that looks good to you.

South of Rosarito the toll highway travels along **spectacular cliffs** offering some great views. Watch for the viewpoints that have room to pull larger RVs off the highway to take a picture or two.

PUERTO NUEVO IS FAMOUS FOR ITS RESTAURANTS SPECIALIZING IN LOBSTER

If you are following Mex 3 south from Tecate you will have the opportunity to visit the **wineries in the Guadalupe Valley**. This is Mexico's premier wine-growing area.

Ensenada is a popular destination for folks from north of the border. It offers shopping and restaurants and has a much more relaxed atmosphere than Tijuana. See the *Ensenada* section below for more information.

Golf

If you enjoy golf there are a number of possibilities in this region.

In Tijuana there is the **Club Campestre de Tijuana**. It is an 18-hole course near central Tijuana and is located just off the Boulevard Agua Caliente.

As you drive south along Mex 1D watch for the **Real del Mar Golf Resort** near Km 19.5. It has 18 holes and is associated with a Marriott hotel.

Farther south along the same road, near Km 78, you'll find the **Bajamar Ocean Front Golf Resort**. There are 27 holes here divided into three 9-hole courses. You pay for 18 holes and pick the two sections you want to play.

Just south of Ensenada is the **Baja Country Club** which has 18 holes.

Finally, to the east near Mexicali is the **Club Campestre de Mexicali**. It has 18 holes and is located south of town.

ENSENADA'S ESTERO BEACH CAN BE CROWDED AT HOLIDAYS

Beaches and Water Sports

While there is some surfing on Rosarito Beach you'll find more surfers to the south from about Km 33 on Mex 1 Libre at Punta el Descanso south to Punta Mesquite. Off the campground at San Miguel is Punta San Miguel, one of the most popular surfing spots in Baja California.

People from Ensenada generally head for the beaches south of town at Estero Beach. Several campgrounds offer access to these beaches and are listed in the *Ensenada* section.

Fishing

Many people come to Ensenada for charter fishing trips. Big boats from Ensenada range far to the south along the Pacific Coast of the Baja Peninsula. They're after yellowtail and albacore tuna. Smaller boats also run out of Ensenada on day trips after bottom fish like rockfish and halibut.

Surf-casting is popular along many of the beaches along the upper northwest coast. One sandy beach where this is popular is the one in front of the Clam Beach and Baja Seasons RV resorts.

Backroad Adventures

See the *Backroad Driving* section of *Chapter 2 - Details, Details, Details* for essential information about driving off the main highway on the Baja and for a definition of road type classifications used below.

🚐 **From Km 55 on Mex 3 between Ensenada and San Felipe** - A national park, **Parque Nacional Constitución de 1857**, is accessible from Mex 3 east of Ensenada. A road goes north to the shallow **Laguna Hanson**, the distance to the lake is 20 miles (32 km). There are primitive campsites at the lake and hiking trails. This is usually a Type 2 road. This lake is also accessible from Mex 2 to the north but that road is sometimes a Type 3. It meets Mex 2 between Tecate and Mexicali near Km 72, the distance to the lake from this direction is about 40 miles (65 km).

THE ROUTES, TOWNS, AND CAMPGROUNDS

TIJUANA (TEE-HWAN-AH), BAJA CALIFORNIA
AND CHULA VISTA, CALIFORNIA
Population 1,800,000

Tijuana is Mexico's fifth largest metropolitan area and perhaps the fastest growing city in North America. That means that the atmosphere can be somewhat chaotic, particularly if you are driving an RV. It's a great city to visit, but not in your own vehicle.

We think that the best base for visiting Tijuana is actually on the north side of the border in the U.S. The **Tijuana Trolley**, a light rail line, runs from San Diego to a

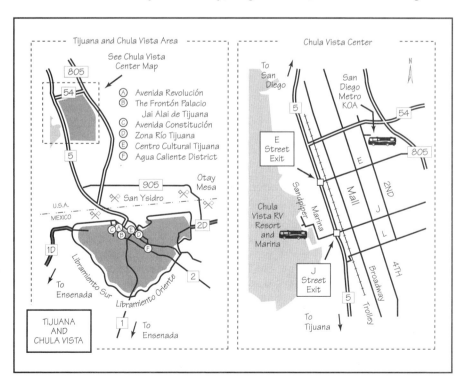

station right at the border. Several campgrounds are located near the line. From them you can board the trolley and travel effortlessly to the border, walk across, and then either walk or use taxis to visit the city's attractions.

The border crossing between San Ysidro and Tijuana (the main Tijuana-area garita or gate) is said to be the busiest border crossing anywhere in the world. This presents a challenge for automobile travelers, but pedestrians find the crossing pretty easy.

Once in Mexico you are within walking distance of **Avenida Revolución**. Most visitors who walk across the border never get beyond this area. It's marked by the Tijuana Arch, much like the one in St Louis. It has some excellent restaurants, shops, and galleries.

About a mile east of the La Reforma district is the **Zona Río**. This is an area of nicer restaurants, hotels, and large shopping centers. The **Centro Cultural Tijuana** (CECUT) is a cultural center and museum with an Imax theater, a performing-arts theater, and crafts shops.

Nearby is the **Mercado Hidalgo,** a large traditional food and crafts market like those found in most Mexican towns and cities. It's fun to shop and try the food in the market and the surrounding streets.

Tijuana Campgrounds

Tijuana actually has no campgrounds, but there is good access from campgrounds north of the border in Chula Vista and San Diego. These campgrounds double as excellent bases for preparation for your trip south of the border.

CHULA VISTA RV RESORT AND MARINA
(Open All Year)

Address:	460 Sandpiper Way, Chula Vista, CA 91910
Telephone:	(800) 741-6878
Fax:	(619) 422-8872
Email:	info@chulavistarv.com
Website:	www.chulavistarv.com

GPS Location: 32.62806 N, 117.10472 W, Near Sea Level

This is a first class, very popular campground in an excellent location for preparing to enter Mexico. Chula Vista is a convenient small town with all the stores and facilities you'll need, and both San Diego and Tijuana are close-by.

This campground is located adjacent to and operated in conjunction with a marina. There are 237 back-in and pull-through sites with 50-amp power and full hookups including TV. Parking is on paved drives with patios, sites are separated by shrubbery. Large RVs and slide-outs fit fine. The bathroom facilities are excellent and there is a nice warm pool as well as a spa, small store, and meeting rooms. The marina next door has two restaurants and a shuttle bus provides access to central Chula Vista, stores, and the local stop of the Tijuana Trolley. Paved walkways along the water are nice for that evening stroll. This is a very popular, and expensive, RV resort. Reservations are essential.

Take the J Street Exit from Highway 5 which is approximately 7 miles north of the

San Ysidro border crossing and about 8 miles south of central San Diego. Drive west on J Street for 2 blocks, turn right on Marina Parkway, and drive north to the first street from the left (about 1/4 mile) which is Sandpiper, turn left here and drive one block, then follow the street as it makes a 90 degree right-angle turn, the entrance will be on your left.

SAN DIEGO METRO KOA *(Open All Year)*

Address:	111 North 2nd Ave, Chula Vista, CA 91910
Reservations:	(800) KOA-9877
Telephone:	(619) 427-3601
Email:	info@sandiegokoa.com
Website:	koa.com/campgrounds/san-diego/

GPS Location: 32.65694 N, 117.08167 W, Near Sea Level

This large campground in Chula Vista also makes a good base for exploring Tijuana and San Diego. It has about 270 spaces. It's a well-equipped park with everything you would normally expect at an upscale KOA including a pool, spa, playground, and store. There's a shuttle to the San Diego (Tijuana) Trolley. Many caravans to Mexico use this campground as a starting point. It is suitable for any size RV. Reservations are necessary, it is extremely popular.

To reach the campground take the E Street Exit from I-5 in Chula Vista. Travel east on E Street until you reach 2nd Ave. Turn left here on 2nd and proceed about .7 mile. The gate is on the right.

TIJUANA TO ROSARITO
17 Miles (27 Km), .5 Hour (From San Ysidro crossing via Mex 1D)

There are two roads south from Tijuana to Rosarito and points south. One is the toll road, Mex 1D. The other is a free road called Mex 1. The toll road is much easier to reach from the border crossing so it is usually the preferred route, especially among those with big rigs.

Mex 1D, the toll road, is most easily accessed by crossing the border in Tijuana at the San Ysidro border crossing and then following the major access route westward just south of the fence that divides Mexico and the U.S.

As you cross the border zero your odometer. An off-ramp makes getting on the road along the south side of the border fence a snap. Stay in the far right lane. Follow signs for "Scenic Road – Rosarito & Ensenada" and "Cuota". The off-ramp goes right and connects to the westbound road just south of the border fence. At 2.5 miles (4.0 km) you start a long uphill grade. Then at 3.5 miles (5.6 km) you reach the top of the hill and start to descend. At 3.9 miles (6.3 km) at the bottom of the hill take the exit to the right for 1D and merge onto a 4-lane highway heading west. Get in the left lane within a mile. At 5.2 miles (8.4 km) the highway splits, take the left fork. You'll soon arrive at the first toll booth on Mex 1D. In another 12.6 miles (20.3 km) you'll reach the northern Rosarito exit. You can join the free road here and drive through Rosarito, or you can continue south on the toll road toward Ensenada.

The free road from Tijuana to Ensenada heads south from the inner Libramiento or ring road that circles the southern border of Tijuana. If you were following the direc-

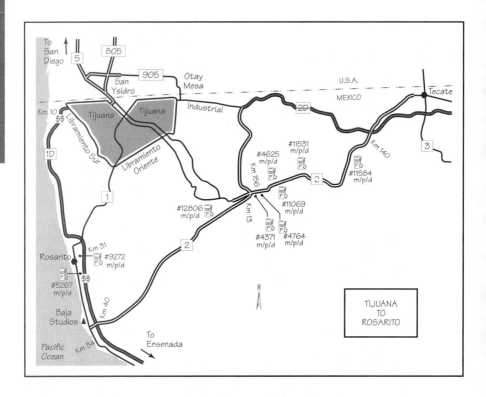

tions given above for reaching the toll road you would be on the inner Libramiento if you had gone straight instead of turning onto the toll road after leaving the border fence. While the Libramiento is better than most surface streets in Tijuana it can still be a challenge, that's why the toll road is the preferred route.

The free road branches off the inner Libramiento (watch for signs for Rosarito or Mex 1 or "Libre") and from that point it is only a short 7.3 mile (11.8 km) drive until you cross over the toll road and enter Rosarito. The free road is the main drag through Rosarito, watch for the many stop signs, there are dozens of them.

Some folks like to cross the border at another crossing to the east of Tijuana called Otay Mesa. See *Crossing the Border* in the *Details, Details, Details* chapter for more information.

Tijuana now has a new outer Libramiento, Mex 2. This major east-west highway has been extended to pass south of Tijuana and connect Tecate with the free Mex 1 south of Rosarito near Km 34. That's just south of the Baja Studios, about 3 miles (5 km) south of Rosarito.

ROSARITO (ROW-SAH-REE-TOE)
Population 72,000

Rosarito is a nice beach party town close to the U.S. and Tijuana. On school breaks

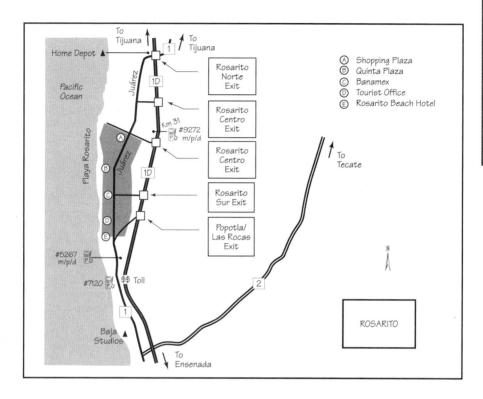

and weekends, particularly during the summer, Rosarito is a busy place. At other times, particularly during the winter, the town and stretch of small towns along the free road to the south is much more quiet. Virtually everything in town except the beach is right on Avenida Benito Juárez, the main road, so a drive through will give you a good introduction. Watch for the many stop signs!

Rosarito has large supermarkets so if you are not planning to go as far as Ensenada you may want to stop and do some shopping there. The town also has curio and Mexican crafts stores, just like Tijuana and Ensenada so you can do some shopping if you haven't yet had a chance.

For many years the most famous place in town has been the **Rosarito Beach Hotel**. It has been around since the 20s, and has grown over the years. On the wide beach nearby is the Rosarito Pier for fishing or just taking a walk.

ROSARITO TO ENSENADA
51 Miles (82 Km), 1 Hour

Mex 1 (Libre) meets the toll highway Mex 1D at the north end of Rosarito. The free highway runs through town while the toll road bypasses it, then they meet and run side by side for about 25 miles (41 km) south. There are lots of developments of various types along this double road. Just after leaving Rosarito off to the right you'll spot the **Baja Studios** where *Titanic* was filmed. Another interesting attraction is

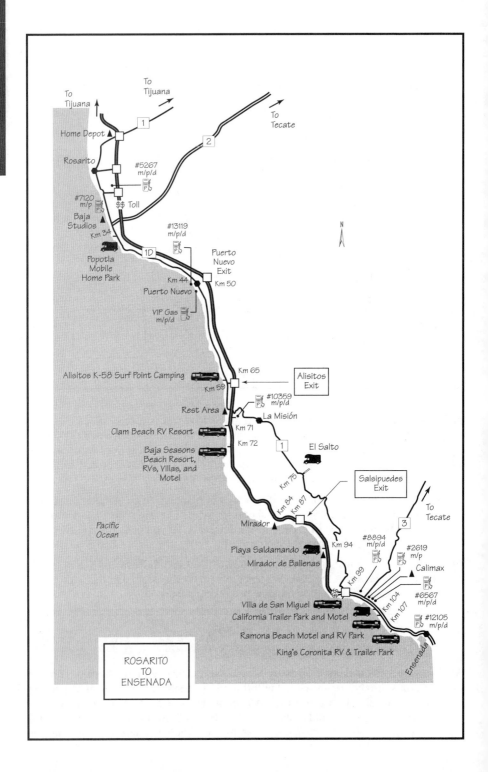

To Tijuana

To Tijuana

To Tecate

1

2

Home Depot ▲

Rosarito

#5267
m/p/d

#7120
m/p

$$ Toll

Baja
Studios

Km 34

#13119
m/p/d

N

Popotla
Mobile
Home Park

1D

Km 44

Puerto
Nuevo
Exit

Km 50

Puerto Nuevo

VIP Gas
m/p/d

Km 65

Alisitos K-58 Surf Point Camping

Km 59

Alisitos
Exit

#10359
m/p/d

Rest Area ▲

La Misión

Clam Beach RV Resort

Km 71

Km 72

1

El Salto

Baja Seasons
Beach Resort,
RVs, Villas, and
Motel

Km 75

Km 84

Km 87

Salsipuedes
Exit

To
Tecate

3

Pacific
Ocean

Mirador ▲

Km 94

#8894
m/p/d

#2619
m/p

Playa Saldamando

Calimax

Mirador de Ballenas

Km 99

#6567
m/p/d

Villa de San Miguel

Km 104

California Trailer Park and Motel

Km 107

#12105
m/p/d

Ramona Beach Motel and RV Park

King's Coronita RV & Trailer Park

Ensenada

ROSARITO
TO
ENSENADA

Puerto Nuevo, about 13 miles (21 km) south of Rosarito. This has become the place to go to get a lobster dinner, there are about 30 restaurants in the small town, they cover the spectrum in price and quality.

For access to campgrounds immediately south of Rosarito we recommend that you stay on the free road. Otherwise stay on the toll road to make much better time. Near La Misión the free road passes under the toll road and heads inland. From that point south all coastal campgrounds are accessible from the toll road only. You'll have to get on the toll road at a point somewhat north of the point it passes under the freeway, the southernmost on-ramp is at Km 59 of the free road (and Km 66 of the toll road) and is called Alisitos.

Rosarito to Ensenada Campgrounds

POPOTLA MOBILE HOME PARK *(Open All Year)*

Address: Km 34 Carr. Tijuana-Ensenada Libre, Rosarito
CP 22710, B.C. México
Reservations: PO Box 431135, San Ysidro, CA 92143-1135
Telephone: (661) 612-1502
Email: recepcion@popotla.mx
Website: www.popotla.mx

GPS Location: 32.27789 N, 117.02869 W, Near Sea Level

This is a large gated RV park mostly filled with permanent residents, but is has a nice area set aside for short-term campers. It's a gated park with a manned entrance station. We usually find these sites mostly empty, perhaps surprising considering the location next to the ocean, but probably reflecting the fact that we visit mostly during the winter.

There are 46 spaces here for overnighters, all with ocean views. Some are large back-in spaces to 36 feet with full hookups. More are smaller spaces but should take RVs to 30 feet. Electrical outlets are 20 amp and all sites have cement patio pads. Some sites are set near the water in a small valley, others are above along the bluff. There are bathrooms with hot showers and a swimming pool. Wi-Fi is available only at the office. The campground is fenced and secure and there is a bar and restaurant on the grounds. Daily rates are $35 depending upon the parking area, monthly rates are $580.

The campground is located near Km 34 on the free road about 7 km (4 miles) south of Rosarito Beach.

ALISITOS K-58 SURF POINT CAMPING *(Open All Year)*

Location: Km 59 Carr. Tijuana-Ensenada Libre, B.C., México
Telephone: (664) 636-1169

GPS Location: 32.12338 N, 116.88519 W, Near Sea Level

This is primarily a surfing spot but during weekends and holidays it is also full of tent campers from Tijuana. There's a big red K58 painted on their water tank and visible from the highway. This is a basic no-frills place to park on a bluff above the ocean. There is a large open field with no hookups, plenty of room and easy access make it suitable for any size RV. There are flush toilets and cold showers available and the owners seem to make an effort to keep the place clean. A small tienda out front has basic supplies and there is also a restaurant nearby. Rates work out to be about $11 for automobiles, $14 for a small RV, and $17 for a motorhome. A paved access walk with stairs leads down to a sand and gravel beach.

The entrance is located near the Km 59 point of the free road south of Rosarito Beach.

🚐 EL SALTO *(Open All Year)*
   Telephone: (664) 407-7751

   $$ ▲ 🧊 🛒

   GPS Location: 32.03681 N, 116.77391 W, 800 Ft.

Unlike the other campgrounds in this section the El Salto is far from the beach. It's a small rural campground used mostly by Mexican families, more suitable for tents than RVs. In fact, we wouldn't recommend it for anything larger than a van.

There are about 20 campsites set in a small valley with a stream. Sites have barbeque stands and are set under low trees. Access in the campground is difficult for taller rigs, and the trees and uneven ground severely limit the parking sites. There is an open parking area above the valley that can accommodate small RVs but leveling is difficult and maneuvering room limited. There are flush toilets and cold showers as well as a small store. A hiking trail leads to a nearby waterfall, or salto. A manager lives on the property.

From the Alistos exit off Mex 1D zero your odometer and drive south on Mex 1. In 1.5 miles (2.4 km) the road curves left and goes under Mex 1D. At odometer 2.9 miles (4.7 km) you enter and pass through the village of La Misión. At odometer 10.5 miles (16.9 km) turn left at a sign for El Salto onto a dirt road and in another .8 miles (1.3 km) you'll reach the campground entrance.

🚐 CLAM BEACH RV RESORT *(Open All Year)*
   Address: La Salina Beach, Km 71 Carr. Tijuana-Ensenada, B.C., México
   Telephone: (646) 155-0977 or (664) 666-2635
   Email: clambeachrv@gmail.com

   GPS Location: 32.07520 N, 116.87926 W, Near Sea Level

For many years this was a primitive campground called Rancho Mal Paso on the same beach as Baja Seasons which is located to the south. Now there's a modern new RV park as well as primitive beach camping but with modern restrooms.

The new park has 82 back-in paved sites off paved access roads. Utilities include 50/30/20 amp outlets at each site, also water and sewer. They're big sites with lots of maneuvering room, some are as long as 65 feet. There are beautiful restroom buildings with hot showers and laundry facilities. These are now some of the nicest facilities in any Mexican campground. Wi-Fi can be received throughout the RV area. Rates for the RV park start at $36 year round. Monthly rates run from $405 to $685.

The primitive camping remains at the north end of the property. Camping there is on an area of solid fill. Sites are not delineated, RVs of any size park overlooking the beach. A new building has flush toilets and hot showers dedicated to this area. Rates for this area are $24 per day.

Access to the campground is directly from the south-bound lanes of the toll road at the 71 Km marker. There's no access from the north-bound lanes, you'll have to drive north to the Alisitos exit and return to reach the campground. There is a walking overpass right beyond the exit so watch for it so you don't miss the turn.

🚐 **BAJA SEASONS BEACH RESORT, RVS, VILLAS, AND**
   MOTEL *(Open All Year)*

Address:	Carretera Escénica Tijuana-Ensenada Km 72.5, La Salina, Ensenada, B.C., México	
Telephone:	(800) 791-6562 (U.S. Res.) or (800) 824-1704 (Mex)	
Fax:	(646) 155-4019	
Email:	reservacionebs@yahoo.com.mx or reservaciones@bajaseasons.net	
Website:	www.bajaseasons.net	

GPS Location: 32.06500 N, 116.87806 W, Near Sea Level

The Baja Seasons is a large beachside RV park within reasonable driving distance of Ensenada. It's located on La Salina Beach, the Clam Beach RV Park described above is on the same beach to the north. The drive into Ensenada is about 30 miles (50 km) on good four-lane highway.

The campground has about 80 nice back-in camping spaces with electricity (some 50-amp, the rest 30-amp), sewer, water, paved parking pad, patios and landscaping. The streets are paved, they even have curbs. We have seen tent campers here but it's not an ideal spot, sites are paved and there aren't good places to set up a tent. It's a very popular big-rig campground. There's a huge but slightly run down central complex with a restaurant and bar, swimming pool, spa, mini golf, game room, library and coin-op laundry. There are also restrooms with hot showers, they could use a refurb. Wi-Fi is available in the clubhouse. Prices are about $24 in winter and $34 in summer for a site away from the water, higher on holidays. Monthly rates run from $366 to $671. Reservations are accepted and are a good idea, particularly on holidays and summer weekends.

The campground is right next to Mex 1D just south of the Km 72 marker. Going south watch the kilometer markers and turn directly off the highway. Going north you will see the campground on your left but cannot turn because of the central divider. Continue north 4.1 miles (6.6 km) to the Alisitos exit to return.

🚐 **PLAYA SALDAMANDO** *(Open All Year)*

Location:	Km 94 Carr. Escénica No. 1 Tijuana-Ensenada, B.C., Mex.	
Telephone:	(619) 857-9242 (U.S., for reservations), (646) 118-5974 (Mexico mobile number)	
Email:	reservations@playasaldamando.com	
Website:	www.playasaldamando.com	

GPS Location: 31.93306 N, 116.75444 W, Near Sea Level

This campground has a steep access road. The owner says it's fine for RVs to 32 feet but maneuvering room is tight, roads narrow, and the drop from the highway steep. It would be tough for trailers. Note that the campground closes if it rains. With prior arrangement management can open another gate for larger RVs.

There are many camping sites spread along a mile of rocky coastline with a few small beaches. Roads and campsites are lined with white-painted rocks. Someone has put in a lot of time with a paintbrush. Most sites are pretty well separated from

ALMOST ALL THE SITES AT PLAYA SALDAMANDO HAVE EXCELLENT VIEWS

each other and sport picnic tables. Almost all have excellent view locations, you can watch the waves and surfers below. It's a great tenting campground and also excellent for small RVs. There are no hookups, both pit toilets and flush toilets are available. Cold showers are free, there is a charge for hot ones.

The access road to this campground is at Km 94 from the southbound lanes, just north of the Mirador de Ballenas. Be alert so you don't accidentally miss it. Going north you must use the Salsipuedes off-ramp about 3 miles to the north and return on the southbound lanes About 0.4 mile (0.6 km) down the steep hill is an attended entrance gate where the fee is collected.

VILLA DE SAN MIGUEL *(Open All Year)*

Location:	Km 99 Carr. Tijuana-Ensenada
Telephone:	(646) 174-7948 (Mexico)
Email:	villadesanmiguel@hotmail.com
Website:	www.villadesanmiguel.com

GPS Location: 31.90137 N, 116.72951 W, Near Sea Level

This campground is very popular with surfers. The point just to the west is Punta San Miguel, this is one of the most popular surfing locations along the northern Baja coastline.

The campground itself is little more than a large gravel parking lot next to the beach. Many folks set up tents in front of the parking area on a sandy area behind the rocky beach. There is a small building with very basic flush toilets and cold showers, not nearly enough facilities for the number of folks who often are camped here. Above the beach area are a large number of permanently-situated trailers.

The campground is located off the four-lane coastal highway just south of the southernmost toll station. The exit is marked San Miguel and is near the Km 99 marker. Northbound is tougher. While there is an exit near Km 100 it requires driving through an underpass (marked as 3.7 meters) to reach the ocean side of the highway. Tall rigs will want to follow a different route as follows. Northbound, take the exit for Mex 1 Libre to Tijuana before you reach the toll booths. After the road heads inland you'll spot a wide gravel pull-off that people obviously use as a turnaround route. Turn around here and follow the signs to get back on Mex 1 in the direction of Ensenada. Just after you have regained Mex 1 take the immediate exit to the right, then follow a gravel and dirt local access road back north again to the campground entrance. There is an entrance gate where the fee is collected, then the road descends to the beach. The entrance road and campsite are used by the largest RVs but that entrance road requires care.

CALIFORNIA TRAILER PARK AND MOTEL *(Open All Year)*

Address:	Km 103-700 Carretera Tijuana-Ensenada,
	Ensenada CP 22480 B.C., México
Telephone:	(646) 174-6033
Email:	reservaciones@motel-california.com
Website:	www.motel-california.com

GPS Location: 31.88454 N, 116.68651 W, Near Sea Level

This is a small hotel with just a few campsites for RVs to about 30 feet. The sites are back-in, most with paved patios, there are 7 of them. They have 15-amp power outlets, water and most have sewer hookups. The restrooms are small but offer flush toilets and hot showers. There's an entrance barrier controlled from the office and Wi-Fi is usable at the office and nearer sites.

The motel is located on the ocean side of the 4-lane highway north of Ensenada near the Km 104 marker. Reservations are accepted.

RAMONA BEACH MOTEL AND RV PARK *(Open All Year)*

Address:	PO Box 6591, Chula Vista, CA 91909
Location:	Carr. Transp. Km 104, Ensenada, B.C., México
Telephone:	(646) 174-6045

GPS Location: 31.88312 N, 116.68596 W, Near Sea Level

The facilities and maintenance at this campground are much improved since our last visit. It's a waterfront campground with a low bluff above the water. It is located just south of the Motel California and next to the upscale Belio Restaurant. You leave the highway and enter the campground through the restaurant entrance and parking lot. The office is next to the campground entrance.

Access is good and the 30 or so sites are suitable for large RVs. The sites have paved patios. Hookups include 15-amp outlets, water, and sewer. Good restrooms with hot showers are located in the same building that house the manager's office. Wi-Fi from the office reaches about half the sites. The monthly rate here is $350.

KING'S CORONITA RV & TRAILER PARK *(Open All Year)*
Address: Hwy Tijuana-Ensenada Km 107, Ensenada CP
                 22860 B.C., México
Reservations: PO Box 5515, Chula Vista, CA 91912
Telephone: (646) 174-4540 or (646) 174-4391

GPS Location: 31.86619 N, 116.66401 W, Near Sea Level

This is an older well-kept campground that is almost full of permanently located RVs. There arc generally about 30 sites available for overnighters but you would do well to call ahead if you wish to stay here, particularly in the summer.

Campsites have full hookups, most with 30-amp outlets and cement patios. This is a gated campground with a mechanical gate. Access to the campground is not a problem for larger RVs and most sites will take RVs to 45 feet. There are no restrooms so rigs must be self-contained. The campground is located on a bluff above a marina, but sites for overnight RVs would be back from the bluff and would not offer much in the way of views.

The campground is located on the ocean side of the four-lane coastal highway near Km 107.

ENSENADA (EHN-SEH-NAH-DAH)
Population 500,000

Ensenada is the Baja's third most populous town and one of the most pleasant to visit. It is an important port and is more than ready for the tourist hordes that make the short-and-easy 68 mile (109 km) drive south from the border crossing at Tijuana or disembark from the cruise ships that anchor in Todos Santos Bay. There are many, many restaurants and handicrafts stores in the central area of town, English is often spoken so this is not a bad place to get your feet wet if you have not visited a Mexican city before. Try walking along **Calle Primera**, also called Avenida López Mateos. It is lined with restaurants and shops and is located just one block inland from the coastal Blvd. Costero (also known as Blvd. Gral. Lázaro Cárdenas). There are also many supermarkets and Pemex stations so Ensenada is the place to stock up on supplies before heading down the peninsula. Many banks and larger stores have ATM machines so you can easily acquire some pesos.

When you tire of shopping and eating, Ensenada has a few other attractions. The best beaches are south of town and at **Estero Beach** which also has several campgrounds, they are discussed below. The **fishing** in Ensenada is good, charters for yellowtail, albacore, sea bass, halibut and bonito can be arranged at the fishing piers downtown or at Marina Coral north of town. Ensenada has the largest fish market on the Baja, it is called the **Mercado Negro** (black market) and is located near the sport fishing piers. Nearby is a nice **Malecón** or waterfront walkway where you can take a good look at the fishing fleet and at a group of sea lions lined up in the water near the fish market. The waterspout at **La Bufadora**, located south near Punta Banda (see below) is a popular day trip. **Whale watching trips** are a possibility from December to March.

Important fiestas and busy times here are **Carnival, spring break** for colleges in the U.S. during late March, the **Rosarito-Ensenada 50-Mile Fun Bicycle Ride** and

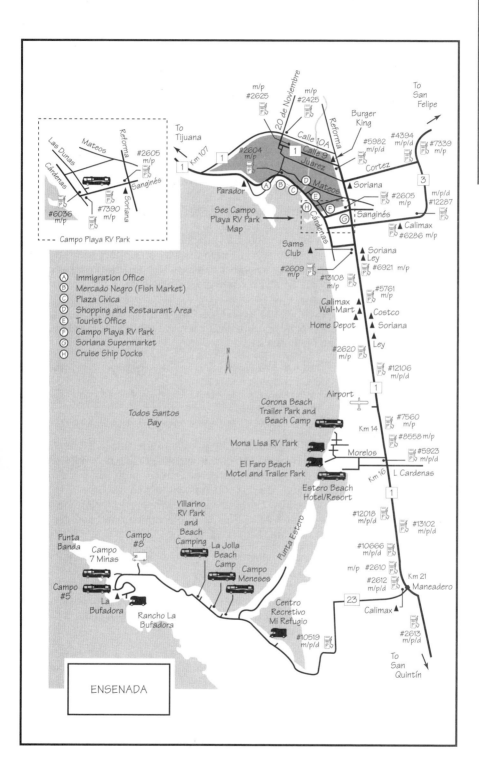

To Tijuana

To San Felipe

To San Quintín

Campo Playa RV Park

Las Dunas
Mateos
Reforma
Cárdenas
Soriana
Sanginés
#2605 m/p
#6036 m/p
#7390 m/p

m/p #2625
m/p #2425
20 de Noviembre
Reforma
Burger King
#5982 m/p/d
#4394 m/p/d
#7339 m/p
Calle 10A
Calle 9
#2604 m/p
Juarez
Cortez
Parador
A B C D Mateos E
H F
G Sanginés
Cárdenas
Soriana
#2605 m/p
#12287 m/p/d
Calimax
#6286 m/p

(A) Immigration Office
(B) Mercado Negro (Fish Market)
(C) Plaza Civica
(D) Shopping and Restaurant Area
(E) Tourist Office
(F) Campo Playa RV Park
(G) Soriana Supermarket
(H) Cruise Ship Docks

Sams Club
#2609 m/p
#13108 m/p
Soriana
Ley
#6921 m/p
#5761 m/p
Calimax
Wal-Mart
Home Depot
Costco
Soriana
Ley
#2620 m/p
#12106 m/p/d

Todos Santos Bay

Airport
Km 14
#7560 m/p
#8558 m/p
#5923 m/p/d
Morelos
L Cardenas
Km 16
Corona Beach Trailer Park and Beach Camp
Mona Lisa RV Park
El Faro Beach Motel and Trailer Park
Estero Beach Hotel/Resort

#12018 m/p/d
#13102 m/p/d
#10666 m/p/d
m/p #2610
#2612 m/p/d
Km 21
Maneadero
Calimax
#2613 m/p/d

Punta Banda
Campo 7 Minas
Campo #8
Villarino RV Park and Beach Camping
La Jolla Beach Camp
Campo Meneses
Campo #5
La Bufadora
Rancho La Bufadora
Punta Estero
Centro Recretivo Mi Refugio
#10519 m/p/d

ENSENADA

Tommy Bahama Newport to Ensenada Yacht Race in April, the **SCORE-Tecate Baja 500** off-road race in June, **Fiesta de la Vendimía Bajacaliforniana** (a wine festival) in August, **Mexican Surf Fiesta** in October at Playa de San Miguel, and the **Score–Tecate Baja 1000** off-road race in November.

The **Estero Beach** area is really a suburb of Ensenada. The road to Estero Beach leads west from near the Km 15 marker of Mex 1 about 7 miles (11 km) south of Ensenada. It's an older downscale resort area with waterfront trailer parks and more and more residences.

Punta Banda is another small area that is virtually a suburb of Ensenada. To get there follow the road west from near the center of Maneadero near the Km 21 marker, about 11 miles (18 km) south of Ensenada on Mex 1. It is then another 8 miles (13 km) out to Punta Banda. Punta Banda has grown up around the large RV parks here. A few miles beyond Punta Banda is the La Bufadora blowhole. There are several small campgrounds without hookups or much in the way of services near La Bufadora. At La Bufadora itself there are a number of decent restaurants as well as lots of tourist souvenir shops serving the many visitors to the blowhole.

Ensenada Campgrounds

This section includes campgrounds in Ensenada itself and south to Maneadero. This includes Estero Beach and Punta Banda.

⊞ CAMPO PLAYA RV PARK *(Open All Year)*

Address:	Blvd. Las Dunas No 570-300 & Calle
	Delante, CP 22880 Ensenada, B.C., México
Email:	campo-playa-sa@hotmail.com

GPS Location: 31.85028 N, 116.61389 W, Near Sea Level

The Campo Playa is the only RV park actually in urban Ensenada and is a place to stay if you want to explore the town. The downtown area is about 2 miles distant, the campground is right on the preferred route that you will probably be following through town, and there is a large Soriana supermarket just up the street. There are also a number of restaurants nearby. Unfortunately, there are nearby bars and discos and they close very late – about 3 A.M. This is an old campground and gets little maintenance or care. Many sites are used for vehicle storage.

There are about 50 spaces here set under shade trees and palms. Most are pull-thrus that will accept big RVs with slide-outs. The spaces have 15-amp outlets, sewer, water and patios. There are also some smaller spaces, some with only partial utility availability. The restrooms are showing their age but are clean and have hot showers. The campground is fenced but the urban location suggests that belongings not be left unattended. The monthly rate here is $330.

The campground lies near the easiest route through Ensenada. Entering town from the north on Mex 1 make sure to take the right fork marked Ensenada Centro just south of the Km 107 marker and the left fork at Km 109. You'll come to a stop light and see Pemex #2604 on the left. Zero your odometer here. You'll pass a plaza on the right with statues of three heads. At 1.2 miles (0.9 km) turn left onto Calle Agustin Sanginés, Pemex # 6036 is on the corner. Drive one block and turn left into Blvd. Las Dunas. The trailer park will be on your right after the turn.

THE ESTERO BEACH RV PARK IS ONE OF THE FINEST IN MEXICO

⛺ ESTERO BEACH HOTEL/RESORT *(Open All Year)*

Reservations:	482 W. San Ysidro Blvd., PMB 1186, San Ysidro, CA 92173
Telephone:	(646) 176-6230, (619) 245-4308, (818) 602-4817
Fax:	(646) 176-6925
Email:	information@hotelesterobeach.com
Website:	www.hotelesterobeach.com

GPS Location: 31.77806 N, 116.60417 W, Near Sea Level

The Estero Beach Hotel has long been one of Mexico's finest RV parks. This is really a large complex with a hotel as the centerpiece and many permanent RVs in a separate area from the RV park. Reservations are recommended, particularly in summer.

The modern RV park has 38 big back-in spaces with 30-amp outlets, sewer, and water. There is also a very large overflow area for parking if you don't want utilities. The parked RVs look across an estuary (excellent birding) toward the hotel about a quarter-mile away. There's a paved walkway along the border of the estuary to the hotel. Wi-Fi reaches the RVs. Rates are currently $45 during October to March, $60 for the remaining months and holidays. There is a 10% discount for month-long stays.

The resort also has a restaurant, bar, museum, several upscale shops, boat launching ramp, tennis courts, and playground. There is a large main swimming pool as well as a beautiful pool and hot tub for the RV park. There's also a public beach adjoining the resort on the far side of the grounds from the RV park.

To reach the Estero Beach Hotel turn west onto Calz. Gral. Lázaro Cárdenas from Mex 1 some 2.7 miles (4.4 km) south of the Walmart. This is the stoplight two blocks south of Pemex #5923. Northbound, it's the second stoplight after you climb the hill from the flats 3 miles (5 km) north of Maneadero. Drive .7 mile (1.1 km) west to a T, now turn left. You'll soon come to a gate. There is a very long entrance drive and then a reception office where they'll sign you up and direct you to a campsite.

EL FARO BEACH MOTEL AND TRAILER PARK *(Open All Year)*

Address:	Entrada principal No. 24 Ex-Ejido Chapultepec, Ensenada, BC Mexico
Telephone:	(646) 177-4620 or (646) 177-4630
Email:	farobeachotel@gmail.com

GPS Location: 31.78000 N, 116.61778 W, Near Sea Level

The El Faro is a popular destination for beach-goers from Ensenada. Busses bring loads of them to the small public beach that is located between the El Faro and the Estero Beach Hotel. It's a popular place because the beach is very clean and well kept.

This is a simple place, RV parking is right next to the beach on a sandy lot separated from the water by rip rap and a low wall. Tenters can pitch on the beach out front. There are about 30 RV spaces. Maximum RV length should be about 30 feet. Restrooms are nearby.

To reach the El Faro turn west onto Calz. Gral. Lázaro Cárdenas from Mex 1 some 2.7 miles (4.4 km) south of the Walmart. This is the stoplight two blocks south of Pemex #5923. Northbound, it's the second stoplight after you climb the hill from the flats 3 miles (5 km) north of Maneadero. Drive .7 mile (1.1 km) west to a T. Turn right and drive .1 mile (.2 km) to a stop sign. Turn left here and take the left fork of the Y at .6 miles (1 km). The El Faro is at the end of the road.

MONA LISA RV PARK *(Open All Year)*

Address:	Playa Monalisa S/N, Chapultepec, Ensenada, B.C., México 22785
Telephone:	(646) 177-4920 or (646) 177-5100
Email:	jesusmolina1113@gmail.com
Website:	www.monalisabeach.com

GPS Location: 31.78444 N, 116.61722 W, Near Sea Level

This is a interesting campground, a fun place to visit. The name apparently comes from the murals painted on every available wall. They depict scenes from Mexico's history and are themselves worth a special trip to the Mona Lisa.

The campground has 8 fairly large back-in spaces to 35 feet. All are paved and some have palapa-shaded tables. All also have 50-amp outlets, sewer, and water. The restrooms are old, dark, and poorly maintained. Tent camping is on sand near the office and restrooms overlooking the ocean. The Mona Lisa is just north of a beach but rock rip-rap fronts the actual RV park property. The current RV sites don't overlook

SOUTH TO ENSENADA

the water. There's also a playground. Wi-Fi can be used near the office. The monthly rate here is $400.

To reach the Mona Lisa turn west onto Calz. Gral. Lázaro Cárdenas from Mex 1 some 2.7 miles (4.4 km) south of the Walmart. This is the stoplight two blocks south of Pemex #5923. Northbound, it's the second stoplight after you climb the hill from the flats 3 miles (5 km) north of Maneadero. Drive .7 mile (1.1 km) west to a T. Turn right and drive .1 mile (.2 km) to a stop sign. Turn left here and take the right fork of the Y at .6 miles (1 km). In another .2 miles (.3 km) turn left and you'll see the Mona Lisa ahead.

🚐 CORONA BEACH TRAILER PARK AND BEACH CAMP
(Open All Year)

Address: PO Box 1149, Ensenada, México
Telephone: (646) 173-7326

GPS Location: 31.78944 N, 116.61472 W, Near Sea Level

This is a long-time beach camp with many permanently located units, and small casitas. The RV parking area is a large flat interior area with no view of the beach. There is parking for 28 RVs of any size with 15-amp outlets and water. There is also a dump station. A few additional full-hookup sites are occasionally available in spaces where older permanent units have been removed. They're a little more costly but some are waterfront sites. The restrooms are clean and have cold water showers. A small grocery store sits next to the camping area but is often not open in winter. While the waterfront of this park is a rip-rap storm barrier there's a long and usually quiet beach to the north of the campground. Easy access to it is one of the best features of this park.

To reach the Corona Beach turn west onto Calz. Gral. Lázaro Cárdenas from Mex 1 some 2.7 miles (4.4 km) south of the Walmart. This is the stoplight two blocks south of Pemex #5923. Northbound, it's the second stoplight after you climb the hill from the flats 3 miles (5 km) north of Maneadero. Drive .7 mile (1.1 km) west to a T. Turn right and drive .1 mile (.2 km) to a stop sign. Turn left here and take the right fork of the Y at .6 miles (1 km). At .3 miles (.5 km) the road makes a quick right and then left to continue straight. In another .2 mile (.3 km) you turn left into the entrance road.

🚐 CENTRO RECREATIVO MI REFUGIO *(Open All Year)*
Address: Carretera a la Bufadora Km 8.5, Poblado Punta
                Banda, Ensenada, B.C.
Telephone: (646) 154-2756, Cell (646) 136-8567
Email: Alicia_311_leyva@hotmail.com

GPS Location: 31.69833 N, 116.63500 W, Near Sea Level

As you drive out toward La Bufadora you may notice a castle on the right, complete with crenellated towers. If you walk down the entrance road you'll find a nice little RV park right alongside. The castle is really a home and the whole establishment is obviously a labor of love, an unusual one.

On the upper level the campground has 10 full-hookup sites with 15-amp outlets, water, and sewer. These are small pull-in or back-in sites, some are suitable (with careful maneuvering) for RVs to about 30 feet. You'd be well advised to walk in and look before entering in anything over 30 feet because turning around could be difficult and the entrance is steep. Some sites directly overlook the estero. If you turn left after descending the entry road you'll find another 20 sites suitable for tent campers, some of these have palapas. There are two restroom buildings in the campground, both with hot showers. Mi Refugio fronts on an estuary, when the tide is out there are mudflats out front. There's no charge for the Wi-Fi here, ask for the code when you check in. The monthly rate for RVs is $250.

The campground is on the road to La Bufadora which leaves Mex 1 in Maneadero. The road goes right at a stoplight next to Calimax supermarket some 6.5 miles (10.5 km) south of the Walmart in Ensenada. You will see the campground on the right 5.5 miles (8.9 km) after taking the cutoff.

🚐 CAMPO MENESES *(Open All Year)*

Address:	Km 12 Carret. Maneadero a la Bufadora, Punta Banda, CP 22791 Ensenada, B.C., México
Telephone:	(646) 194-5532

GPS Location: 31.71639 N, 116.66194 W, Near Sea Level

This campground is a long lot running from the road to the beach. There is room for perhaps 50 RVs to park along the central divider. Facilities include water, a dump station, and restrooms with toilets and cold showers.

Take the road toward La Bufadora from Mex 1 at the stoplight in Maneadero, it's about 6.5 miles (10.5 km) south of the Walmart in Ensenada. You will see the Campo Meneses on the right 7.5 miles (11.9 km) from the cutoff.

🚐 LA JOLLA BEACH CAMP *(Open All Year)*

Address:	Apdo. 102, Km 12.5 Carret. Maneadero a la Bufadora, Punta Banda, CP 22794 Ensenada, B.C., México
Telephone:	(646) 154-2005
Fax:	(646) 154-2004
Email:	lajollabeach_54@hotmail.com

GPS Location: 31.71667 N, 116.66500 W, Near Sea Level

The La Jolla Beach Camp is a big place. There are a lot of permanently-located trailers here but most of the transient trade is summer and holiday visitors using tents or RVs. A large dirt lot has room for about 200 groups. During the winter this area is practically empty. You can park along the waterfront and run a long cord for low-amp electricity from a few outlets near the restroom buildings. There is room for large RVs when the campground is not crowded. Water is available and there's a dump station. Restrooms are very basic, like what you'd expect next to a public beach, but there are hot showers available in a restroom located in the group of permanent trailers. There's also a launch ramp, it's only suitable for light boats since it's really just access to the sandy beach. The campground has a small grocery and Wi-Fi is only useable near the office. Winter rates of $15 do not include electricity. That's $4 more, and hot showers cost $3.50.

Take the road toward La Bufadora from Mex 1 at the stoplight in Maneadero next to the Calimax, it's about 6.5 miles (10.5 km) south of the Walmart in Ensenada. You will see the La Jolla on the right 7.8 miles (12.6 km) from the cutoff.

VILLARINO RV PARK AND BEACH CAMPING
(Open All Year)

Address: Km 13 Carr. la Bufadora, Punta Banda,
                 B.C., México
Telephone: (619) 819-8358 (US), (646) 154-2045
Email: villarvpark@prodigy.mx

GPS Location: 31.71694 N, 116.66667 W, Near Sea Level

This campground with lots of permanents also has a good-size transient area. It's close to Ensenada, on the beach, and a little off the beaten path.

Behind a glass-fronted terrace overlooking the beach is a large packed dirt area with some trees and about 25 larger hookup sites. Some sites have 15-amp outlets, sewer, and water and some have only electricity and water. There are a few pull-thrus. Most sites have picnic tables, some have fire rings. After careful maneuvering through the entrance and access road many of the sites in this campground will take big RVs. The restrooms are very clean and well maintained, they have hot showers. In front of the campground is a small store, a post office, a coffee/sandwich shop and a public phone. Wi-Fi is available in front of the sandwich shop at tables. There's also a small boat ramp, it's only suitable for small light boats since you must cross the soft beach. Rates here are slightly higher on weekends.

Take the road toward La Bufadora from Mex 1 at the stoplight in Maneadero at the Calimax, it's about 6.5 miles (10.5 km) south of the Walmart in Ensenada. You will see the Villarino on the right 7.9 miles (12.6 km) from the cutoff.

CAMPO 7 MINAS *(Open All Year)*

GPS Location: 31.73342 N, 116.71206 W, 500 Ft.

This is an easy place to find, the RV parking area is in a lot behind a convenience store near the highway. If you park here you have convenient access to the restrooms and even Wi-Fi. There are additional no-facility boondocking sites in remote locations, just ask for directions.

Take the road toward La Bufadora from Mex 1 at the stoplight in Maneadero at the Calimax, it's about 6.5 miles (10.5 km) south of the Walmart in Ensenada Some 11.2 miles (18.1 km) from the junction you'll see the store on the right.

CAMPO #5 *(Open All Year)*

GPS Location: 31.72944 N, 116.72250 W, 400 Ft.

This is the most obvious of several ejido or Campo campgrounds along the road out to la Bufadora. It's difficult to miss since it's right alongside the road. The views here are spectacular, you're hundreds of feet up the mountain overlooking the ocean. There are no hookups but a dilapidated restroom building has a toilet and cold shower. Any size RV will fit just fine. A trail leads down to a secluded beach.

Take the road toward La Bufadora from Mex 1 at the stoplight in Maneadero at the Calimax, it's about 6.5 miles (10.5 km) south of the Walmart in Ensenada Some 11.9 miles (19.2 km) from the junction you'll see the campground on the right.

EVERYBODY LOVES THE LA BUFADORA WATERSPOUT

RANCHO LA BUFADORA *(Open All Year)*

GPS Location: 31.72583 N, 116.71667 W, Near Sea Level

This is really just a parking area where RV camping is allowed for a fee. Tents are often pitched out front. It's located along the rocky shore just below the parking lots at La Bufadora blowhole. There's a small rocky beach. There is a restroom building with flush toilets. To reach the parking area you must brave the crowded parking lots for the blowhole. Ignore the people waving you in to a parking space and watch for the sign for Rancho La Bufadora a bit down a side road to the left. This is the turn, follow the road down and around to the left. There's a gate a short distance down the hill with an attendant during the day. Just beyond you'll find yourself in the camping lot.

TECATE (TEH-KAW-TAY)
Population 65,000

Tecate is one of the most relaxed and pleasant border towns in Mexico. Besides being a great place to cross into Baja (there are decent roads south to Ensenada and east to Mexicali) the town is well worth a short visit.

In the past Tecate was an agricultural center. Now it's a maquiladora border town with many factories turning out products for the U.S. The center of town is dominated by the **Plaza Parque Hidalgo** which is just a few blocks from the border crossing.

Probably the most famous tourist attraction here is the **Tecate brewery** which has a beer garden offering a free beer and tours.

Coming into Mexico here from the U.S. is pretty easy. It's probably the best crossing for RVs coming south onto the Baja. To pick up the essential FMMs (tourist permits) we suggest that you park on the U.S. side and walk over to get them at the crossing, it's much easier to find a parking place on the U.S. side. Many people overnight on the U.S. side, leave the RV in a campground, drive their tow car to the crossing for the card, and then return to pick up the RV and cross.

Once you do cross with your RV just drive down the hill four blocks to Av. Juárez (the street just before the park), jog one block left, and then turn right and head south, you're on the road to Ensenada. Watch carefully for stop signs, police in this town can be predatory.

Crossing back into the U.S. is pretty easy too. The line to cross the border north-bound is on a road along the border fence east of the crossing. To get on it you must travel east of the city to a new entrance road. It's about .6 miles (1 km) east of the crossing and accessible from Mex 2 (not the toll road). Turn north toward the border at the sign for Garita Tecate, the road name is Manuel Moreno. When you reach the fence you'll turn left. Get in the left lane, big RVs can make the necessary turn into the gate area much more easily from the left lane. If you wait too long you won't be able to get over. This setup is much better than in the past with less chance of running

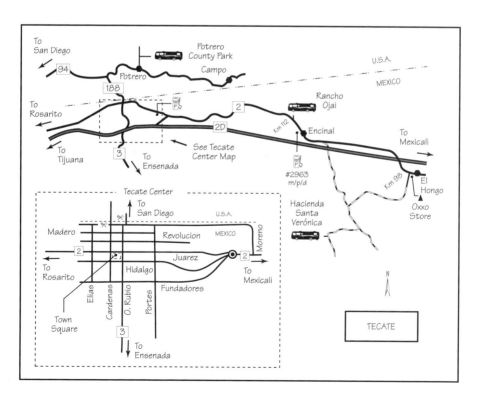

afoul of the local police. Once across you'll need to find a place to park and go back to the Migración office to turn in your FMMs. The crossing is open every day from 5 a.m. to 11 p.m.

Tecate Campgrounds

POTRERO COUNTY PARK *(Open All Year)*

    Address: 24800 Potrero Park Dr., Potrero, CA 91963
    Telephone: (Reservations) (877) 565-3600,
                     (Info) (619) 478-5212
    Website: www.sdparks.org

GPS Location: 32.61278 N, 116.59472, 2,300 Ft.

This is a good campground on the U.S. side of the border near Tecate. If you are headed south and want to get an early start in the morning consider spending the night here. It is only 5 miles (8 km) from Tecate, the small nearby town of Potrero offers a small country store. Another nearby town, Campo, has an interesting railroad museum.

There are 39 back-in sites to 40 feet with electrical and water hookups set under oak trees for shade and also 7 tent sites. Large RVs will find plenty of room in most RV sites. Drives are paved and so are the sites. Picnic tables and fire pits are provided. Areas are also set aside for tents and there are hot water showers (extra charge). There is a dump station. Other amenities include an outside wash-up area for dishes, playground, pavilion, and a nature trail. Reservations are accepted but usually not necessary during the winter season.

Follow Hwy. 94 from San Diego toward Tecate. Zero your odometer where Hwy. 188 to Tecate cuts off to the right but continue straight. Drive 2.3 miles (3.7 km) to the outskirts of Potrero and turn left. Then after another 0.3 miles (0.5 km) turn right on the entrance road to the campground.

RANCHO OJAI *(Open All Year)*

    Address: Km 112 Carretera Libre Mexicali-Tecate,
                     Tecate, B.C., México
    Telephone: (665) 655-3014 or (665) 110-8351
    Fax: (665) 655-3015
    Email: reservations@campinginbaja.com
    Website: www.campinginbaja.com

GPS Location: 32.55917 N, 116.43611 W, 3,000 Ft.

Rancho Ojai is something a little different in Baja campgrounds. This is a former working ranch located in the rolling hills just east of Tecate off Mex 2. It's about two miles from the U.S. border as the crow flies. The facilities are modern and nicely done. This is normally a summer destination, the area is known for its mild summer weather, but winters have an occasional frost.

This was formerly an award-winning KOA, for several years the only KOA in Mexico. KOA no longer operates in Mexico but this is still an outstanding park. There are 36 RV sites with full hookups with 30 and 50-amp outlets, sewer, and water. Most are large flat pull-thrus suitable for large RVs. There are also tent camping sites. The tiled restrooms are new and clean with hot water showers. The ranch offers a ranch-style clubhouse, a barbecue area, swimming pool, spa, grocery shop, sports areas for volley ball and horseshoes, mini-golf, bicycle rentals and a children's playground. Wi-Fi can be used at the clubhouse. The campground is fenced and there is 24-hour security.

The Rancho is located about 13 miles (21 km) east of Tecate on the north side of the free highway near the Km 112 marker. It is not accessible from the toll highway. There is a stone arch entrance near the highway and you can see the camping area across the valley.

HACIENDA SANTA VERÓNICA *(Open All Year)*

Address:	Blvd. Agua Caliente No. 4558, C-2 despacho 3 y 4
	Torres de Agua Caliente, CP 22420 Tijuana, B.C.,
	México
Telephone:	(664) 686-4110 (Reservations), (665) 521-0017 (On Site)
Email:	haciendasantaveronica@hotmail.ca
Website:	www.hsantaveronica.com

GPS Location: 32.45944 N, 116.36306 W, 3,000 Ft.

Slightly farther east of Tecate than Rancho Ojai is Hacienda Santa Verónica. To get there you must negotiate a rough and partially paved back road but once you've reached the campground you're likely to want to spend some time. This is a 5,000 acre rancho. It is described in its own brochures as rustic, but other than the almost no-hookup camping area it is really surprisingly polished. The rancho is very popular with off-road motorcycle riders and also offers quite a few amenities: rental rooms, a swimming pool, tennis courts, a nice restaurant and bar, horseback riding, and occasionally even a bullfight. This is a popular summer destination, in the winter things are pretty quiet except on weekends.

The camping area is a grassy meadow with big oak trees for shade. Spaces are unmarked, you camp where you want to. Any size RV will find room. A few low-amp electrical outlets are near the restroom and picnic area but were not in service when we visited. There are marginal restrooms with toilets but no showers near the camping area and warm showers near the pool.

To find the hacienda head east on Mex 2 from the Rancho Ojai to the small town of El Hongo, a distance of 8.7 miles (14 km) from Rancho Ojai. Near the center of town there is a small paved road heading south through the village, it is marked with an easy-to-miss Hacienda Verónica sign and just before an Oxxo store. The paved road soon turns to dirt. After 1.1 miles (1.8 km) the road curves right and leaves town. You'll reach a Y after 4.7 miles (7.6 km) take the right fork and you'll reach the gate in another 1.5 miles (2.4 km).

TECATE TO ENSENADA ON HIGHWAY 3
67 Miles (108 Km), 2 Hours

See the information in the Tecate section just above about crossing the border either way.

Highway 3 is a good two-lane paved road that runs 63 miles (102 km) south from Tecate to meet with the four-lane coastal road just before it enters Ensenada. The route is suitable for larger RVs and the road is recently widened and straightened.

WINE TASTING IN THE GUADALUPE VALLEY

Some 45 miles (73 km) south of Tecate the road passes through the **Guadalupe Valley**, Mexico's premier wine-growing region. There are now over 100 wineries in this area, many are signed off the main highway. There are also a lot of excellent restaurants. It can be difficult to search out the best places so a good guidebook is essential. See our section titled *Travel Library* in Chapter 2 for some recommendations.

Tecate to Ensenada on Highway 3 Campground

RANCHO SORDO MUDO *(Deaf Ranch) (Open All Year)*

Address:	PO Box 1376, Chula Vista, CA 91912 or Apdo. 1468, Ensenada, B.C., Mex.
Telephone:	(646) 155-2223
Email:	ranchosordomudo@hotmail.com
Website:	www.ranchosordomudo.org

GPS Location: 32.11186 N, 116.54689 W, 1,200 Ft.

If you decide to follow the inland route on Mex 3 south from Tecate to Ensenada you might decide to spend the night at Rancho Sordo Mudo, about 24 miles (39 km) north of Ensenada in the Guadalupe Valley. The ranch is actually a school for deaf children, the campground was originally constructed for the use of visitors helping at the school. The income from the RV park goes to a good cause and the surroundings are very pleasant. There is no fixed price, donations are accepted.

There are 27 pull-thru and back-in spaces in a grassy field, they have electric and water hookups. Oranges grow on the trees between sites, you're welcome to help

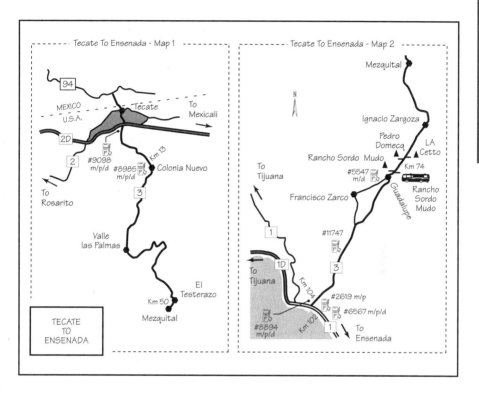

yourself to a few. When we visited a gift shop was under construction and there are plans to have a full-time manager living in the campground. This is a decent campground in an increasingly popular area and it is well-signed on Mex 3. Driving south start watching as you pass the Domecq winery, the campground will be on your left right next to the highway just after the Km 74 marker. Heading north it is even easier to spot just north of the village of Guadalupe.

ENSENADA TO SAN FELIPE ON HIGHWAY 3
117 Miles (189 Km), 3.5 Hours

Highway 3 also connects Ensenada with San Felipe. The intersection where Mex 3 heads west for Ensenada is 30 miles (48 km) north of San Felipe near the Km 141 marker.

This is a two lane paved road suitable for RVs driven carefully at moderate speeds. It climbs up and over the mountainous spine of the peninsula so you should expect many grades and curves. The highest point is at about 4,000 feet.

Along the way the highway passes through a farming area known as Valle de Trinidad. Small dirt roads head north and south connecting with some camping destinations for those with smaller high-clearance vehicles. They are described below.

BEAUTIFUL SCENERY AT LAGUNA HANSON

Ensenada to San Felipe on Highway 3 Campgrounds

LAGUNA HANSON *(Open All Year)* $$$

Telephone: (646) 554-5470 (Off-site Information)

GPS Location: 32.04243 N, 115.92206 W, 5,200 Ft.

Laguna Hanson is primitive camping area in the Parque Nacional Constitución de 1857. It is located in the dry mountains to the northeast of Ensenada and is known for its remote location and excellent birding. The area is covered with pines and there are numerous granite boulders and rock outcrops. In winter there's sometimes snow.

The park has a number of camping areas scattered around the two shallow, muddy lakes. These are groups of unimproved parking sites under pine trees, most have a nearby outhouse. Visitors to the park must pay a fee to the rangers who are usually on-site. Although this is a park the area is also used for grazing cattle so you may have company.

From near Km 55 on Mex 3 between Ensenada and San Felipe (about 50 km east of Ensenada) drive north on the signed road. This is a Type 2 (see *Backroad Driving in Chapter 2* for the definition) sand and dirt road. If you zero your odometer when you leave the highway you'll come to the first fork at 2.8 miles (4.5 km), go left. At 3.9 miles (6.3 km) there's a second fork, this time go right. At 13.4 miles (21.6 km) there's a third fork, follow the main road to the left. At 16.3 miles (26.3 km) there's a fourth fork, go left. You'll pass through Rancho Amona which has a small store and restaurant. You'll enter the park at 19 miles (30.6 km). At another fork at 19.4 miles (31.3 km) go left and at mile 20.1 (32.4 km) you'll reach a collection of buildings at

Laguna Minor where you'll probably find a ranger and can pay your fee of 100 pesos for a day visit (for two people) or 150 pesos for overnight camping. The larger lake and campgrounds are just beyond.

MIKE'S SKY RANCHO *(Open All Year)*

$$ Δ

> **Address:** PO Box 1948, Imperial Beach, CA 92032
> **Telephone:** (664) 681-5514 (Tijuana)

GPS Location: 31.10962 N, 115.63587 W, 3,900 Ft.

Mike's is a well-known remote rancho popular with off-road enthusiasts. There are hotel rooms, a family-style restaurant and bar, a swimming pool, restrooms with hot showers, plenty of room to park and camp (no defined spaces), and many trails in the surrounding area suitable for off road driving and riding. From Mike's a rough Type 3 (see *Backroad Driving* in Chapter 2 for the definition) track climbs over a ridge to access Rancho El Coyote (see page 91) and the access road to San Pedro Mártir National Park. It's 12 miles (19 km) to Rancho El Coyote. Ask at the ranch about the condition of this road before attempting it.

Easiest access to Mike's is from Mex 3 near Km 137, about 82 miles (133 km) east of Ensenada. Follow the signed sandy Type 2 road (see *Backroad Driving* in Chapter 2 for the definition) southward. At 3 miles (4.8 km) there's a Y, stay right. At 11.2 miles (18.1 km) there's a Y, stay left on the main road. At 13.6 miles (21.9 km) there's a Y, go left following the sign for the rancho. At 16 miles (25.8 km) there's a Y, stay right. You'll reach Mike's at 19.9 miles (32.1 km).

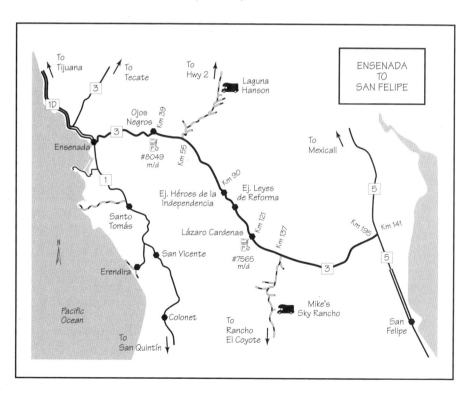

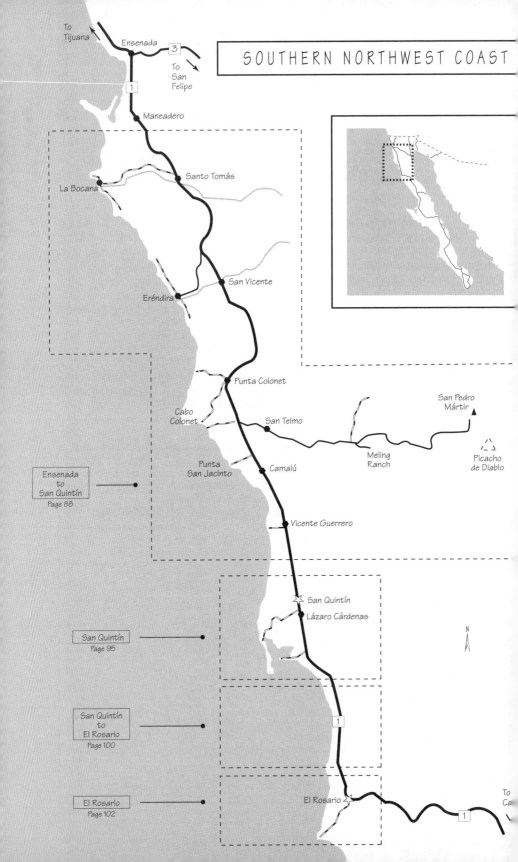

SOUTHERN NORTHWEST COAST

To
Tijuana

Ensenada

3

To
San
Felipe

1

Maneadero

Santo Tomás

La Bocana

San Vicente

Eréndira

Punta Colonet

Cabo
Colonet

San Telmo

San Pedro
Mártir

Punta
San Jacinto

Camalú

Meling
Ranch

Picacho
de Diablo

Vicente Guerrero

Ensenada
to
San Quintín
Page 88

San Quintín

Lázaro Cárdenas

N

San Quintín
Page 95

San Quintín
to
El Rosario
Page 100

1

El Rosario
Page 102

El Rosario

1

To
Ca

Chapter 5
Southern Northwest Coast

INTRODUCTION

South of Maneadero the character of the Baja changes considerably. There are far fewer people and less traffic. In the beginning the road climbs into coastal hill country, much of it is covered with greenery. One of the valleys you will cross is the Santo Tomás Valley, known for its vineyards. After some time the road flattens out and runs along a coastal plain. There is much irrigated farming in this fast-growing region with occasional roads toward the ocean which is out of sight to the west. Near San Quintín dirt roads lead west to Bahía San Quintín, a sheltered estuary offering a place to launch boats and also some history. Finally the road climbs to cross a barren mesa and then descends steeply into the town of El Rosario.

Enjoy the hustle and bustle of the fast-growing farming towns that often line the road. At the south end of this section you will be turning inland and driving through some of the Baja's most remote countryside.

Highlights

The **Santo Tomás Valley**, about 22 miles (35 km) south of Ensenada, is another of Mexico's wine regions. Many of the grapes from this area go to the Santo Tomás Winery, Mexico's largest, which is located in Ensenada. The ruins of the old **Misión Santo Tomás de Aquino** are located near the Balneario El Palomar.

Bahía San Quintín, about 110 miles (177 km) south of Ensenada, is a popular fishing destination. The bay provides a protected place to launch boats and the fishing outside the bay is excellent. Wide sandy beaches are easy to reach from the highway just to the south of Bahía San Quintín. In the 1890s an English company failed in an attempt to develop an agricultural town in the area, remains of a pier and cemetery are all that remain.

Inland from this stretch of road is the **Parque Nacional Sierra de San Pedro Mártir** (Mountains of San Pedro Mártir National Park). Access to this high pine country is via a long, steep, and fairly narrow paved road. See this chapter's *Backroad Adventures* for information about visiting this park.

One hundred and forty-six miles (235 km) south of Ensenada the road turns sharply left and heads inland. The small town here, **El Rosario**, is traditionally the spot to get fuel and prepare for the isolated road to the south.

Roads and Fuel Availability

Much of the road in this section of the book is built to the narrow Baja Peninsula standard of just over 19 feet wide. Additionally, there are seldom any shoulders. That means that all drivers much be cautious, particularly those driving large RVs. See the *Roads and Driving in Mexico* section in the *Details, Details, Details* chapter.

This section of Mex 1 is marked by kilometer markers that begin in Ensenada and end at Lázaro Cárdenas near Bahía San Quintín with Km 196. There the numbers start over and reach Km 59 in El Rosario.

Gasoline is not hard to find in this part of the Baja. There are several stations in Maneadero and also stations in most small towns along the route. The stations south of Maneadero, the distances between them, and the type of fuel sold are as follows: **Santo Tomás**, 18 miles (29 km) gas; **San Vicente**, 24 miles (39 km), gas and diesel; two stations in **Punta Colonet**, 23 miles (37 km), gas and diesel; three stations in **Camalú**, 12 miles (19 km), gas and diesel; **Emiliano Zapata**, 5 miles (8 km), gas and diesel; **Vicente Guerrero**, 3 miles (5 km), gas and diesel; two stations in **San Quintín**, 5 miles (8 km), gas and diesel; three stations in **Lázaro Cárdenas**, 3 miles (5 km), gas and diesel; **Ejido El Papalote**, 4 miles (6 km), gas and diesel; **Rancho los Pinos**, 4 miles (6 km), gas and diesel; **El Pabellón**, 2 miles (4 km), gas and diesel; and **El Rosario**, 27 miles (44 km), gas and diesel.

A word of warning is in order about fuel. It is very important to fill up with gas or diesel either near San Quintín or in El Rosario at the south end of this section. There will probably be no fuel available from filling stations until you reach Villa Jesús María, some 22 miles (35 km) north of Guerrero Negro. This is a gas gap of 195 miles (315 km). There are old Pemex filling stations at Cataviña and at the Bahía de L.A. Junction but they have been closed down and the pumps removed. Individuals with drums of gasoline in the back of their pickups often sell fuel at these stations, but we wouldn't want to have to count on these guys being around if we were in dire need. The Hotel Mision Cataviña in Cataviña also has a pump for gasoline but it is usually not open. In an emergency you should stop and ask, they might have some fuel and be willing to open up. There is also now fuel in Bahía de los Angeles, 39 miles (63 km) east of the Bahía de L.A. Junction.

Sightseeing

The Parque Nacional Sierra de San Pedro Mártir is located high in the sierra east of the highway. It is an area of pine forest that is so free from human interference that there is actually an astronomical observatory at 9,300 feet in the park. You can drive to the observatory, tours are given from 10 am to 1 pm. Picacho Diablo, the highest mountain in Baja California at 10,150 feet, is accessible to climbers from the park. See *Backroad Adventures* in this chapter for more information about this road. See also the campground listings for *Parque Nacional Sierra de San Pedro Mártir, Meling Ranch,* and *Rancho El Coyote* in the *Ensenada to San Quintín Campgrounds* listing.

The ruins of several Dominican missions can be viewed as you travel down the peninsula in this section. Since all were constructed of adobe they have suffered from the occasional rain over the years and give the appearance of having melted. At Santo Tomás the ruins of Misíon Santo Tomás de Aquino are actually located on the grounds of a campground, the Balneario El Palomar. Ask for directions for finding them at the office. The ruins of Misíon San Vicente Ferrer are located in the town of San Vicente, about 43 miles (69 km) south of the La Bufadora cutoff in Maneadero. To find them take the dirt road west from about Km 88. Near Vicente Guerrero is the Misíon Santo Domingo. It is accessible by taking a road east at about Km 169 to the village of Santo Domingo. Finally, near El Rosario there are the ruins of Misíon el Rosario. The directions for finding the mission can be found in the *Backroad Adventures* section below.

The late 19th century wheat-farming scheme at San Quintín left a few remnants that you might want to track down. East of the bay is the restored grist mill and southeast around the bay is the old pier. Just south of the latter is the Old English Cemetery.

Beaches and Water Sports

There are miles of long sandy beaches along this section of coast. The primary activities are surfing and surf fishing. Road access is actually not bad, see *Backroad Adventures* below for some ideas. Since many of the back roads lead to beaches in this area we've discussed the attractions in that section. Water temperatures along the coast are cool but that just makes the fishing better.

South of the mouth of the San Quintín estuary is a long beach called **Playa Santa María** at the north end and **Playa Pabellón** farther south. Both surfing and fishing are popular, access is from the Cielito Lindo and the two El Pabellón RV parks, see the campground descriptions below for directions.

Fishing

From Punta Banda at the north end of the area covered by this chapter and south for about 200 miles upwelling water from the ocean depths brings nutrients that make fishing near the shore extremely good. The problem with this area is that it is unprotected and not really very safe for small boats. Launching sites for larger boats are scarce.

One way around this problem is to beach cast. Surf fishing is good along much of the coast. Another solution is to hire a panga and guide to take you out. You can do this at Puerto San Isidro near Eréndira, Puerto Santo Tomás near La Bocana, or at San Quintín at the launch near the Don Eddie's Landing RV Park or the Cielito Lindo, also an RV park.

If you do decide to use your own boat the best launch site is San Quintín. However, from there you must find your way out through the weeds of the estuary, not easy to do for someone without local knowledge. There are also poor launch ramps at Puerto San Isidro and Puerto Santo Tomás that might be usable for small boats if the tide and weather are just right.

Backroad Adventures

See the *Backroad Driving* section of *Chapter 2 - Details, Details, Details* for essential information about driving off the main highway on the Baja and for a definition of road type classifications used below.

In the area covered by this chapter there are many small roads branching off the highway to the west and east. Most of those to the west are headed for the coast, one to the east is headed up into the Sierra de San Pedro Mártir and the national park there. There are quite a number of people living between the highway and the coast, that means that there are a great number of roads of varying quality. Many of them are farm roads but they often reach the coast in places that offer good surf fishing and surfing. High clearance vehicles, especially with four-wheel drive are your best bet. The condition of these roads changes, we advise getting local information about road conditions before heading out.

Some places to try roads like this are as follows. In Santo Tomás near Km 51 a road leads to the coast at Punta San José and southwards all the way to Eréndira. The area is popular for surf fishing and surfing. There is also a web of roads west of Punta Colonet. They reach the long beach at San Antonio del Mar which is good for surf fishing and also Bahía Colonet, Punta Colonet, and Punta San Telmo. Surfing is popular south of the points, particularly south of Punta San Telmo which is widely known as "Quatro Casas". Consider these roads to be Type 3 roads unless you have local knowledge. More possibilities follow.

From Km 47 Near Santo Tomás - One and nine tenths miles (3.1 km) north of the El Palomar campground a gravel road goes along the Santo Tomás valley to **La Bocana** and then north along the coast to **Puerto Santo Tomás**. La Bocana is at the mouth of the Santo Tomás River and is 16.1 miles (26.0 km) from Mex 1. Puerto Santo Tomás is about 2.6 miles (4.1 km) to the north. This is a Type 2 road. See also the campground listing for *La Bocana Camping* in the *Ensenada to San Quintín Campgrounds* section.

From Km 78 between Santo Tomás and San Vicente - A paved but sometimes potholed road leads about 11 miles (18 km) to the coast at the ejido town of **Eréndira**. The road continues up the coast to **Puerto San Isidro** and beyond. Eventually it crosses the coastal mountains to reach Santo Tomás. The paved road to Eréndira is OK for any RV, beyond Eréndira the road is unpaved and usually Type 2 and may become a Type 3 as it crosses the mountains. See also the campground listings for *Coyote Cal's Hostel*, and *Coastal Camping North of Eréndira* in the *Ensenada to San Quintín Campgrounds* section.

From Km 141 North of San Quintín - About 34 miles (55 km) north of San Quintín a road goes east to San Telmo, the **Meling Ranch**, and the **Parque Nacional Sierra de San Pedro Mártir**. The road is paved all the way to the park. The first 31 miles (50 km) as far as the Meling Ranch cutoff is usually a Type 1 road. Beyond the ranch to the park entrance gate at 53 miles (85 km) the road is narrow and steep and is a Type 2 road (but OK for low clearance vehicles) despite being paved. The road continues to an astronomical observatory at 62 miles (100 km). You should be aware that the road may be closed due to snow in the winter. See also the campground listings for *Parque Nacional Sierra de San Pedro Mártir, Meling Ranch,* and *Rancho El Coyote Meling* in the *Ensenada to San Quintín Campgrounds* section.

From the southern border of the town of Lázaro Cárdenas - A road runs past **Bahía Falsa** to the coast where there are oyster farm and the village of La Chorera. The distance to La Chorera is 11 miles (16 km) along a graded gravel and sand road that is normally a Type 2 road. Bahía Falsa is the outer bay of the San Quintín estuary, the road takes you around the north end of Bahía San Quintín and past the volcanic cones that protect the bay. There are other less developed sand and dirt roads along the outer peninsula. The outer coast is a popular surfing destination. We list one camping area in La Chorera.

From the 90-degree turn in the town of El Rosario - Heading south the highway takes a sharp left. If you go right here, then almost immediately left you will cross the river and within a mile reach the village of El Rosario de Abajo (Lower

SOUTHERN NORTHWEST COAST

SWEEPING VIEWS FROM THE PAVED ROAD TO SAN PEDRO MÁRTIR

El Rosario). The ruins of **Misión el Rosario** are in this town on the right side of the road. Roads lead about 10 miles (16 km) out to the coast from here to Punta Baja and points south along the Bahía Rosario. The sandy beach along the bay is a popular surf-fishing location. This is usually a Type 3 road. The road is suitable for high-clearance vehicles only, the river crossing right at El Rosario is sometimes a problem as the bridges tend to wash out. Fortunately you will reach this less than a mile from the highway so you won't waste much time if the crossing is not possible.

THE ROUTES, TOWNS, AND CAMPGROUNDS

ENSENADA TO SAN QUINTÍN
116 Miles (187 Km), 4 Hours

Mex 1 as it leaves Ensenada runs through some 7 miles (11 km) of suburbs until it reaches the town of Maneadero. Toward the north end of Maneadero is a stop light and the road west out to La Bufadora. You'll find several campgrounds along the La Bufadora road, they are described in the preceding chapter.

Leaving the south edge of Maneadero the road climbs into brush-covered hills. This is a scenic section of road but exercise caution because the road is busy, hilly, and only two lanes. Fifteen miles (24 km) after leaving Maneadero the road descends into the Santo Tomás Valley.

For a few miles the road runs along the valley floor which is used to grow grapes and olives. Then it once again climbs steeply into the rolling hills. You'll pass through the small farming towns of San Vicente and Punta Colonet.

After Punta Colonet the road runs along a broad coastal plain which is covered with irrigated farmland. The ocean is occasionally visible in the distance to the right. It's really not far away and is accessible via the occasional rough dirt side road. Along this section are the villages of Camalú, Vicente Guerrero, San Quintín, and Lázaro Cárdenas. These last two towns almost seem to be one as they merge into one another along the highway, they and the bay that almost adjoins them to the west form the area that for the sake of convenience is often called San Quintín.

Ensenada to San Quintín Campgrounds

LAS CAÑADAS CAMPAMENTO *(Open All Year)*

> **Address:**   Km 31.5 de la Carretera Ensenada-San Quintín
> **Telephone:**   (646) 153-1055 or (800) 027-3828
> **Email:**   info@lascanadas.com
> **Website:**   www.lascanadas.com

GPS Location: 31.66181 N, 116.51887 W, 400 Ft.

This is a large modern swimming resort or balneario which caters to the crowds from Ensenada and Tijuana to the north. There are swimming pools, water slides, pedal boats, a fishing lake, zip lines, teepee rentals and a store. It also is a campground. There are seven full hookup sites suitable to any size RV. These have 20-amp power, water and sewer hookups as well as large patios, picnic tables, and barbeques and are

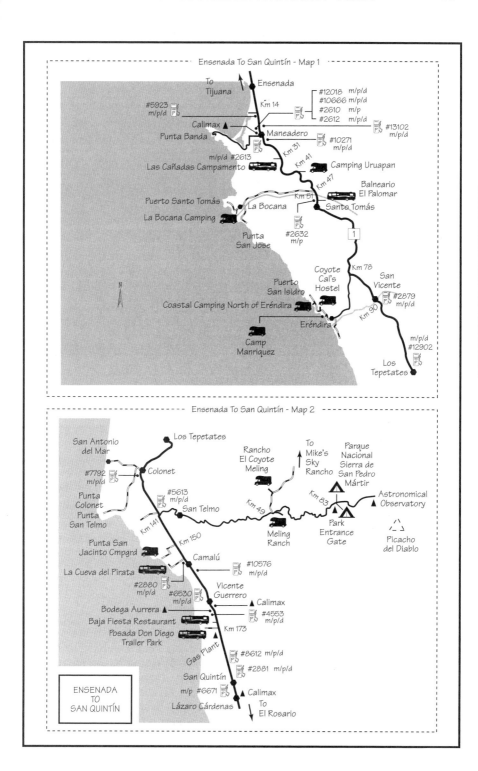

Ensenada To San Quintín - Map 1

To Tijuana
Ensenada
Km 14
#12018 m/p/d
#10666 m/p/d
#2610 m/p
#2612 m/p/d
#5923 m/p/d
Calimax
Punta Banda
Maneadero
#10271 m/p/d
#13102 m/p/d
m/p/d #2613
Km 31
Las Cañadas Campamento
Km 41
Camping Uruapan
Km 47
Balneario El Palomar
Km 51
Puerto Santo Tomás
La Bocana
Santo Tomás
La Bocana Camping
Punta San Jose
#2632 m/p
1
N
Coyote Cal's Hostel
Km 78
San Vicente
Puerto San Isidro
#2879 m/p/d
Coastal Camping North of Eréndira
Km 90
Eréndira
Camp Manriquez
m/p/d #12902
Los Tepetates

Ensenada To San Quintín - Map 2

Los Tepetates
San Antonio del Mar
Rancho El Coyote Meling
To Mike's Sky Rancho
Parque Nacional Sierra de San Pedro Mártir
#7792 m/p/d
Colonet
Astronomical Observatory
Punta Colonet
#5613 m/p/d
San Telmo
Km 49
Km 83
Park Entrance Gate
Picacho del Diablo
Punta San Telmo
Km 141
Meling Ranch
Punta San Jacinto Cmpgrd
Km 150
Camalú
La Cueva del Pirata
#2880 m/p/d
#6530 m/p/d
Vicente Guerrero
#10576 m/p/d
Bodega Aurrera
Calimax
Baja Fiesta Restaurant
#4553 m/p/d
Posada Don Diego Trailer Park
Km 173
Gas Plant
#8612 m/p/d
#2881 m/p/d
ENSENADA TO SAN QUINTÍN
San Quintín
m/p #6671
Calimax
Lázaro Cárdenas
To El Rosario

SOUTHERN NORTHWEST COAST

SOUTHERN NORTHWEST COAST

THE MODERN FULL HOOKUP RV PARK AT LAS CAÑADAS

located above and away from the crowded water park. There is also tent camping on grass in large areas nearer the water park. Restrooms for the tent camping area offer hot showers. The pools are closed October 22 to March 15 but the camping stays open. There's a small grocery store at the entrance. This facility struggles with how to charge RVers, particularly the ones with no interest in the swimming and other recreational facilities. For an RV camping-only rate you must arrive after 6 p.m. and leave before 9 a.m.

The balneario is located directly off Mex 1 some 3 miles (5 km) south of Maneadero near Km 31.

CAMPING URUAPAN *(Open All Year)* $$ △ ⬚
   Address: Mex 1, Km 41

   GPS Location: 31.61806 N, 116.45194 W, 600 Ft.

This is a small rustic camping area and river swimming hole (very shallow) run by the ejido in Uruapan. The two parking/camping areas are shaded with big trees, they and the uneven ground make use by RVs over about 25 feet in length impractical. There is a restroom building with flush toilets. Much of the time the campground is unattended but someone comes by to collect. There is no security and we do not recommend camping here with just one RV. The campground is on the east side of Mex 1 near Km 41 some 8 miles (15 km) south of Maneadero.

🚐 LA BOCANA CAMPING *(Open All Year)*

GPS Location: 31.53681 N, 116.65842 W, Near Sea Level

This is a simple campground near the beach at La Bocana, west of Santo Tomás. The village there is just a few buildings, then the road turns north to follow the cliffs for a few miles to Puerto Santo Tomás.

The campground is a grassy field, the only amenities are outhouses. A nice sandy beach is nearby. Some people also camp a short distance past the formal camping area where the road climbs to a bluff overlooking the ocean.

The road to La Bocana and Puerto Santo Tomás leaves Mex 1 at Km 47, about 1.9 miles (3.1 km) north of Balneario El Palomar in Santo Tomás. It's a gravel Type 2 road as far as La Bocana, the distance is 16.1 miles (26.0 km). See *Backroad Driving* in Chapter 2 for an explanation of road classifications in this book.

🚐 BALNEARIO EL PALOMAR *(Open Winter Only)*

Address:	Km 51 al Sur de Ensenada, Delegación de Santo Tomás
Telephone:	(646) 153-8002
Email:	vivepalomar@gmail.com
Website:	balnearioelpalomar.com

GPS Location: 31.55667 N, 116.41194 W, 600 Ft.

Balnearios (swimming resorts) are very popular in Mexico, they often make a good place to camp. This is a good example although it is much less popular now that Las Cañadas (see above) has opened.

The El Palomar has six pull-thrus large enough for RVs to about 40 feet (but take a look at the steep entrance ramp before trying to enter in a large RV) and 20 or so very small back-in spaces. All have 15-amp outlets, sewer, water, patios and barbecues. Many also have picnic tables. Two restroom buildings are provided, they have hot showers. There are two swimming pools near the camping area and a small lake and water slide about a half-mile away. Swimming areas are only open in summer. There's also a small zoo, tennis courts, and large areas for picnicking. Across the street in the main building there is a store, a restaurant, and a small gas station. Wi-Fi is only available in the restaurant. The store has a good collection of Mexican handicrafts. You should be aware that this is a very popular place with people from Ensenada on weekends during the summer and on holidays. At other times this place seems to be very, very quiet.

The El Palomar is at the north entrance to the town of Santo Tomás about 30 miles (49 km) south of Ensenada on Mex 1. The office is on the west side of the road and the campground on the east.

🚐 CAMP MANRIQUEZ *(Open All Year)*

GPS Location: 31.28888 N, 116.40069 W, Near Sea Level

Camp Manriquez is a backyard campground along the coast just beyond Eréndira. Sites are placed right above a small beach, a pleasant location. They are not delineated, you park or pitch where you want. Facilities are limited to an outhouse and there is firewood for sale. This is a small place with only room for a few vans, pick-ups, or tents.

To reach the campground leave Mex 1 just south of the Km 78 marker on the road toward Eréndira. Follow the paved road for 10.7 miles (17.3 km) to Eréndira. Continue straight through town and the road becomes gravel. It reaches the ocean and turns right. About a mile beyond that turn, 12.9 miles (20.8 km) from Mex 1, you'll see a sign for camping on the left.

COYOTE CAL'S HOSTEL *(Open All Year)*

Telephone:	(646) 154-4080
Email:	bajabuddies@coyotecals.com
Website:	www.coyotecals.com

GPS Location: 31.29401 N, 116.41232 W, 100 Ft.

Coyote Cal's is a hostel located overlooking the coast to the north of Eréndira. It has both private and dorm rooms, a bar, cooking facilities, and bathrooms with showers. It also has an area out front for tent campers and enough room for a small camping van or two. Campers have full use of the cooking area, bathroom facilities, and bar.

To reach the campground leave Mex 1 just south of the Km 78 marker on the road toward Eréndira. Follow the paved road for 10.7 miles (17.3 km) to Eréndira. Continue straight through town and the road becomes gravel. It reaches the ocean and turns right. About two miles beyond that turn, 13.8 miles (22.3 km) from Mex 1, you'll see the sign for Cal's on the right as the road make a sharp left.

COASTAL CAMPING NORTH OF ERÉNDIRA *(Open All Year)*

GPS Location: 31.29401 N, 116.41528 W, Near Sea Level

Once you get beyond Coyote Cal's (see above for directions) the road follows the coast for several miles. There are numerous places to pull off on side roads and boondock above the rocky shore. While this is generally a quiet area there's no security and no safety guarantees. It's best to camp only in groups.

PARQUE NACIONAL SIERRA DE SAN PEDRO MÁRTIR *(Open All Year)*

GPS Location: 31.00028 N, 115.55694 W, 8,200 Ft.

Parque Nacional Sierra de San Pedro Mártir is located high on the mountainous spine of the peninsula. See also the information about the park under *Sightseeing* and *Backroad Adventures* above.

This is a large and mostly undeveloped park. It's in a pine forest at the altitude of 8,000 to 9,000 feet so it's very cool in winter and often has snow. It's primarily a summer destination. There is a road through the park up to the observatory and also rough tracks requiring high clearance and sometimes four-wheel drive to other areas of the park, also lots of hiking. You can camp in several designated areas, the only camping facilities are outhouses, tables, and raised barbeque grills. Most campsites are near the entrance gate where there are also some buildings and the ranger's offices.

The road to the park begins near Km 141 about 34 miles (55.5 km) north of San Quintín. The entire road is now paved. RVs to 35 feet can travel the road as far as the Meling Ranch cutoff at about 31 miles (50 km). Beyond the ranch to the park entrance gate at 53 miles (85 km) the road is narrow and sometimes very steep letting only smaller camping vehicles (vans and pickup campers) and cars comfortably reach the park. The entrance fee in 2017 was 64 pesos per person per day, that includes camping. Inside the park the road continues to an astronomical observatory at 65 miles (106 km). You should be aware that the road may be closed due to snow in the winter.

RANCHO EL COYOTE MELING *(Open All Year)*

Telephone:	(616) 166-0086 (México) or (619) 390-0905 (U.S.)
Email:	ranchoelcoyotemeling1950@gmail.com
Website:	www.ranchoelcoyote.com

GPS Location: 31.04019 N, 115.76382 W, 2,800 Ft.

Owned by the same family as the Meling Ranch (see next entry), Rancho El Coyote is very similar but is some distance off the paved road.

This ranch has tent camping on grass as well as RV camping in their parking area. It has restrooms with hot showers as well as a nice swimming pool and a restaurant. Horses are available for rent. From El Coyote a Type 3 track (see page 19 for road classification information) leads 12 miles (19 km) to Mike's Sky Rancho. Check at El Coyote for information about the road condition before heading out that way.

To reach the rancho follow the road to Parque Nacional Sierra de San Pedro Mártir from near Km 141 of Mex 1. At about Km 49 turn north on a dirt road marked for Rancho El Coyote. Follow this Type 2 (see *Backroad Driving* in Chapter 2 for an explanation of road classifications in this book) dirt road for 4.6 miles (7.4 km). Turn left into the ranch access road, the ranch is .4 miles (.6 km) from the entrance.

MELING RANCH *(Open All Year)*

Telephone:	(646) 120-2590 (Reservations)
Email:	info@ranchomeling.com
Website:	www.ranchomeling.com

GPS Location: 30.97210 N, 115.74563 W, 2,000 Ft.

Meling is one of the oldest guest ranches on the Baja. The ranch sits in a broad valley and is easily accessed from the paved road up to Parque Nacional Sierra de San Pedro Mártir. Tent camping is on a nice lawn near a swimming pool. RV camping is in the large dirt parking lot nearby. There are no hookups but there is a nice modern restroom building with hot showers as well as a swimming pool and family-style restaurant. With 24-hour notice horses are available for rent. While the ranch location is before the steepest sections of the road up to the park it's still not a major highway, the access route to get here is best for RVs no longer than 35 feet. This can be a good place to leave moderately large rigs while driving a tow vehicle up to the park.

The road to Parque Nacional Sierra de San Pedro Mártir and the Meling Ranch leaves Mex 1 near Km 141, about 34 miles (55.5 km) north of San Quintín. It's a paved road. The entrance for Meling Ranch is at 31 miles (50 km). There's a mile long dirt road to the gate.

THE "SHIPWRECK" IS A FAVORITE PLACE WITH SURFERS

PUNTA SAN JACINTO CAMPGROUND *(Open All Year)*

GPS Location: 30.86122 N, 116.16660 W, Near Sea Level

This is a popular surfing location. There's a wrecked ship just off the beach, surfers call the location "Shipwreck".

The campground is a fenced compound with many permanently located trailers and small cottages owned by surfers. There's a watchman on site living in an old trailer near the entrance, he'll collect your money. Visitors can park to the north of the permanent area near the beach. There are a few fire rings and not much else. It is possible to travel out here and park in any size RV although visitors are mostly surfers in smaller vehicles. Facilities are limited to pit toilets, cold showers may be available.

To reach the campground leave the highway near Km 150 and head west on a rough dirt road. At 1.2 miles (1.9 km) you'll enter a small village and see the Playa sign pointing left. Follow the sign and in another 0.2 mile (0.3 km) another sign will take you right. The road will take you out of town to the beach area and then bear right and in 3.1 mile (5 km) you'll arrive at the campground gate.

LA CUEVA DEL PIRATA *(Open All Year)*
Telephone: (616) 107-8805 or (616) 165-4485

GPS Location: 30.82227 N, 116.08842 W, Near Sea Level

This is a hotel with a restaurant. It's above the beach west of Camalú, an easy drive from the highway. There are no RV amenities here, just parking on gravel in the big cleared area surrounding the building. Camping is free if you eat in the restaurant. Views of the rocky beach and nearby headland are excellent.

From the Mex 1 in Camalú at Pemex #2880 drive toward the beach on the good gravel road. It's 2.3 miles (3.7 km) to the hotel.

BAJA FIESTA RESTAURANT *(Open All Year)*

    Address: Av. Benito Suarez Sur, Vicente Guerrero, B.C., México
    Telephone: (616) 166-4011

        GPS Location: 30.71892 N, 115.98882 W, Near Sea Level

This is a very popular Mexican restaurant located in Vicente Guerrero just north of the entrance road for the Posada Don Diego Trailer Park (below). It has a large lot behind the restaurant, RVers are welcome to spend the night (no hookups) if they have dinner. There are bathrooms and showers (30 pesos for showers) and someone is on-site all night. There is free Wi-Fi in the restaurant. Baja Fiesta is at the south end of Vicente Guerrero on the west side of the highway, just north of Km 173.

POSADA DON DIEGO TRAILER PARK *(Open All Year)*

    Address: Carr. Transpeninsular Km 174,
                 CP 22920 Vicente Guerrero, B.C., México
    Telephone: (616) 166-2181
    Email: info@posadadondiego.com
    Website: www.posadadondiego.com

       GPS Location: 30.71211 N, 115.99773 W, Near Sea Level

This Col. Vicente Guerrero trailer park is very popular with caravans, it is roomy and has lots of spaces, in fact it is the only conventional large RV campground with full hookups in this area.

The campground has 60 spaces, about a third of these have non-functional hookups.. Most of the available slots are large enough for big RVs with slide-outs, they have 15-amp outlets, water, and patios. A few are pull-thrus, most are back-ins. About half have sewer, there is also a dump station available. Tent campers usually pitch in an undeveloped area to the north of the RVs. The restrooms are older but in good repair and clean, they have hot water showers. The campground also has a restaurant/bar, a meeting room and a playground. Wi-Fi is available at some of the sites near the restaurant, ask for the code, there is no charge. There is a night watchman.

To reach the Posada Don Diego follow the road going west from just north of the gas plant at Km 173. This is just south of Col. Vicente Guerrero. The campground is about 0.5 miles (0.8 km) down this sometimes rough but passable gravel road.

SAN QUINTÍN (SAHN KEEN-TEEN)
Population 40,000 in the area

San Quintín is an interesting place, both geological and historically. The area is a large salt water lagoon system which fronts a fertile plain. Long sandy beaches stretch north and south. The lagoon and plain probably would have eroded away long ago except that there are eight small volcanoes (seven onshore and one an island off-

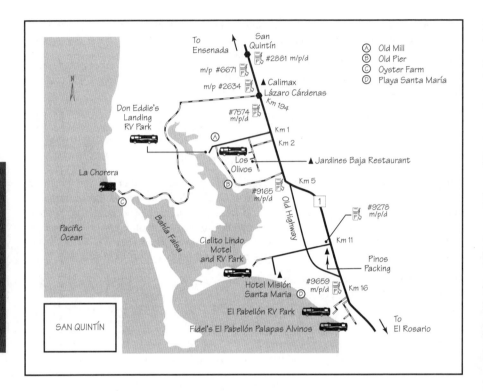

shore) that shelter the area from the sea. For the last few decades the plain has been heavily farmed, unfortunately there is not enough fresh water in the aquifer and salt water has started to displace the fresh water. Farming is gradually retreating to the east side of Mex 1.

Farming is also responsible for the interesting history of the area. During the late 19th century the region was the focus of a settlement scheme by an American company and then later an English company under a grant from Mexican President Porfirio Díaz. The plan was to grow wheat but it turned out that there wasn't enough rainfall. Today there are several ruined structures to remind visitors of the colony, they include the Molino Viejo (old mill), the Muelle Viejo (old pier), and the English cemetery.

Outdoorsmen love the area. Goose and duck hunting is good in the winter, fishing offshore is excellent. The protected waters are a good place to launch a trailer boat if you've pulled one south, but the shallow waters of the bay are difficult to navigate and the offshore waters can be dangerous.

The large influx of workers into this area from throughout Mexico to work on the farms, particularly single males, has meant that the area has a crime problem. Camping outside campgrounds is definitely not recommended throughout this region or in the neighboring areas to the north and south.

San Quintín Campgrounds

LA CHORERA *(Open All Year)* $$ ▲ COLD

GPS Location: 30.45931 N, 116.03677 W, Near Sea Level

If you like to explore and don't mind several miles of very rough road here's a camping location for you. It's in the village of La Chorera on the outside of the line of volcanoes that form the western side of Bahía San Quintín and Bahía Falsa.

The camping area is located in the small village of La Chorera. Once you find the campground (you may have to ask for Don Alvaro's place) see Don Alvaro or his sons. They'll most likely be happy to have you visit, it's pretty informal. There's room for rigs to about 30 feet but probably nothing larger than a van or pickup camper would want to brave the rough washboard road. There's a pit toilet and rustic cold showers. To the south is an area of grassy dunes and rocky beach good for hiking. Or you could climb one of the volcanoes. Ask the owner about buying seafood if that sounds good. There's no set fee here, but insist on paying a reasonable amount.

The road out to the campground leaves Mex 1 at the southern end of Lázaro Cárdenas. It's the first road south of the Calimax supermarket. Head west on the dirt road. It soon becomes very rough with a washboard surface. The road goes west and then south to go around the south end of the string of volcanoes, then reaches the coast and goes north. The coast here is busy, it's used for oyster farming. After 11 miles (18 km) you'll reach La Chorera, a small village. Forge ahead slowly and when you see the Modulo de Salud go down toward the water along the road on the left or southern side of it. The road curves down to the left to the Alvaro family compound and parking on cliffs above the ocean.

DON EDDIE'S LANDING RV PARK *(Open All Year)*

Location:	Bay of San Quintín, Baja, Mexico
Telephone:	(616) 632-5417 or (866) 989-6492
Email:	doneddie@hotmail.com

GPS Location: 30.48635 N, 115.97727 W, Near Sea Level

Don Eddie's Landing RV Park is primarily a fishing destination. It is located some 3 miles (5 km) off Mex 1 . The formerly rough but now paved entrance road made it unpopular for overnight stays but now RVs often overnight here.

The campground has 20 large back-in-spaces. They are separated by rail fences. Parking is on gravel and sand and all sites are full-hookup. Restrooms with hot showers are available. The sites are associated with a motel and restaurant/bar and there is another restaurant/bar next door. Wi-Fi only reaches the sites near the restaurant/bar. Fishing is good in open water outside the bay. There's a boat launch if you've brought your own trailer (large and seaworthy) boat or you can hire a boat and guide.

The access road to Don Eddie's Landing leads west from Mex 1 south of Col. Lázaro Cárdenas. It is well-signed at the 1 Km marker. The wide paved road leads west for 3.3 miles (5.3 km), then you'll see signs pointing to the restaurant and RV park. Turn here, drive .4 km (.2 mile), turn right, and you'll see the entrance to Don Eddie's on your left almost immediately.

SOUTHERN NORTHWEST COAST

ONE OF THE NICE SEAFOOD RESTAURANTS AT DON EDDIE'S LANDING

🚐 LOS OLIVOS *(Open All Year)*

Address:	Anillo Periférico #1010, Las Granjas, J.M. Salvatierra, San Quintín, B.C., México
Telephone:	(616) 111-3205 or (604) 819-4272
Email:	LosOlivosRVpark@hotmail.com
Website:	www.losolivosrvpark.com

GPS Location: 30.48883 N, 115.93913 W, Near Sea Level

The newest campground in the San Quintín area is also the most unusual. Los Olivos is a balneario built in an olive grove. The facility is extremely neat and well kept and includes two swimming pools (open April - Oct) as well as a well equipped children's playground.

Camping is in two areas. Tent campers are in the middle of the olive orchard with water provided from six spigots. This area is lighted at night and well away from the play areas. The RV sites are at the back of the park beyond the swimming pool. There are 6 pull-thru sites with 15-amp electrical outlets and water. Large RVs may have to unhook to enter the sites as it's a tight turn to enter the pull-thrus. This area also has a dump station as well as restrooms with hot showers. There's a nice fairly upscale restaurant, the Jardines Baja, just down the road.

To reach the campground turn toward the west off Mex 1 on the same road that leads to Don Eddie's Landing, at Km 1 south of Col. Lázaro Cárdenas. Follow the road west for 1.1 miles (1.8 km) and turn left. The entrance will be on your right in .3 mile (.6 km).

CIELITO LINDO MOTEL AND RV PARK
(Open All Year)

Telephone: (616) 103-3169
Email: cielitolindos@hotmail.com

GPS Location: 30.40884 N, 115.92326 W, Near Sea Level

The Cielito Lindo Motel has been around for a long time. It is well-known for its restaurant and fishing charters can be arranged. The long and sandy Playa Santa María is a short walk from the campground.

The motel camping area has 8 back-in slots with water and sewer hookups. The sites are suitable for big RVs and there's lots of maneuvering room. There is a row of pine trees to provide shade and some shelter from the frequent wind in this area. The restaurant/bar is pretty good, some people come here just because of the food. Restrooms with hot showers are located in a building on the north side of the central courtyard area.

The Cielito Lindo is located near the Hotel Misión Santa Maria. The paved road with lots of potholes leads west from Mex 1 near the Km 11 marker, just south of Pemex #9278. It is signed for both the Hotel Misión Santa Maria and the Cielito Lindo. Follow the road west for 2.8 miles (4.5 km) past the Hotel Misión Santa Maria entrance (where the road turns to gravel) to the Cielito Lindo entrance, .8 miles beyond the Hotel Misión Santa Maria entrance.

EL PABELLÓN RV PARK
(Open All Year)

GPS Location: 30.37417 N, 115.86917 W, Near Sea Level

Miles of sand dunes and ocean. That's El Pabellón RV Park. This is a large graded area set in sand dunes close to the ocean. There are 12 pull-thru RV sites as well as lots more space for no-hookup camping. The hookup sites have 15-amp-style outlets but 30-amp breakers and water. Half of them also have sewer hookups. The restrooms are good, they're clean and have flush toilets and hot showers. Tent campers pitch in the dunes in front of the campground or behind rows of trees that provide some shelter if the wind is blowing. There is water in the faucets at this campground but it is salty so don't fill your tanks with it. This campground is suitable for any size RV. There is seldom an attendant at the entrance gate but someone will come around to collect. You can also purchase firewood.

The turn for El Pabellón is between Km 16 and 17 south of San Quintín. Turn south at the sign and follow the 1.2 mile dirt and gravel road to the campground.

FIDEL'S EL PABELLÓN PALAPAS ALVINOS
(Open All Year)

GPS Location: 30.37150 N, 115.86346 W, Near Sea Level

This campground appears to be an extension of El Pabellón. At first they seem to be virtually identical with Palapas Alvinos adjoining El Pabellón to the east. They are separated by a chain-link fence so you cannot drive between them.

WELCOME TO THE EL PABELLÓN RV PARK

Like El Pabellón this campground is a large parking area adjoining the beach and suitable for any RV. Water hookups run in a line with the water trucked in so that it is not brackish. Restrooms are good with hot showers and there is a dump station here. Unlike El Pabellón there is generally someone, usually Fidel the owner, on-site 24 hours a day. Fidel has installed a several low-amp electrical outlets so you can keep those batteries charged. There are also a few small palapa shelters fronting the beach, some with electricity. Fidel's house serves as an informal restaurant, wood for fires can be purchased.

You'll find a large sign marking the entrance near Km 16.5, about 0.2 miles (0.3 km) east of the El Pabellón entrance. The signs will take you toward the ocean along power lines and then turn right toward the campground, the distance is 1 mile (1.6 km) and the road is generally solid and fine for even big RVs.

SAN QUINTÍN TO EL ROSARIO
37 Miles (60 Km), 1.25 Hours

After leaving San Quintín the road continues southward along the coastal plain. It soon crosses a long bridge over the Río Santa María, which is usually dry. After a few more miles the ocean is within sight to the west, occasionally a small track leads to the bluff above the ocean. About 40 miles (65 km) south of Lázaro Cárdenas the road turns inland into the San Quintín Canyon and begins to climb to the top of El Rosario Mesa. Soon after reaching the top of the mesa the road descends steeply into the town of El Rosario. If you haven't filled with fuel lately, do so here. You won't find another Pemex until you reach Villa Jesús María, about 195 miles (315 km) to the south. Watch for the town's Pemex on the left as you descend in to El Rosario from the north.

San Quintín to El Rosario Campground

🚐 **PLAYA DEL SOCORRO**

GPS Location: 30.30937 N, 115.81612 W, Near Sea Level

This is a simple parking place above a rocky beach. The only amenity is a barely useable pit toilet. It can take any size rig. Although it is located next to a small slowly developing housing development it's really a pretty lonely place. We recommend camping or parking here only with others.

Driving south from San Quintín watch the kilometer markers. Just south of Km 25 you'll see a sign for camping. Turn toward the beach here and drive for .3 mile (.5 km), turn left to go around a small housing development, and you'll find a lot for parking near the ocean.

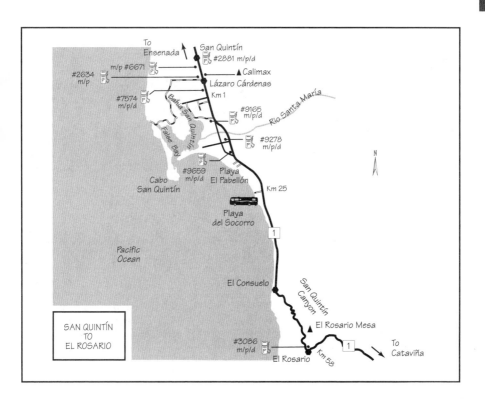

EL ROSARIO (EL ROE-SAHR-EEYOH)
Population 4,000

For many years El Rosario was as far south as you could drive unless you were an off-roader. Today's road turns inland here and heads for the center of the peninsula, it won't return to the west coast until it cuts back to Guerrero Negro, and even there it won't stay for long. **Espinosa's Place**, a local restaurant, has been famous for years for its seafood burritos (lobster and crab meat). The town of El Rosario is actually in two places, El Rosario de Arriba is on the main highway, El Rosario de Abajo is 1.5 miles (2.4 km) away down and across the arroyo (river bed). Each has the ruins of an old mission, the first was in El Rosario de Arriba, it was abandoned when the mission moved to El Rosario de Abajo. Little remains of the first except the foundations, there are still visible ruined piles of adobe walls at the second, which was abandoned in 1832. See *Backroad Adventures* in this chapter for directions to the mission.

El Rosario Campground

🚐 **HOTEL SINAHI RV PARK** *(Open All Year)*

Address:	Carret. Transp. Km 56 #1056, El Rosario, B.C., México
Telephone:	(616) 165-8818
Email:	hotelsinahi@hotmail.com

GPS Location: 30.06670 N, 115.71551 W, 100 Ft.

THE MISSION RUINS AT EL ROSARIO DE ABAJO

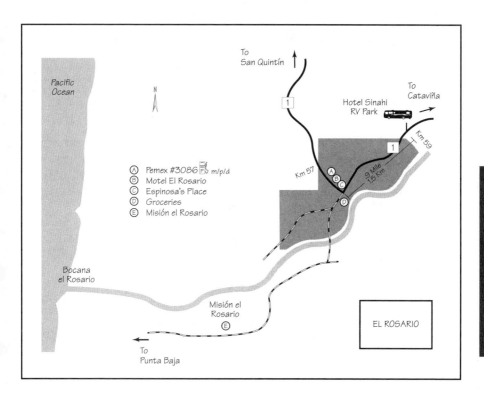

The Hotel Sinahi in el Rosario has 33 RV or tent camping sites on a plateau behind the hotel and in the yard below. There are 25 sites for RVs or tent campers up a ramp above the hotel, but they are so close together that there will probably be room for fewer campers most of the time. All sites have electricity (15 amp), water and sewer drains are available to most of them. There are also eight sites below in a large lot adjacent to the hotel. There is a toilet cubicle and two little shower rooms with hot water in the hotel buildings that are available to campers. There is plenty of room for big RVs to maneuver and sites are flat. The hotel also has a little restaurant. Wi-Fi is only available in the restaurant.

The Motel Sinahi is near the eastern outskirts of El Rosario on the north side of the highway. It is 0.9 miles (1.5 km) east of the 90-degree turn in the middle of town.

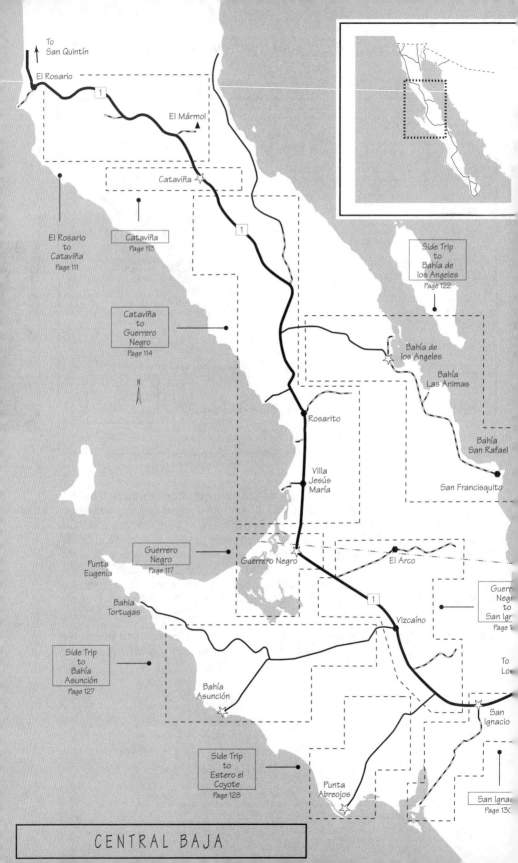

To
San Quintín

El Rosario

1

El Mármol

Cataviña

1

N

Side Trip
to
Bahía de
los Angeles
Page 122

Bahía de
los Angeles

Bahía
Las Animas

Rosarito

Bahía
San Rafael

Villa
Jesús
María

San Francisquito

Guerrero Negro

El Arco

Punta
Eugenia

Bahía
Tortugas

1

Vizcaíno

To
Lo

Bahía
Asunción

San
Ignacio

Punta
Abreojos

CENTRAL BAJA

Chapter 6
Central Baja

INTRODUCTION

This central section of the Baja Peninsula is much different than that to the north. The area has far fewer people, and the landscape is definitely desert. In fact, the area from El Rosario to the cutoff to Bahía de los Angeles has some of the most scenic and interesting desert country in the world.

Highlights

The desert country around **Cataviña** is filled with huge granite boulders. Between them grow a variety of desert cactus, this is great country for short hikes and photography. In this area you'll see a unique type of cactus, the **cirio** or boojum tree. These large cactus look like upside-down green carrots - big ones! The Baja is the only place in the world that you are likely to see them.

The **Ojo de Liebre** lagoon near Guerrero Negro is one of only three places on the Baja where you can get right up close to **California gray whales**. They give birth to their young in the lagoon, you can see them from January to March each year. A second location for this is **Laguna San Ignacio**, accessible from San Ignacio and also described in this chapter.

Bahía de los Angeles is beautiful, you'll want to see it. The bright blue bay and string of islands offshore are a real spectacle as you approach on the highway. The town itself can be a bit of a letdown, but there are some very popular primitive but accessible camping sites near town and excellent summer fishing locations some distance to the south.

Roads and Fuel Availability

The main road, Mex 1, from El Rosario to Guerrero Negro and on to San Ignacio is in good condition. The countryside is made up of rolling hills so the road rises and falls and snakes around looking for the best route. This may be the area where you really begin to notice the relatively narrow highway. Just keep your speed down and watch for traffic. When you meet someone, or when someone wants to pass you, slow to a safe speed and get as near the right edge of the pavement as you safely can.

Kilometer markers in this section are in three segments. The first two count up as you go south: El Rosario to a point near the Bahía de los Angeles Junction (60 to 280) and Bahía L.A. Junction to the Baja Sur Border (0 to 128). From the border to San Ignacio (and for the rest of the trip south) the kilometer markers run from south to north. They begin at the border with Km 221 and reach Km 74 at San Ignacio.

There is exciting new road work in this section of the Baja. The old road from San Felipe far to the north on the Sea of Cortez connects with Mex 1 near Km 233 between Cavatiña and the road out to Bahía de Los Angeles. It's not finished, but it should be within the next few years. When that happens we suspect that most RVers headed for the southern peninsula will cross the border at Mexicali and drive south through San Felipe. At this point the unpaved and very rough section is only 23.5 miles (37.9 km) long. The junction is just north of the Laguna Chapala flats. You'll see a very busy tire repair shop marking the junction. See much more about this road in *Chapter 11 – San Felipe*.

Farther south the road out to Bahía de los Angeles is paved and for many years was in very poor condition with lots of potholes. The entire 42 mile (68 km) length has been repaved and is in excellent condition.

This section of the peninsula is home to the famous "Baja Gas Gap". It is the one place on the Baja highway where even cautious travelers might run in to trouble. From the gas station at El Rosario to the gas station at Villa Jesús María just north of Guerrero Negro is a distance of 195 miles (315 km). If either the gas station at El Rosario or the one at Villa Jesús María was temporarily out of fuel the gap would be even larger. Even so, few vehicles are permanently lost in the "gas gap", just be sure to fuel up before entering it.

Fuel locations, types available, and distances between stations is as follows: **El Rosario**, gas and diesel; **Villa Jesús María**, gas and diesel, 195 miles (315 km); **Guerrero Negro**, several stations, gas and diesel, 19 miles (31 km); **Vizcaíno**, gas and diesel, 44 miles (71 km); and **San Ignacio**, gas and diesel, 43 miles (69 km). There are also two stations in **Bahía de los Angeles**, both gas and diesel are available.

Sightseeing

El Mármol is an abandoned onyx mine located in the desert about nine miles north of the highway. From the early 1900s to about 1950 this was the world's major source of onyx, if you have some this is probably where it came from. Today the place is abandoned but there is a well-known onyx-walled schoolhouse and blocks of onyx scattered around. See the *Backroad Adventures* section below for driving instructions.

Near **Cataviña** there is an area of extremely photogenic cactus set among rounded granite boulders. The highway goes right through the middle of this area so you can't miss it.

From late December to about the middle of April the **California gray whales** come to the Baja. They congregate in shallow bays along the west coast where their young are born. It is possible to take a ride in a panga out to see them up close. There are three places where this is done: Guerrero Negro, Laguna San Ignacio, and Bahía Magdalena. This is discussed in much more detail in the sections about Guerrero Negro and San Ignacio later in this chapter.

Misión San Fernando Velicatá, Misión Santa Maria, and **Misión San Borja** are located in the area covered by this chapter. See the *Backroad Adventures* section below for detailed information about visiting the sites.

The **28ᵗʰ Parallel** forms the border between the states of Baja California and Baja California Sur. The spot is marked by a huge metal statue of an eagle, also by a huge Mexican flag at the military base located at the base of the statue. The road runs right by both so you'll have a good look.

San Ignacio appears to be a classic desert oasis, and it really is. The town has thousands of date palms, as well as an attractive square bordered by the Misión San Ignacio. There is also a museum describing the cave paintings found in the surrounding Sierra de San Francisco, they're known as **rupestrian art**. Guides are available in Guerrero Negro, San Ignacio, Mulegé, Loreto and also near some of the sites and are required. You must also register to visit many of the sites at the museum in San Ignacio.

Beaches and Water Sports

Surfing in this area, of course, is limited to the Pacific Coast. Since the main highway runs far from the coast, road access to surfing generally requires long drives on pretty poor roads. Exceptions are the places accessible from El Rosario in the north and also where the road nears the coast north of Rosarito.

One of the popular surfing spots near Rosarito is Punta Santa Rosalillita, also known as "The Wall". See *Backroad Adventures* below for more about this location. This is also a popular sailboarding location, it is sometimes called "Sandy Point".

A few miles south is Punta Rosarito, also a surfing destination. To the south of the point is the long Altamara beach. See *Backroad Adventures* below for driving instructions.

Still farther south, near Villa Jesús María a roads lead out to Laguna Manuela. This is a popular fishing destination, but there is a long beach called Playa Pacheco to the north of the lagoon. Between the beach and the lagoon is Morro Santo Domingo, a high headland ringed with small coves. There's also a small beach near the fish camp at the end of the road at the lagoon, it is often used by the folks from Guerrero Negro for picnics. Watch for soft sand, access to the long Playa Pacheco is very sandy and requires 4WD or a walk. See *Backroad Adventures* below for more about this road.

Kayaking is popular on the Gulf of California coast. Winds tend to be from the north so long-distance kayakers usually travel from north to south. Bahía de los Angeles makes a good place to explore with beaches for camping that don't require long passages.

Fishing

Since much of this route is inland fishing possibilities are limited to Bahía de los Angeles and areas on the Pacific coast reached by a variety of side roads.

The **Bahía de los Angeles** area is probably the most popular destination on the Baja for fishermen with large and small trailer boats. There are good boat launches, a reasonable number of fish, and the weather is much warmer than on the west side of the peninsula at this latitude.

Unfortunately, boating conditions can be dangerous here. A combination of often very strong winds (generally either from the north or the west) and very active tidal currents can make boating a challenge.

The best fishing is in the summer and fall and the most popular fishing is for yellowtail. Expect daytime temperatures to 100 degrees Fahrenheit in the middle of the summer.

The fishing is not as good as it once was due to commercial overfishing. Your best fishing opportunities are north and south of the bay. Access to the north by vehicle is nonexistent much past Playa La Gringa, but to the south there are several fishing destinations for those with the RVs to travel rough roads. Destinations include Bahía las Animas (30 miles south), Playa San Rafael (45 miles south of L.A. Bay with good shore fishing), and Bahía San Francisquito (85 miles south of L.A. Bay). See the *Backroad Adventures* of this section for more information about access to these locations.

Farther south is Laguna Manuela. You reach it on a marked road heading westward from Villa Jesús Maria. You can launch small boats across the beach here and fish the lagoon for bass, halibut, sierra, and corvina. See *Backroad Adventures* for road information.

South of Guerrero Negro there are a number of fishing towns reached by newly paved roads, often fairly long ones. These include Bahía Asunción and Estero El Coyote/Punta Abreojos, both of which have nearby campgrounds. See the *Side Trip to Bahía Asuncion* and *Side Trip to Estero El Coyote* sections below for more.

Backroad Adventures

See the **Backroad Driving** section of **Chapter 2 - Details, Details, Details** for essential information about driving off the main highway on the Baja and for a definition of road type classifications used below.

From Km 121 Between El Rosario and Cataviña - The ruin of **Misión San Fernando Velicatá** is a short distance off the highway on this road east of El Rosario. This is usually a Type 2 road, the distance is about 3 miles (5 km). The GPS location of the mission is 29.97106 N, 115.23682 W.

THE OLD SCHOOL HOUSE AT EL MÁRMOL BUILT ENTIRELY OF ONYX

From Km 149 Between El Rosario and Cataviña - The virtually abandoned onyx mining area called **El Mármol** makes an interesting day trip. The access road is about 19 miles (31 km) west of Cataviña. This is a graded road that is about 9.5 miles long, it is usually a Type 1 road. Take a look at the old school house built entirely of onyx. The mine was very active in the early part of the century, the quarried onyx slabs were shipped by water from Puerto Santa Catarina about 50 miles west on the Pacific coast. The GPS location of the mine is 29.97006 N, 114.80957 W.

From Km 38 Between L.A. Bay Junction and Guerrero Negro - A good road leads west to the small community of Santa Rosalillita, Bahía Santa Rosalillita, and Punta Santa Rosalillita. It leaves Mex 1 near Km 38, some 8 miles (13 km) north of Rosarito. The road leads 9.5 miles (15 km) to the village. At about 8 miles (13 km) a side track leads north toward the community of San José de las Palomas giving access to many more beaches. The road to Santa Rosalillita is paved and suitable for any vehicle, the others in the area vary, some are Type 2 or even 3, watch for soft sand. See also the campground description for *Santa Rosalillita Surfer Camping* in the *Cataviña to Guerrero Negro Campgrounds* section.

From Km 52 Between L.A. Bay Junction and Guerrero Negro - Another mission, **Misión San Borja** is also accessible if you have four-wheel drive or a lightly loaded pickup with good ground clearance. From Rosarito, located about 97 miles (158 km) south of Cataviña on Mex 1 drive east, roads leave the highway both north and south of the bridge over the arroyo. At about 15 miles (24 km) the road reaches Rancho San Ignacio, the mission is beyond at about 22 miles (36 km). Misión San

Francisco de Borja was built in 1759 and has been restored by the government. A family lives on site and gives tours. This is usually a Type 2 road.

From Km 69 Between L.A. Bay Junction and Guerrero Negro - A short 3.1 mile (5.5 km) road leads to a beach which is popular for surfing, board sailing, and surf fishing. This is normally a Type 2 road. The beach is called El Tomatal.

From Km 96 Between L.A. Bay Junction and Guerrero Negro - From the town of Villa Jesús María a road heads 7 miles westward to the Laguna Manuela. This area is popular for fishing, primitive camping, and the beach. Drive about a mile west on a paved road, then turn south on a graded dirt road, you'll reach the lagoon in another 6 miles (10 km). This is usually a Type 1 road.

From Bahía de los Angeles - A road leads south from Bahía de los Angeles for many miles. Along the way it passes beaches on the southern curve of Bahía de los Angeles, an abandoned silver-smelting operation at Los Flores, a side road to Bahía las Animas, Bahía San Rafael, and eventually reaches Punta and Bahía San Francisquito. The road is a badly washboarded Type 1 for about 10 miles (16 km), then becomes a bad Type 2 road.

From Km 189 Between Guerrero Negro and San Ignacio - From 16 miles east of Guerrero Negro a road that was paved at one time goes north to the almost-abandoned mining town of **El Arco**. The distance is 26 miles (42 kilometers). The road continues beyond El Arco for 23 miles (37 km) to **Misión Santa Gertrudis**, which is being restored. The road to El Arco is usually a marginal Type 1, the one to the mission usually a Type 3 road.

From Km 144 Between Guerrero Negro and San Ignacio - There's a junction here at Ejido Vizcaíno for a road that runs southwest to the coast at **Bahía Tortugas.** Much of this road is now paved, the remainder is a Type 1 road often with soft sand in places. The distance to the coast is about 107 miles (173 km) Type 2 and 3 side roads allow you to travel on to Punta Eugenia and other coastal locations. Also accessible on this road is the paved road to Bahía Asunción and the campground there, see *Side Trip to Bahía Asunción* for more information and the campground description.

From Km 118 Between Guerrero Negro and San Ignacio - This is a 22-mile (35 km) drive into the Sierra San Francisco to the village of **San Francisco**. This is a cave-art location, **Cueva Ratón** is located near the village, you must have a guide from the village to get in the locked gate. Guides can take you to other caves too, some trips require several days. Before visiting you must register in San Ignacio. This is usually a Type 2 road.

From Km 97 Between Guerrero Negro and San Ignacio - A paved road leads out to the coast at Punta Abreojos and then a dirt road continues on to La Bocana and on up the coast to eventually reach Bahía Asunción. It's 51 miles (82 km) to Punta Abreojos, another 11 miles (18 km) to La Bocana, and another 46 miles (74 km) all the way to Bahía Asunción. The section beyond Punta Abreojos isn't paved and the condition varies, it's sometimes a Type 2 road and sometimes a Type 3. Check in Punta Abreojos before you head north. Just short of Punta Abreojos is Estero el Coyote and Campo Rene, they are described in the section below titled *Side Trip to Estero el Coyote.*

From San Ignacio - This 40-mile (65 km) road leads southeast from the village to **Laguna San Ignacio**. This is one of the best California gray whale observation sites on the peninsula. Most people opt to leave their RVs in San Ignacio and ride down with a van tour. The first 30 miles (48 km) of the road is paved. The remainder of the road, 10 miles (16 km) to the bay is a sandy Type 2 road with a few short stretches of soft sand. See also the description of *Antonio's Ecotours* and *Ecoturismo Kuyima* in the *San Ignacio Campgrounds* section for more information.

THE ROUTES, TOWNS, AND CAMPGROUNDS

EL ROSARIO TO CATAVIÑA
73 Miles (118 Km), 2.25 Hours

From El Rosario the highway heads northeast for about four miles (6 km) along the north side of the El Rosario River. It then crosses and follows a climbing canyon into rolling hills that can be surprisingly green during the winter. This is the beginning of the longest mountainous section of Mex 1 as the highway passes along the western edge of the Peninsular Range for some 180 miles (290 km) but never crosses to the Gulf of California side.

From this point until well past Cataviña the scenery is fascinating, you are in what

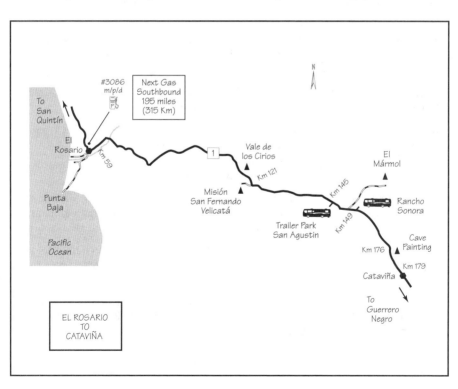

is known as the Sonoran Desert Vegetation Region. You'll soon see your first cirios (boojum trees) and as you drive along there will be more and more of them. Other cactus include huge cardóns, barrel cactus, chollas, and agaves. Many of these cactus are found only in this area.

Near Km 121 a short road runs south to the ruins of Misión San Fernando Velicatá. See *Backroad Adventures* for more information about this road.

Near Km 149 is the cutoff to the north to El Mármol. See the *Backroad Adventures* section above for a description of this road and destination.

As you near Cataviña, near Km 160, you enter a region of large granite boulders. These are known as the Cataviña boulder fields. Around and among them grow all types of cactus, and together they are extremely photogenic. You'll be tempted to pull off and camp on one of the short roads leading into the boulders, but you'll be much safer at one of the inexpensive campgrounds just a few miles ahead.

El Rosario to Cataviña Campgrounds

TRAILER PARK SAN AGUSTIN *(Open All Year)* $$$

GPS Location: 29.92148 N, 114.97980 W, 1,900 Ft.

This appears to be another of the old government campgrounds that were set up when the highway was built in the 70s. Over the years this one has been open for camping at times but also totally abandoned at other times. For the last few years it has again been open.

The campground has about 10 sites. These are long pull-thrus with drains, no other hookups. Restrooms have bucket-flush toilets, no showers. The fee, at $15, is pretty high for this kind of place

The campground is on the south side of Mex 1 near Km. 145. This is 52 miles (84 km) east of El Rosario and 21 miles (34 km) west of Cataviña.

RANCHO SONORA *(Open All Year)* $$
Address: Carret. Transpeninsular Km 149, Cataviña, El Rosario
Telephone: (555) 151-9446

GPS Location: 29.91417 N, 114.93889 W, 2,100 Ft.

This is a great place to stay if you are in an RV and want to visit El Mármol in a smaller tow vehicle. It's also a convenient place to overnight if you can't quite make Cataviña. The gift shop sells all sorts of things made of onyx.

Facilities are minimal, just a place to park next to the building and an outhouse. RVs can park in the large lot to the left of the buildings or in what appears to be a more secure area to the right of them..

The campground is located near Km 149. This is a few hundred yards from where the road out to El Mármol leaves the highway. It's 55 miles (89 km) from El Rosario and 18 miles (29 km) from Cataviña.

Cataviña (cat-ah-VEE-nya)

You can't really call Cataviña a town. There is little more here than a motel, now called the Hotel Misión Cataviña, an abandoned Pemex, an old government-built campground, a small store, and a few shacks and restaurants. The area, however, is one of the most interesting on the Baja. The Cataviña boulder fields are striking. The road threads its way for several miles through a jumble of huge granite boulders sprinkled liberally with attractive cacti and desert plants. It is a photographer's paradise.

Cataviña Campgrounds

Parque Natural Desierto Central Trailer Park $$ △ ⬛ 🚌 BIG RIGS
   (Open All Year)

GPS Location: 29.73111 N, 114.7222 W, 1,800 Ft.

This is one of the fenced compounds that were built by the government soon after the road south was finished. None of the hookups other than sewer work any more, but the facility continues to offer an overnight haven to passing RVers. The landscaping has boulders and cactus, just like the surrounding area. Sites are large, most are pull-thrus. There are bathrooms with toilets that are flushed with a bucket of water but no showers. Many people use this campground, perhaps because they don't know about Rancho Santa Inez (see below). It's a noisy place at night because it's right next to the highway.

CACTUS AND DESERT PLANTS ON THE DRIVE THROUGH CATAVIÑA

The campground is located in Cataviña off Mex 1 just west of the Hotel Misión Cataviña and the abandoned Pemex, it's on the south side of the road.

🚐 **RANCHO SANTA INEZ** *(Open All Year)* $$ A 🚰 🍴 🚌

GPS Location: 29.72930 N, 114.69680 W, 1,900 Ft.

Many folks drive right by the entrance road to this camping spot, and that's a mistake. We think it is the best place to stay in this area.

The camping area is a large flat dirt lot with only a few trees for shade. There's room for lots of RVs of any size, that's why many of the caravans stay here. Other facilities include a water faucet and a small building with a flush toilet. Best of all is the small restaurant. An advantage here is that the campground is quiet because it is off the main highway.

To reach the campground turn north on the well-marked road near Km 181, less than a mile east of the Hotel Misión Cataviña. Follow the paved side road for about 0.8 miles (1.3 km), the camping area is on the left.

CATAVIÑA TO GUERRERO NEGRO
145 Miles (234 Km), 4.25 Hours

The two-lane highway continues snaking its way southeastwards from Cataviña. It passes signs for a few small ranchos, along the road is the occasional small restaurant, often with a truck or two parked out front. Eighteen miles (29 km) from Cataviña on the right side of the road you'll see a very large pile of rocks. The small mountain is called **Cerro Pedregoso** (rocky hill). It has long been a landmark for travelers along the highway.

About 15 miles (24 km) beyond Cerro Pedregoso the highway descends and runs along **Laguna Chapala**. This is a large dry lake bed, before the current highway was completed a very rough road followed pretty much the same route in this region. Here it ran over the dry lake bed, it was very dusty and often heavily rutted.

Just north of the lake bed, near Km 233 you may see a road headed northeast. It is signed for San Felipe and Calamajué, they're both on the Gulf of California. This will be the new route to the border through San Felipe. See Chapter 11- San Felipe for more information about this route. At this time the first section is very rough and under construction.

Thirty miles beyond the dirt road to San Felipe is the cutoff to Bahía de los Angeles, often called the **L.A. Bay Junction**. The road to Bahía de los Angeles and the attractions there are discussed in a separate section later in this chapter. In the past there was a gas station at this junction, the buildings remain but the pumps are gone. Sometimes you will find an entrepreneur here in a pickup with gas drums in the back, a welcome sight if you are low on fuel.

South of the L.A. Bay Junction the road begins to gradually approach the west coast. There are roads out to the coast at Km 38 to **Santa Rosalillita**, Km 69 for **El Tomatal**, and Km 96 for **Laguna Manuela**. See *Backroad Adventures* above for more about all of these roads.

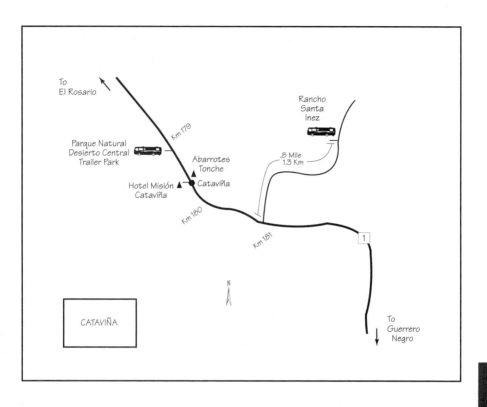

In Rosarito, 33 miles (53 km) south of the L.A. Bay Junction there is a back road northeastwards to the **Misión San Borja**. See *Backroad Adventures* for more about this trip.

Fifty-six miles (90 km) from the L.A. Bay Junction you will reach the small town of Villa Jesús Maria which has a Pemex gas station with both gas and diesel. This is also the cutoff for the road out to Laguna Manuela.

Twenty-two miles (35 km) beyond Villa Jesús Maria is the border between Baja California and Baja California Sur. The **border** is marked by a huge metal **statue of an eagle**, as you approach the border you can see it for miles, it looks like a giant tuning fork from this direction. At the border there is a military base with a huge flag, a motel, a restaurant with RV parking behind, and a former RV park. A checkpoint at the border sometimes checks tourist cards and always fumigates the wheels of your RV. They recently were charging 20 pesos for doing this. They'll also take citrus fruits (except small limes), apples, potatoes, avocados and perhaps other fruits and vegetables to combat the spread of farm diseases so plan to have used them all up by the time you reach this crossing. Just a short distance beyond the checkpoint is the side road in to the town of Guerrero Negro.

Baja California Sur observes Mountain time while Baja California observes Pacific time so you will have to change your clocks at the border.

CENTRAL BAJA

Cataviña to Guerrero Negro Campgrounds

⧆ RESTAURANT SAN IGNACITO
(Open All Year)

Telephone: (616) 163-9346 or (616) 103-8584

GPS Location: 29.65925 N, 114.64336 W, 2,200 Ft.

This is a small restaurant whose owners welcome RVers and campers. They have quite a bit of parking room behind the restaurant and in front. A flush toilet and cold showers are available. There are no hookups.

Watch for the restaurant on the east side of the highway near Km 191 of Mex 1.

⧆ PUNTA PRIETA RV PARK AT THE L.A. BAY JUNCTION
(Open All Year)

GPS Location: 29.04750 N, 114.15361 W, 1,100 Ft.

This is another of the old government campgrounds. It is often closed, but occasionally the gates are open and someone is operating the place. It has the standard nice desert plant landscaping, as well as the standard non-functional hookups. Recently a large communal palapa roof and several smaller palapa shades at individual sites have been added. There's room for large RVs. Toilets are flushed using a bucket of water if there's enough on hand and there are no showers.

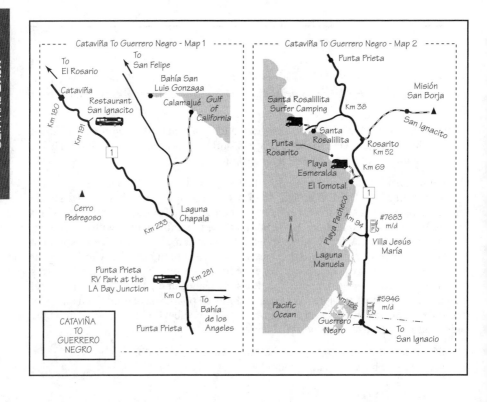

CENTRAL BAJA

The campground is very near the cutoff to Bahía de los Angeles, just to the north on Mex 1. While we wouldn't depend on it being open on the way south we might stop here going north if we had noticed that it was open on our southward journey.

⛺ SANTA ROSALILLITA SURFER CAMPING *(Open All Year)*

GPS Location: 28.66411 N, 114.24486 W, Near Sea Level

This campground is little more than surfer beach access along the coast to the north of the marina at Santa Rosalillita. This huge new marina is designed to be part of the Escalera Maritima project. The idea is that pleasure boats from the states will be taken out of the water here and trucked across the peninsula to Bahía de Los Angeles. The plan originated under a previous presidential administration and progress toward completion now is stalled. The beautiful paved road from Mex 1 to Santa Rosalillita and the pavement to Bahía de los Angeles are part of the same project.

The entrance road here leads to beach camping and surfing locations along the coast to the north. There are miles of sandy roads and places to park. There are no facilities. While the roads are fairly hard at first, watch for soft spots, four-wheel drive is best if you're going far. For security It's best to have more than one rig if you're going to overnight here.

To reach the campground drive west on the beautifully paved road to Santa Rosalillita. It leaves Mex 1 near Km 38, about 23 miles (37 km) south of the intersection with the road to Bahía de los Angeles. From Mex 1 follow the paved road eastward. Nearing the coast you'll see a few buildings ahead and the road forks. Take the right fork, marked for Escalera Maritima. The entrance to the camping area is 10 miles (16 km) from Mex 1. Watch for a rough dirt road on the right toward the beach as the big marina complex comes in to sight ahead.

GUERRERO NEGRO (GEH-RER-ROW NEH-GROW)
Population 13,000

The 28th parallel is the dividing line between the states of Baja and Baja South. You'll know when you pass over the line because it is marked by a very large statue of a stylized eagle. Most people think it looks like a tuning fork and it is visible for miles. Two miles (3 km) south of the eagle the road to Guerrero Negro goes west.

Guerrero Negro is one of the newest towns on the Baja, and it's a company town. Founded in 1955 the town owes its existence to the Exportadora de Sal (ESSA) salt works. Large flats near the town are flooded with seawater which quickly evaporates leaving salt. This is gathered up using heavy equipment and shipped on barges to Isla Cedros offshore where there is enough water to allow cargo ships to dock. Tours of the **salt works** can be arranged through the Malarrimo RV park, they are reasonably priced.

More recently the town has gained fame for the **California gray whales** that congregate each winter in the nearby Ojo de Liebre or Scammon's Lagoon. There is now a lively tourist industry catering to the many people who come to visit the whales.

CENTRAL BAJA

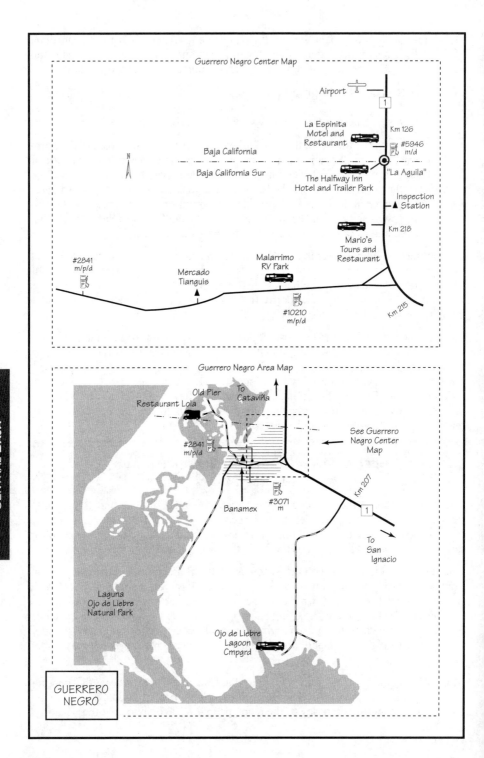

A GRAY WHALE GETS AN UP CLOSE LOOK AT A TOURIST AT SCAMMON'S LAGOON

It's interesting to the general public, and fascinating for birders to drive out the gravel road north of town to the abandoned salt loading pier. The road runs through an area of salt water marshes usually full of birds. It's 6.8 miles (11 km) from town out to the former salt loading facility. There's also a small restaurant nearby that allows campers to overnight, see *Restaurant Lola* described below.

The town itself is small and the places of interest, restaurants and stores, are almost all arranged along the main street. Guerrero Negro has small supermarkets, a bank with an ATM machine, and also a Pemex.

Guerrero Negro Campgrounds

🚐 **LA ESPINITA MOTEL AND RESTAURANT**
   (Open All Year)

GPS Location: 28.00639 N, 114.01222 W, Near Sea Level

This is a restaurant and small store along the road just north of the border between Baja Norte and Baja Sur. Unfortunately, when we last visited there was no one around and it appeared to be closed. The facilities, however, seemed to be unchanged. Perhaps it is just a temporary closure. There are 8 RV sites with 15-amp electricity and water. The restrooms have hot showers ($2.00) and you can dry camp for $5. There are also motel rooms for about 250 pesos per night.

La Espinita is 0.2 mile (0.3 km) north of the giant eagle that marks the border.

CENTRAL BAJA

THE HALFWAY INN HOTEL AND TRAILER PARK *(Open All Year)*

Address: Carretera Transpeninsular, Paralelo 28, Guerrero Negro B.C.S.
Telephone: (615) 157-1305 or 1304
Website: www.halfwayinnhotel.com

GPS Location: 28.00167 N, 114.01378 W, Near Sea Level

This hotel is located almost on the line between Baja California and Baja California Sur. It's been here for years under different names. Now it has a Trailer Park sign. For now it has only RV parking for free but there are plans to put in sites. There are no facilities for RVs other than a bathroom with no showers off the lobby. Let's hope the RV hook-ups soon appear. When they do the price is bound to go up.

Watch for the hotel on the west side of the road next to the eagle monument at the border.

MARIO'S TOURS AND RESTAURANT *(Open All Year)*

Address: Carretera Transpeninsular Km 217.3, CP 23940
              Guerrero Negro, B.C.S.
Telephone: (615) 157-1940
Email: mariostours@hotmail.com or mail@mariotours.com
Website: www.mariostours.com

GPS Location: 27.98333 N, 114.01333 W, Near Sea Level

Mario's is a large palapa-style restaurant located along Mex 1 between the border station and town. That means, of course, that access to town is easy, you don't have to pass through the border station.

The restaurant has 42 large pull-thru camping sites in the rear, they're about 70 feet long. They have electricity (30-amp outlets), water, and sewer hookups. Watch your electrical power at this campground. There's a restroom with showers behind the restaurant dedicated to the RV park. Wi-Fi is available only in the restaurant. Mario's also offers good whale-watching tours.

The restaurant is located on the west side of Mex 1 near the Km 218 marker some 0.6 mile (1 km) south of the border between Baja California and Baja California Sur.

MALARRIMO RV PARK *(Open All Year)*

Address: Blvd. Emiliano Zapata S/N, Col. Fundo Legal,
              CP 23940 Guerrero Negro, B.C.S., México
Reservations: PO Box 284, Chula Vista, CA 91912
Telephone: (615) 157-0100
Fax: (615) 157-0100
Email: info@malarrimo.com
Website: www.malarrimo.com

GPS Location: 27.96778 N, 114.03000 W, Near Sea Level

The Malarrimo is generally considered the best place to stay in Guerrero Negro. Not only are the campground facilities pretty good, the restaurant is the best in this section of Baja.

There are 20 RV spaces with 15-amp electrical outlets and 30-amp breakers, sewer, and water. A few parking spaces are paved. Large RVs can crowd into a few sites up front. It is possible to park RVs to 40 feet with careful maneuvering. Guerrero Negro electricity is marginal, watch voltage while hooked up to avoid damage to your RV. Restrooms are older but clean and have hot water showers. A Wi-Fi signal is usable from many of the sites. This is an efficiently run place and English is spoken. They run tours to see the gray whales and cave art, and even have a gift shop. There's also a convenience store along the street out front. Many people make a special point to overnight in Guerrero Negro so they can eat at the restaurant. There's a slightly reduced rate here of $11 for vans and pickup campers, tent campers pay $9.

To find the campground drive in to Guerrero Negro from the east. Almost immediately after entering town, 1 mile (1.6 km) from the turn off Mex 1, you will see the Malarrimo on the right.

RESTAURANT LOLA (Open All Year)

$$ ▲ COLD ¶¶

GPS Location: 28.01608 N, 114.11787 W, Near Sea Level

This small lagoon-side restaurant offers camping possibilities for those wanting to be away from town, perhaps to take advantage of the awesome birding possibilities out toward the old port.

This is a small restaurant on the beach. There are several palapas where you can pitch a tent or park a rig. Nearby is a restroom with flush toilets and cold showers. Fishermen also use this area for loading and unloading so there can be quite a bit of activity when they are working.

To reach the restaurant zero your odometer at Malarrimo RV Park and drive west into town. In 1.8 mile (2.9 km) turn right and head out toward the old salt loading dock. You'll soon be driving on a gravel road through salt water marshes. At odometer 7.7 miles (12.4 km) turn left and off the main road and at 8.6 miles (13.9 km) you'll see the restaurant on the left.

OJO DE LIEBRE LAGOON CAMPGROUND

(Open Dec 20 to April 15 – Varies)

$$ ▲ HOT ¶¶
CEL (WI FI FREE BIG RIGS

Telephone:	(615) 155-4114
Email:	benitojuarez08@hotmail.com
Website:	www.ballenatours.com

GPS Location: 27.74889 N, 114.01167 W, Near Sea Level

One of the top attractions of the Baja Peninsula is a whale-watching trip. One way to do this is to drive across the salt flats to the edge of Laguna Ojo de Liebre (Scammon's Lagoon). It costs a little less to take a tour here than from in town, and camping along the edge of the lagoon is excellent. This place is only accessible during the whale-watching season, approximately the last third of December to the middle of April.

When you arrive at the lagoon there is an entrance kiosk where a 90 peso fee is collected. This covers overnight parking (camping) but not the use of a palapa. There is a large parking lot where visitors on whale-watching trips can park. A large building houses the tour ticket sales as well as a souvenir store, and restaurant with Wi-Fi.. There are campsites to the right overlooking the water with palapas (some with low-amp electricity) as well as spots for RVs to park (no electricity). The use of palapas requires an additional payment. Buildings with toilets (they have fantastic views) and hot showers are located at the back of the large parking area.

To reach the lagoon turn westward from Mex 1 at about Km 207. This is 5 miles south of the turnoff for the town of Guerrero Negro. The turn is marked with a large sign for Laguna Ojo de Liebre. The road for the first 1.9 miles (3.1 km) is paved, then turns to graded dirt. It is fine for even the largest RVs. At 3.7 miles (6 km) you will reach an entrance gate where your name will be recorded as you enter the salt flats working area. You may see heavy equipment collecting the salt from the flats. At 13.7 miles (22.1 km) there is a Y, go right as indicated by the sign. Finally, at 15.0 miles (24.2 km) you will reach the entrance gate at the lagoon.

SIDE TRIP TO BAHÍA DE LOS ANGELES
42 Miles (68 Km), 1.75 Hours

From a junction on Mex 1 a paved road runs 42 miles (68 km) down to the coast at Bahía de los Angeles. This is an excellent road so this is a simple and very worthwhile trip.

BAHÍA DE LOS ANGELES (BAH-HEE-AH DAY LOES AHN-HAIL-ACE)
Population 500

The Bahía de los Angeles (Bay of the Angels) is one of the most scenic spots in Baja

SEA LIONS OFFSHORE FROM BAHÍA DE LOS ANGELES

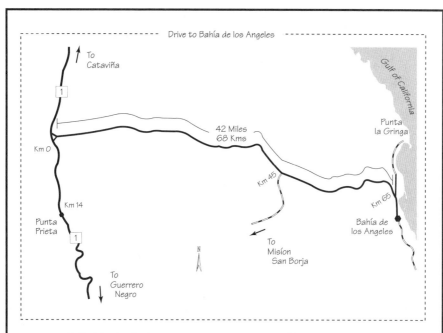

Drive to Bahía de los Angeles

To Cataviña

Gulf of California

Punta la Gringa

42 Miles
68 Kms

Km 0

Km 14

Punta Prieta

Km 45

Km 65

Bahía de los Angeles

To Misíon San Borja

To Guerrero Negro

N

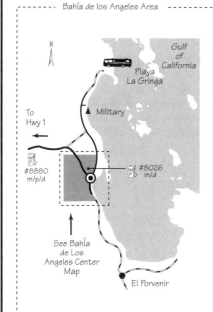

Bahía de los Angeles Area

N

Gulf of California

Playa La Gringa

To Hwy 1

Military

#8880 m/p/d

#8026 m/d

See Bahía de Los Angeles Center Map

El Porvenir

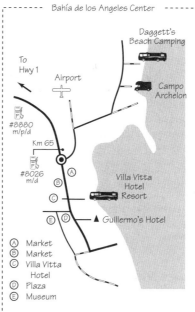

Bahía de los Angeles Center

Daggett's Beach Camping

To Hwy 1

Airport

Campo Archelon

#8880 m/p/d

Km 65

#8026 m/d

Ⓐ

Ⓑ

Villa Vitta Hotel Resort

Ⓒ

Ⓔ Ⓓ ▲ Guillermo's Hotel

Ⓐ Market
Ⓑ Market
Ⓒ Villa Vitta Hotel
Ⓓ Plaza
Ⓔ Museum

SIDE TRIP TO BAHÍA DE LOS ANGELES

CENTRAL **BAJA**

California with blue waters and barren desert shoreline backed by rocky mountains.

The huge bay is protected by a chain of small islands, and also by Isla Angel de la Guarda, which is 45 miles (75 km) long. Even with this protection boating is often dangerous because of strong winds from the north and evening "gravity" winds that whistle downhill from the west. Fishing, boating, diving, and kayaking are good in the bay, among the islands, and offshore and there are several launch ramps in town. Exercise caution, these are considered dangerous waters due to the frequent strong winds.

Whale sharks visit this bay during late summer and early fall. You can arrange a boat tour to go out and swim with them.

Kite surfing can also be good here. The place to be is Playa La Gringa which is described as a camping area below.

It is important when coming to Bahía de los Angeles, to remember that all supplies are trucked in at great expense and services are limited. Arrive with those water tanks full. Also be aware that there is no ATM in town.

Bahía de los Angeles Campgrounds

VILLA VITTA HOTEL RESORT *(Open All Year)*

Telephone:	(619) 630-1680 (Res. in USA) or (664) 120-3301 (Cell)
Email:	gigi@villavitta.com or villavittaresort@gmail.com
Website:	www.villavitta.com

GPS Location: 28.95111 N, 113.55833 W, Near Sea Level

The Villa Vitta RV Park is located across the street from the hotel of the same name. The campground is a flat dirt lot with no landscaping, however, it is right next to the beach with no permanently located RVs out front. There are 38 large sites, 20 are pull-thrus and the others are back-ins along the beach. There are patios and old electrical outlets but electricity is not provided. There is no water but there is a dump station. The only toilets are in the motel across the street, there are no showers. This motel/campground has a launch ramp, it's available for an extra fee. The motel has a restaurant.

You'll find that the Villa Vitta is hard to miss, you'll see the hotel on the right and the RV park on the left soon after entering town. You check in at the motel.

CAMPO ARCHELON *(Open All Year)*

| Email: | archeloncamp@yahoo.com |
| Website: | archeloncamp.com.mx |

GPS Location: 28.97139 N, 113.54694 W, Near Sea Level

This camp is located just north of town along the beach and offers rental cabins as well as a six palapas near the beach for tent campers or RVers in smaller units. There are no hookups and RV size should be limited to about 25 feet. Clean and well maintained toilets are provided as are limited hot water showers.

At the traffic circle near the entrance to town turn left. Follow the paved road for 1.5 miles (2.4 km), you'll see the sign for Camp Archelon on the right.

CENTRAL BAJA

DAGGETT'S BEACH CAMPING *(Open All Year)*

Email: rubendaggett@hotmail.com
Website: www.campdaggetts.info

GPS Location: 28.97556 N, 113.54694 W, Near Sea Level

This is the most popular place to stay in Bahía de los Angeles for tent camping or an RV. There are 20 palapa shelters, some with room to park an RV alongside. There are no hookups but there is a dump station, rustic flush toilets, and hot showers. Electricity may be added in the near future. There are also kayak rentals and fishing, snorkeling, and whale shark charters.

To drive to the campground follow the north beaches road from Bahía L.A. As you enter town turn left at the traffic circle. After 0.8 mile (1.3 km) the road jogs right, than in 0.5 miles (0.8 km) it jogs left to continue north. Three-tenths mile (0.5 km) after this last turn you'll see the sign for Daggett's Beach to the right. Follow the road to the beach and campground.

PLAYA LA GRINGA *(Open All Year)*

GPS Location: 29.04056 N, 113.54472 W, Near Sea Level

This beach is located north of Bahía de los Angeles and has long been a favorite of Baja visitors. It's can be an excellent place for kiteboarding, particularly for beginners. Recently it has been partially fenced off and a fee is being charged – sometimes.

To reach the campground just drive north from town along the north beaches road as described in the descriptions above. Playa La Gringa is 7 miles (11.3 km) north of town, the road is paved for only the first 5.8 miles (9.4 km). The road is passable in any RV, but sections of bad washboard often make it slow going. While big RVs can drive out here they must exercise caution when maneuvering and parking because the surface is soft in places. This can be a remote location, solo camping is not recommended.

GUERRERO NEGRO TO SAN IGNACIO
89 Miles (144 Km), 2.25 Hours

Once you cross the border into Baja Sur north of Guerrero Negro you will note that the kilometer markers are counting down instead of up as they have been doing in the state of Baja California. All sections of kilometer markers on Mex 1 in Baja California Sur go from south to north. The markers for this section of road begin in Santa Rosalía, the town where the highway reaches the coast of the Gulf of California.

About 5 miles from the Guerrero Negro junction you will see a sign and a road headed toward the coast. This is the access road for whale watching at Laguna Ojo de Liebre, or Scammon's Lagoon. The distance is about 17 miles to the lagoon on a road that is usually passable for any RV but often wash-boarded. The road to the lagoon is only open during the whale-watching season from December through some time in April.

The highway from Guerrero Negro to the mountains runs across the Vizcaíno Desert.

CENTRAL BAJA

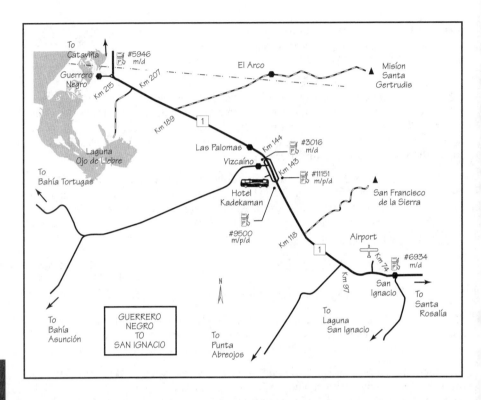

Much of the way you are crossing stabilized sand dunes that have blown eastward from the Laguna Ojo de Liebre area. The most noticeable vegetation is datilillo, a member of the yucca family, and small mesquite trees.

Sixteen miles (26 km) south of the Guerrero Negro junction is the road northeast to an old mining town, El Arco. See *Backroad Adventures* in this chapter for more information about this trip.

Forty-four miles (71 km) from the Guerrero Negro cutoff you will reach the small community of **Vizcaíno**. There's a junction there for a road that runs southwest to the coast at Punta Eugenia and Bahía Tortugas. See the *Backroad Adventures* section above for more information. Also take a look at *Side Trip to Bahía Asuncion* which includes the description of a campground in that town.

The road begins a gradual climb into the Sierra San Francisco that form the spine of the peninsula at about 70 miles (113 km) from the Guerrero Negro junction. The pass through the mountains used by the highway is fairly mild with no major grades on the western slopes. As you near the mountains you will begin to see the large cardón cactus.

Fifty-nine miles (95 km) from the Guerrero Negro cutoff there is a road to the left that leads to the most accessible of the pinturas rupestres or cave painting locations in this section of the Baja. Cueva Ratón is near the small village of **San Francisco de la Sierra**. See the *Backroad Adventures* section above for more information about this road. You must register and obtain information at the cave painting museum in San Ignacio before visiting the cave.

Sixty-eight miles (110 km) from the Guerrero Negro cutoff a good paved highway goes right toward the ocean at Punta Abreojos. See *Side Trip to Estero el Coyote* below for more about this destination including a campground description.

Finally, 86 miles (139 km) from the Guerrero Negro junction you will enter the outskirts of San Ignacio. The road to the right to San Lino is first, then you'll see the side road leading to the village of San Ignacio.

Guerrero Negro to San Ignacio Campground

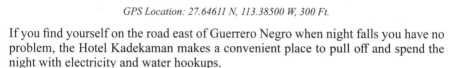

HOTEL KADEKAMAN *(Open All Year)*

Address:	Blvd. Lázaro Cárdenas S/N, CP 23935 Vizcaíno, B.C.S., México
Telephone:	(615) 156-4112
Email:	kadekaman@yahoo.com
Website:	www.kadekaman.com

GPS Location: 27.64611 N, 113.38500 W, 300 Ft.

If you find yourself on the road east of Guerrero Negro when night falls you have no problem, the Hotel Kadekaman makes a convenient place to pull off and spend the night with electricity and water hookups.

This motel has a restaurant out front and five spaces for RVs to park in the back. There are electricity (15 amp) and water hookups but no sewer. A restroom is clean and modern and has a toilet and hot shower. The Wi-Fi signal reaches the RV parking spaces. You'll notice that the entry has an arch that would probably be too low for some rigs so it's best to turn into the lot just to the southeast and enter the motel compound from the side.

The campground is located near the Km 143 marker on Mex 1 in the town of Vizcaíno. It is 0.4 miles (0.6 km) southeast of the Pemex #3016 station.

SIDE TRIP TO BAHÍA ASUNCIÓN
70 Miles (113 Km), 1.25 Hours

From a junction on Mex 1 in Vizcaíno a paved road leads westward to the ocean at Bahía Tortugas. See the description of this road in the *Backroad Adventures* section of this chapter. Using the first 46 miles (75 km) of this road and then taking a 24 mile (69 km) side road will bring you to the coast and the town of Bahía Asunción.

Bahía Asunción is increasingly popular with visitors, particularly now that the access highway is completely paved. This is a small but neat village complete with small stores, a restaurant or two, a gas station, and a baseball park. The population is about 2,400.

Fishing is popular. It's for yellowtail, reef and surf fish and is best during the period from September to December. This is an open coast and launch facilities aren't great, local knowledge is important so it's best to hire a guide and boat.

The long beach out front is great for walking and beachcombing. Most surfing is at

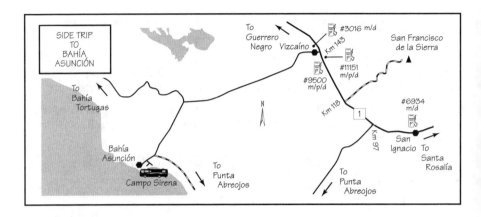

Punta Choros, about 4 miles (6 km) east of town. Access is on sandy roads, four-wheel-drive is recommended.

▧ Campo Sirena *(Open All Year)*
Telephone: (615) 160-0289 or (615) 155-7097 (Cell)
Email: infoasuncion@gmail.com
Website: www.bahiaasuncion.com

GPS Location: 27.14385 N, 114.29105 W, Near Sea Level

Shari Bondi, the owner/manager of this park, is a one-woman tourist and promotional service for the town of Bahía Asunción. She and her husband operate a fishing guide service, motel, bed and breakfast, and this campground. If you check the internet for information about Bahía Asunción you'll most likely end up on one of her websites.

The small campground is simple but adequate. There are low amp electrical outlets and water faucets in a dirt lot on a bluff above the beach near the eastern, end of town. Large rigs can be accommodated since the parking site arrangement is in-formal. A small building has a bathroom with toilet and hot shower and there is a washing machine and loaner library. For an extra fee ($10) there is a nearby dump station. Free Wi-Fi is available in the park. The location is in town and within walking distance of the central area.

As you enter Bahía Asunción the road becomes divided and has light poles down the center island. When you come to the end of this center island, turn left and into the campground. There is a sign on the highway telling you where to turn.

Side Trip to Estero el Coyote
47 Miles (75 Km), 1 Hour

To reach Estero el Coyote you turn toward the coast from Mex 1 at Crucero del Pacifico near the kilometer 97 marker. This is 15 miles (24 km) west of San Ignacio. The road is marked for Punta Abreojos and leads southwest to the Pacific. Forty seven miles (75 km) down this road you reach the coast and the entrance road to Estero el Coyote and Campo Rene.

THE ESTERO EL COYOTE IS EXCELLENT FOR KAYAKING

Estero el Coyote is the next estero to the west from Laguna San Ignacio and its gray whales. It's an extensive 6-mile-long but shallow mangrove-lined body of water that goes almost dry at low tide, then rapidly fills as the tide comes in. There are few if any whales in this shallow lagoon, but fishing and birdwatching are excellent, oysters are available from the local fishermen, and you might even see a dolphin or two. It's also a great kayaking location.

From Campo Rene, which is located on the lagoon, you also have easy access to the nearby Pacific beach. This is a great place to unload the 4-wheelers and enjoy the miles of unpopulated beach and dunes.

CAMPO RENE *(Open All Year)*
Telephone:	(615) 157-2348, (615) 159-3163, (615) 103-0008
Email:	info@sdro.com
Website:	www.camporene.com/

GPS Location: 26.80964 N, 113.46928 W, Near Sea Level

Campo Rene offers a restaurant, cabanas, and tent and RV camping sites on the shore of Estero el Coyote. Guided sport fishing is available. Guests here often visit the nearby processing plant to pick up some oysters and bring them back for preparation at their rigs or in the restaurant.

Camping facilities include 6 palapa shelters along the estero and an additional 6 back-in slots with no palapas. All have low amp electrical outlets, power is produced on site with a generator. There are also 12 cabanas here and restrooms with hot showers are provided. There's lots of room to maneuver so any size rig will fit.

CENTRAL BAJA

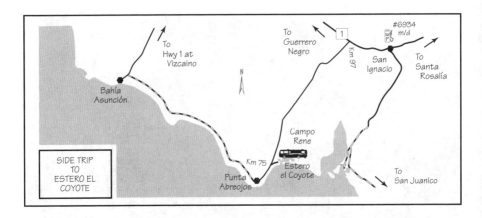

Access is from the paved highway out to Punta Abreojos. From the Crucero del Pacifico intersection on Mex 1 drive to the entrance near Km 75. You'll see a sign on the left. This is the second entrance you'll notice, the first, about a kilometer earlier, is a poorer road. The second access road runs 3 miles (5 km) behind the dunes to the campground. It's a dirt and sand road. Unless it has recently rained or flooded the road should be very firm and OK for any RV.

SAN IGNACIO (SAHN EEG-NAH-SEE-OH)
Population 700

San Ignacio is a date-palm oasis built around lagoons formed by damming a river which emerges from the earth nearby. The town is located just south of Mex 1. The road into town is paved and big RVs should have no problems since they can drive around the main square to turn around. The main square is also the location of the **mission church of San Ignacio**, one of the easiest to reach and most impressive mission churches on the Baja. This one is built of lava rock and has walls that are four feet thick.

From San Ignacio it is possible to take a guided tour to see rock paintings in the surrounding hills. You should visit the rock art museum located just south of the church, next door is where you register to visit rock-art sites. It is also possible to follow the thirty-five mile long partly paved road to **Laguna San Ignacio** to see gray whales from January through March. Two of the campgrounds listed below are at the lagoon. Whale tours are available in San Ignacio, vans are used to take you out to the lagoon.

San Ignacio Campgrounds

RICE AND BEANS OASIS *(Open All Year)*

Address:	Carretera Transpeninsular, Accesso a San Lino, CP 23930 San Ignacio, B.C.S, México
Telephone:	(615) 154-0283

GPS Location: 27.29861 N, 112.90444 W, 600 Ft.

This is San Ignacio's nicest RV park and definitely the best choice for big RVs. The campground also boasts a restaurant, arguably the best place to eat in San Ignacio. Both the RV park and associated restaurant are owned and operated by the same family that has the popular Rice and Beans Restaurant in San Felipe. This place is very popular with the off-road crowd and sees a lot of activity when one of the many races are in progress.

There are 29 spaces all with hookups. About half have sewer. They are located on two terraces overlooking San Ignacio's date palm forest. Tents are allowed but there is no separate area for them. There is no shade and unfortunately the highway runs just above the campground so it can be noisy. Restrooms are separate rooms with flush toilets and hot showers. There is a small swimming pool. The restaurant is at the entrance and the food is good. They have a computer set up in the restaurant for customer use, also Wi-Fi which you can sometimes pick up in the sites that are closest to the restaurant. This is a Passport America campground, cardholders can stay overnight for half price.

The access to the campground is directly off Mex 1 between Km 74 and 75 just west of San Ignacio.

RV PARK EL PADRINO *(Open All Year)*

GPS Location: 27.28556 N, 112.90139 W, 400 Ft.

The El Padrino is the closest RV park to town, you can easily stroll in to the central

VISIT THE ROCK ART MUSEUM NEXT DOOR TO THE MISSION CHURCH IN SAN IGNACIO

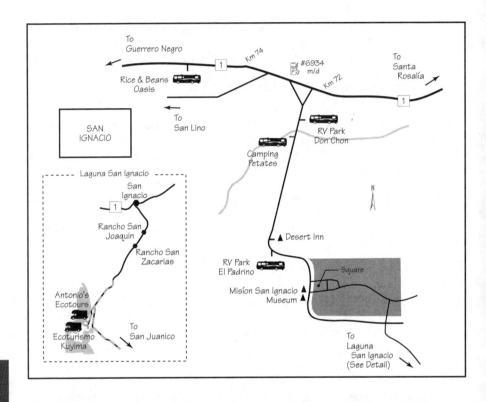

square or over to the nearby motel for dinner. Unfortunately, it has deteriorated to the point where it is really just a place to park with no hookups and unusable toilet facilities.

There are large areas where you can camp with no hookups. A centrally located restaurant also serves as an office when it is open, but it was closed when we visited. Otherwise there is usually a watchman on duty. The campground offers gray whale watching tours to San Ignacio Lagoon which is about one hour away in their van.

Take the San Ignacio cutoff near the Pemex. The campground is just past the Desert Inn, 1.3 miles (2.1 km) from the cutoff.

CAMPING PETATES *(Open All Year)*
   Telephone: (615) 103-5197

GPS Location: 27.29722 N, 112.89778 W, 400 Ft.

This is a camping area in the date palms next to the San Ignacio lagoon. There is room for perhaps 15 RVs here. Bigger RVs will have to exercise caution to avoid the palms. There are no hookups, facilities include waterfront palapas, flush toilets, and hot water showers. The managers are not on-site overnight.

From the San Ignacio cutoff near the Pemex head toward town. In .5 miles (.8 km), just past the lagoon crossing, you'll see the entrance on the right.

RV PARK DON CHON *(Open All Year)* $ ▲ 🄲🄴🄻🄻

GPS Location: 27.29944 N, 112.89417 W, 400 Ft.

This campground is easy to spot as you drive the side road in to San Ignacio. It's a very simple place with parking for any size RV on dirt under date palms next to the lagoon. The only facilities are dilapidated bucket-flush toilets. The campground is often unattended, but recently an attendant has been living on site and spends the night.

To reach the campground take the San Ignacio cutoff near the Pemex. In just 0.2 mile (0.3 km) from the turn you'll see a sign indicating the entrance to the Don Chon on the left.

ANTONIO'S ECOTOURS *(Open Jan 1 to April 15 - Varies)* $$ ▲ 🄷🄾🄣 🍴 📶

Address:	Domocillio Conocido, Laguna San Ignacio, B.C.S., México
Telephone:	(612) 220-8071, (615) 112-5375, (615) 103-3323
Email:	Jasso-2521@hotmail.com
Website:	www.antoniosecotours.com

GPS Location: 26.82893 N, 113.16775 W, Near Sea Level

Antonio's is one of two whale-watching operations with camping located on the shore of Laguna San Ignacio. There are about 5 spaces overlooking the lagoon for RVs. Restrooms have warm solar showers and flush toilets and there is a restaurant with Wi-Fi.

The road out to the Lagoon starts in San Ignacio, it's 40 miles (65 km) to the campground. This road is currently a Type 2 road (see Chapter 2 for information about back-road classifications). When we visited (spring of 2017) the first 30 miles (48 km) had been paved. Beyond that the road was easy to negotiate except for a few short soft sand sections and lots of stutter bumps. The campground is well signed and easy to find once you reach the lagoon.

ECOTURISMO KUYIMA *(Open Jan 1 to April 15 - Varies)* $$$ ▲ 🄷🄾🄣 🍴 📶

Address:	Domocillio Conocido, Laguna San Ignacio, B.C.S., México
Telephone:	(615) 154-0070
Email:	kuyima@prodigy.net
Website:	www.kuyima.com

GPS Location: 26.82458 N, 113.16981 W, Near Sea Level

This is a whale-watching camp on the shore of San Ignacio Lagoon. It's neat and well run, a very professional operation.

Facilities include ten waterfront RV/tent sites outlined in white shells. There are also rental cabañas, toilets, solar showers, a restaurant, and a gift shop. Whale tours can be arranged even if you drive in without reservations.

The road out to the Lagoon starts in San Ignacio, it's 41 miles (66 km) to the campground. Follow the instructions given above to reach Antonio's, Kuyima is about a mile beyond Antonio's and is also well signed.

CENTRAL BAJA

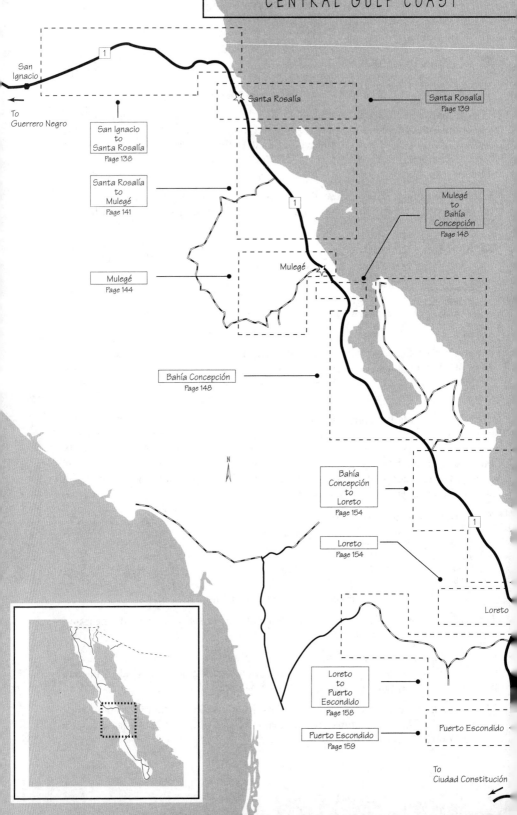

CENTRAL GULF COAST

San
Ignacio

1

To
Guerrero Negro

Santa Rosalía

Santa Rosalía
Page 139

San Ignacio
to
Santa Rosalía
Page 138

Santa Rosalía
to
Mulegé
Page 141

Mulegé
to
Bahía
Concepción
Page 148

1

Mulegé

Mulegé
Page 144

Bahía Concepción
Page 148

N

Bahía
Concepción
to
Loreto
Page 154

1

Loreto
Page 154

Loreto

Loreto
to
Puerto
Escondido
Page 158

Puerto Escondido

Puerto Escondido
Page 159

To
Ciudad Constitución

INTRODUCTION

The section covered in this chapter is one of the most popular areas of the whole Baja Peninsula. Here Mex 1, the Transpeninsular, reaches the warm Gulf of California for the first time. There are tourist resorts, quiet tropical towns, and sandy beaches suitable for RV parking. What more could you want?

Highlights

The sandy beaches lining **Bahía Concepción** are the primary destination for many RVers headed down the Baja. Here you can camp right next to the water, there are enough nearby services so that you can stay for an extended period, and there is plenty to keep you busy with sightseeing trips to the north and south and water sports right at your doorstep.

Loreto, a town toward the southern end of this section, is just about the only fly-in destination with scheduled air service north of La Paz and Cabo. It has hotels, restaurants, a golf course, and resort-type services like guided fishing, diving, and sightseeing trips.

Roads and Fuel Availability

The Transpeninsular is two lanes wide for the length of this section, just as it is along most of the peninsula. It is narrow but relatively uncrowded, so continue to exercise caution and keep the speed down.

Kilometer markers along here decrease as you drive south. The segment from San

Ignacio to Santa Rosalía counts down from 74 to zero. In Santa Rosalía a new segment of kilometer posts begins with 197, it counts down to zero at Loreto. At the Loreto cutoff the kilometer posts start again at 119, these reach zero at the 90 degree corner in Ciudad Insurgentes on the west side of the Sierra de la Giganta where the road turns south toward La Paz and the Cape.

Fuel is readily available in this section. Here are the locations, with types, and distances between stations: **San Ignacio**, gas and diesel; **Santa Rosalía**, three stations with gas and diesel, 45 miles (83 km) (watch these guys!); **just south of Mulegé**, gas and diesel, 41 miles (66 km); and **Loreto**, gas and diesel, 80 miles (129 km). From Loreto to the next station at **Ciudad Insurgentes** is a distance of 74 miles (119 km).

Sightseeing

At the northern end of this section is the coastal town of **Santa Rosalía**. It has an unusual history for a Baja town and some unusual sights, including a church designed by the same man who designed the Eiffel tower, a French-style bakery, and wood buildings dating from the 19th century. See the *Santa Rosalía* section for more information. The town has an active copper mine, newly reopened, and is an anthill of activity.

Mulegé is a date-palm oasis located on an estuary along the Gulf of California. It's a friendly little town that is very accustomed to visitors from north of the border. It also has some interesting sights including an old mission and a jail that only locked the doors at night when it was in operation.

You can visit some missions in this section. One is the **Misión Santa Rosalía de Mulegé** mentioned above. The other is the well-preserved Jesuit **Misión San Javier** in the hills behind Loreto, the road is described in *Backroad Adventures* below. Easiest of all to visit is the **Misión Nuestra Señora de Loreto** right in central Loreto, it also has a museum with exhibits about the Jesuit missions in the region.

There are several **rock-art sites** in the mountains behind the coast. Most popular is probably the one near Rancho La Trinidad. You can find a guide in Mulegé. The drive is described below in the *Backroad Adventures* section.

Golf

Just a few miles south of Loreto is a resort - Nopoló. This is a FONATUR complex. FONATUR is the Mexican governmental agency that has planned and constructed places you are probably more familiar with: Cancún, Cabo San Lucas, Ixtapa, and Bahías de Huatulco. The resort has a golf course, the only one between Ensenada and Cabo San Lucas. It is an 18-hole course and tee-time reservations are easy to get. There is also a driving range and a tennis center.

Beaches and Water Sports

Punta Chivato has a primitive camping beach offering excellent water sports opportunities. The beach is fine for swimming with nice sand. Snorkeling is good along rocky reefs just offshore, winds are good for board-sailing, and the fishing is good too. There is a nearby boat ramp and a sheltered area for small boats right at the campground.

KAYAKERS ESPECIALLY LOVE THE WATERS AT BAHÍA CONCEPCIÓN

The white sand beaches on the west side of **Bahía Concepción** are one of the area's biggest attractions. The waters of the bay are protected and excellent for swimming and water sports. Kayakers especially love the area. Most beaches near the highway are available for camping, they are listed under *Bahía Concepción Campgrounds* below.

Kayakers also like to make 1 to 2 week trips from Mulegé to Loreto or even from Puerto Escondido south to La Paz.

Fishing

It is not too hard to find launching ramps in this section. There are ramps in Santa Rosalía, San Lucas Cove, Punta Chivato, Mulegé, Bahía Concepción, Loreto, and Puerto Escondido. Some are better than others, in fact some are just beaches with hard sand, but you should be able to find a place to launch most any trailer boat along here somewhere.

In this section the two most popular fisheries are probably for yellowtail during December through January and for Dorado in July and August. The winter yellowtail season coincides with great weather for camping.

Pangas can be chartered in many places along this coast so don't think that you can't fish if you don't have a boat.

San Lucas Cove, located between Santa Rosalía and Mulegé, has three campgrounds and is very popular with fishermen. It offers protected waters for your boat at the campgrounds and easy access to 10-fathom water in Craig Channel behind Isla San Marcos.

Backroad Adventures

See the *Backroad Driving* section of *Chapter 2 - Details, Details, Details* for essential information about driving off the main highway on the Baja and for a definition of road types used below.

From Km 169 Between Santa Rosalía and Mulegé - This is a usually Type 2 road that leads 9 miles (14 km) to the village of **San José de Magdalena**. This town is known as the garlic capital of the Baja. You can buy long braids of garlic here from the harvest in March and lasting perhaps to December. The road continues beyond town but deteriorates to a Type 3.

From Km 136 at Mulegé - This road leading westward from near the Mulegé cutoff leads quite a distance into the mountains, but the most popular destination is **Rancho La Trinidad** and nearby cave art in La Trinidad canyon about 12 miles (19 km) from Mulegé. You must use a guide to visit the cave art, ask around for one in Mulegé. The road to the rancho is usually a Type 2 but beyond it deteriorates to Type 3 requiring 4WD. Eventually the road circles around to San José de Magdalena, reaching it 50 miles (81 km) after passing Rancho La Trinidad. From **San José de Magdalena**, of course, you can return to Mex 1 at Km 169 as described above.

From Km 62 Between Bahía Concepción and Loreto - From this point a graded road leads 10 miles (16 km) to the village of **San Nicolas**, then 6 miles (10 km) along the coast northward to **San Sebastian**. This is usually a Type 2 road.

From Km 118 Between Loreto and Puerto Escondido - The **Misión San Javier** is a popular excursion for tourists from Loreto. The distance from the junction to the church is 22 miles (35 km) on a graded Type 2 road with some steep sections. At about 18 miles (29 km) you will pass a cutoff for the long road to San Miguel de Comondú and San Jose de Comondú. That is usually a bad Type 3 road.

It is also possible to pass through San Javier and follow a very long Type 2 road that crosses the spine of the peninsula to hook up with Hwy 53 north of Ciudad Insurgentes. This road is about 45 miles (73 km) of dirt and gravel and follows a fairly flat river-valley route. It requires crossing and recrossing the river some 12 times, often in spots with water and no bridge or markers. Inquire locally about water levels and condition of this road before setting out.

THE ROUTES, TOWNS, AND CAMPGROUNDS

SAN IGNACIO TO SANTA ROSALÍA
45 Miles (73 Km), 1.25 Hours

The road in this section is passing through the Sierra San Francisco. Grades are not difficult, other than the descent to the coast, but the road is sinuous in places so you'll want to keep the speed down.

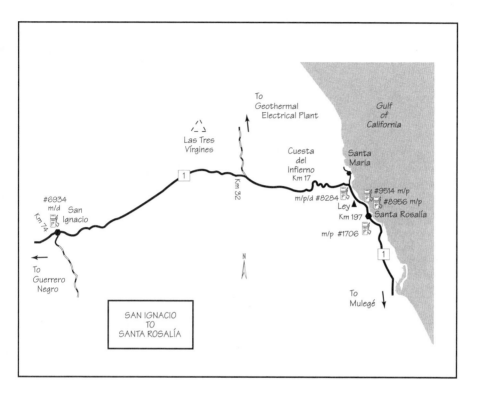

About 20 miles eastward from San Ignacio you may notice that the road is crossing lava flows. They are from **Las Tres Vírgines** (The Three Virgins), a volcanic mountain with three separate cones on the north side of the highway. In a short distance you'll pass the road left to an experimental geothermal electrical plant. The volcano is thought to have last shown significant activity about 1847 in the form of quite a bit of vapor. At about this point the road begins a long descent toward the Gulf of California.

Thirty-five miles from San Ignacio the descent becomes much steeper. This grade is called the **Cuesta del Infierno** (loosely translated as Grade to Hell), it is about 2.5 miles (3.1 km) long and the steepest grade on Mex 1. Be sure to gear down and keep the speed low as you descend, there are many curves. Soon the grade becomes less steep and after another 4 miles (6.5 km) or so you'll reach the coast and turn south to enter Santa Rosalía.

SANTA ROSALÍA (SAHN-TAH ROH-SAH-LEE-AH)
Population 14,000

Don't pass through Santa Rosalía without stopping. This old mining town is unlike any other town on the Baja. Located at the point where Mex 1 finally reaches the

CENTRAL GULF COAST

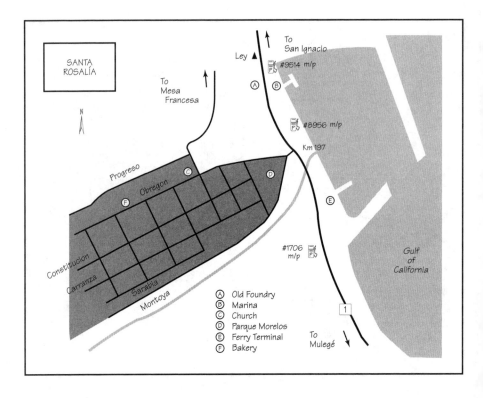

Gulf of California, Santa Rosalía was founded in the 1880s by a French company to extract the large amounts of copper ore located here. The mining operation lasted until the 1950s. For years after that the town was a fishing and ferry port, and a hub for the surrounding area. Just recently the mines have again opened and the mining infrastructure is being upgraded. The town is a hive of activity.

The ferries run from here to Topolobampo, the port for Guaymas on Mexico's west coast. For information see *Ferries* in *Chapter 2 - Details, Details, Details.*

Much of the town is constructed of wood imported from the Pacific Northwest, the building designs are French colonial. **Santa Rosalía's church** is unique, it was designed by A.G. Eiffel who is better known for his tower in Paris. It was prefabricated in France and shipped by boat around Cape Horn. The town also has a well-known **French-style bakery**.

It is best not to drive a large RV in to town, although the town is built on a grid plan the roads are fairly constricted. It is better to park along the highway outside town and then walk in. Be careful where you park, the police here are notorious for giving tickets.

Santa Rosalía Campgrounds

Santa Rosalía no longer has a campground. However, there are campgrounds not far

SANTA ROSALÍA'S UNIQUE CHURCH WAS DESIGNED BY AG EIFFEL

to the south and they make a decent base for visiting the town. Santa Rosalía also makes a good day trip from Mulegé.

SANTA ROSALÍA TO MULEGÉ
37 Miles (60 Km), 1 Hour

Nine miles (15 km) south of Santa Rosalía, is San Lucas. Caleta San Lucas, a large cove just a half mile east of town, is the location of two RV parks popular with fishermen. They are RV Park San Lucas Cove and much smaller RV Camacho, both discussed below. The island offshore is Isla San Marcos, there is a large gypsum mine on the island. Just a bit farther south you'll see the sign for another RV park, Playa Dos Amigos.

Twenty-five miles (41 km) south of Santa Rosalía, near Km 155, is a road leading to the coast and a campground known as Punta Chivato. The road is 11 miles (18 km) long, unpaved and rough, but usually suitable for any RV. The waterfront camping area is very popular with folks who know about it, it is covered below.

You'll arrive at Mulegé 37 miles (60 km) from Santa Rosalía, near Km 136. The roads in town are narrow and not at all suitable for RVs, all of the campgrounds listed below except the second can be reached without entering town. On a first visit it's best to explore town in a tow car or on foot.

CENTRAL GULF COAST

Santa Rosalía to Mulegé Campgrounds

🚐 RV CAMACHO *(Open All Year)*

GPS Location: 27.22056 N, 112.21306 W, Near Sea Level

This is a small campground just north of the much larger RV park called San Lucas Cove. Usually there are no rigs in here, management is limited to a visit in the evening to collect fees and most people are probably more comfortable with the larger campground next door. There are about 5 waterfront sites, two with shade palapas. An area behind the waterfront sites provides lots of room for additional parking, big RVs are fine. There are sometimes hot water showers and flush toilets.

To reach the campground watch for the sign at Km 181 south of Santa Rosalía. The 0.6 mile (1 km) dirt road east to the campground is fine for any size RV.

🚐 RV PARK SAN LUCAS COVE *(Open All Year)*

  Address: Apdo. 50, Santa Rosalía, B.C.S., México

GPS Location: 27.21861 N, 112.21417 W, Near Sea Level

This is a popular waterfront campground that may remind you of those farther south on Bahía Concepción. It is not quite as scenic as those but has a similar ambiance. The fishing in this area is excellent and most of the campers in this park are here for the fishing.

FISHING AT SAN LUCAS COVE IS EXCELLENT

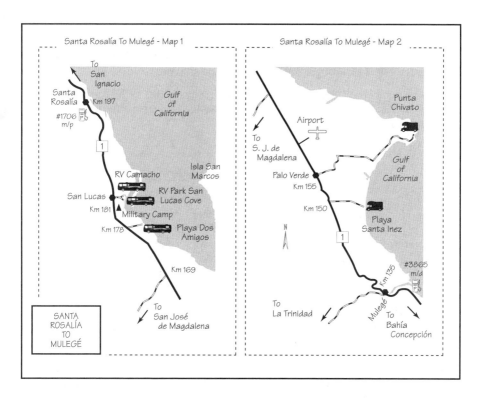

There are about 20 parking sites along the beach and at least 40 more on a large hard-packed sandy area behind. There is lots of room for big RVs. The campground has flush toilets and usually hot water showers as well as a dump station, so it is possible to make an extended visit. Municipal water is now connected to the campground so the water is not salty. There's also a small restaurant/bar with Wi-Fi. Folks either pull their boats up on the beach or anchor them out front.

Access is via the same road as RV Camacho above. It is near Km 181 south of Santa Rosalía. At about 0.5 mile (0.8 km) take the right fork into the campground. The road in to the campground is packed sand and is about 0.6 miles (1 km) long. Big RVs will have no problems negotiating it.

PLAYA DOS AMIGOS *(Open All Year)*

Telephone: (615) 152-1020 (Santa Rosalia) or
(615) 155-4097 (at park)

GPS Location: 27.20250 N, 112.20833 W, Near Sea Level

This camping area is located on the south shore of the Bahía el Islote de San Lucas, RV Camacho and RV Park San Lucas Cove are on the north shore of the same bay. The beach out front of this campground is shallow and very gradually sloping so it's not good for larger boats but fine for kayaks.

The campground is a large field just back from the beach. Permanent units occupy

CENTRAL GULF COAST

the beach. Most travelers must park behind although at times there are some narrow slots for parking along the beach. The restroom building has flush toilets and hot showers. The access road has been improved considerably and is now suitable for any size RV but is still rough. A manager lives on site.

The access road is well marked with billboards, it heads east to the campground just north of the Km 178 marker. It's about 0.6 mile (1 km) long. Near the beach bear left, the large lot to the right is privately owned.

🚐 PUNTA CHIVATO *(Open All Year)*

GPS Location: 27.07269 N, 111.94874 W, Near Sea Level

While this beach area seems remote it is also adjacent to the community of Punto Chivato. Homes overlook the camping area. There is a large parking area behind a sandy beach. A small spit provides enough protection for small fishing skiffs. Sand sometimes drifts into the camping area but when we recently visited there was a large area with a good parking surface. The long access road and limited parking room mean that this is not really a suitable campground for most big RVs although we often see some pretty big ones here. There are no facilities of any kind.

Access to camping area is via a long dirt road. The access road leaves Mex 1 just north of Km 155 between Santa Rosalía and Mulegé in the village of Palo Verde. The distance from Mex 1 to the camping area is 11.3 miles (18.2 km). After 2.1 miles (3.4 km) there is a fork in the road, take the right fork for the new road. The road nears the shoreline at 5.7 miles (9.2 km) and turns left to parallel the shoreline some quarter-mile back from the beach. At about 8.5 miles (13.7 km) from the highway the road turns inland and rounds the end of a runway, then turns again toward the beach. You'll pass a small hotel at 10.1 miles (16.3 km), formerly called El Hotelito, now signed as Hotel Chivato. This hotel has managed the beach in the past but when we last visited was unattended. From the hotel continue another 1.2 mile (1.9 km) east-ward to the camping area. En route you will pass another hotel entrance (it's closed) and then through a row of houses which overlooks the beach and campground.

MULEGÉ (MOO-LAH-HAY)
Population 4,000

Situated near the mouth of the palm and mangrove-lined Río Santa Rosalía, Mulegé is a welcome tropical paradise after the long drive across desert country from the north. In many ways Mulegé may remind you of San Ignacio, both have a definite desert oasis ambiance. Mulegé is a popular RVer destination, many permanents make their seasonal home here. There are five decent RV parks and the beaches and coves of the Bahía Concepción begin only 12 miles (19.6 km) to the south.

Fishing, diving, and kayaking are all popular here. Yellowtail are often thick during the winter and summer anglers go offshore for deep water fish. The nearby Santa Inés Islands are popular diving destinations, dive shops in Mulegé offer trips to the islands and other sites. Kayakers love Bahía Concepción and the coastline north and south.

There are some interesting sights in Mulegé itself. The **Misión Santa Rosalía** is located about 2 miles (3.3 km) upstream from the bridge on the right bank (facing downstream). It is usually locked except during services but the excursion offers excellent views of the town and river. Mulegé is also known for its **prison**. Now closed the prison building houses a museum and you can take a look at the cells. You can drive out to the mouth of the river (if you have a smaller RV or tow car) on the north shore, there you'll find a rock formation and lighthouse known as El **Sombrerito**, you can't miss it.

Mulegé is a base for visiting two cave art sites nearby. These are **La Trinidad** and **San Borjitas**. You must visit with a guide. The easiest way to find a tour including transportation, permits, and a guide is to ask for information at one of the local hotels.

Mulegé is accustomed to visitors and takes them in stride, there's a large Norteamericano population. There are quite a few good restaurants and some small grocery shops. A few miles south of town is a Pemex, it has lots of room for big RVs and is an easy place to fill up.

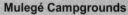

Mulegé Campgrounds

🚐 HACIENDA DE LA HABANA

(Open Oct - June – except Easter week)

Telephone: (615) 103-0935
Email: raysranch@yahoo.com

GPS Location: 26.87278 N, 112.01889 W, 100 Ft.

Hacienda de la Habana is located back in the wide valley behind Mulegé. It's a pleasant well-watered area, very unusual for the Baja.

The hacienda has 24 large full-hookup pull-thru sites with parking on grass. Electrical outlets are the 20-amp style but have 30-amp breakers. There are flush toilets, showers, a swimming pool, and a beautiful lounge area overlooking the pool. The monthly rate in the campground is $300.

Reaching the campground requires driving on dirt roads but they can be traveled in any RV driven slowly. From Mulegé drive west on Icehouse Road. This is the road that goes inland just north of Km 135, about .5 mile (.8 km) north of the bridge over the Río Mulegé. Icehouse Road is also Calle Manuel M De Leon but neither name is signed at the intersection. There may be a sign for the campground, it is also signed (at least from the south) for La Trinidad and Piedras Pinturas. Drive inland for .5 mile (.8 km) and turn left, this turn is just opposite the icehouse. In just .1 mile (.2 km) take the first right. In another .2 miles (.3 km) the road makes a 90-degree left. In .1 miles (.2 km) the road comes to a T, turn right. In another .2 miles (.3 km) at a fork take the right branch. In another .3 miles (.5 km) the road makes a 90-degree turn to the left. Finally, in another .3 miles (.5 km) take a right. Heading west now, in .6 miles (1 km) you'll see a former restaurant building on the left. Turn into the driveway just beyond with a sign for Hacienda de La Habana and follow it to the campsites. It sounds complicated but signs mark most turns, it's only 2.3 miles (3.7 km) from the highway.

HUERTA DON CHANO RV PARK *(Open All Year)*

Address: Calle Playa, H. Mulegé, BCS
Telephone: (615) 153-0720 or (615) 107-5851 (Cell)
Email: manual_romero25@yahoo.com.mx

GPS Location: 26.89806 N, 111.97479 W, Near Sea Level

Although we hesitate to tell people to go through the central part of Mulegé in an RV we would make an exception if you're headed for this park. It's well run and handy to town, so it's worth the effort. The route has no tight turns so should present no problems.

This park is located away from the other RV parks in Mulegé. It's on the north side of the river. The park has about twenty back-in sites, some large enough for rigs to about 35 feet. The campground has quite a bit of shade. Restrooms are provided and they have hot showers. Wi-Fi is also provided and reaches most of the park.

Zero your odometer as you enter Mulegé at the arch off Mex 1. At .1 mile (.2 km) follow the road to the right. Proceed straight down the hill through town, making no turns. You'll end up driving along the river toward the ocean and at 1 mile (2 km) on your odometer you'll see the sign on your left for the campground entrance.

HOTEL CUESTA REAL *(Open All Year)*

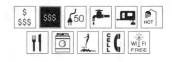

Telephone: (615) 153-0321
Email: mayocuesta@hotmail.com

GPS Location: 26.89670 N, 111.96611 W, Near Sea Level

This little motel and campground are excellent for smaller RVs. It's a great alternative for a stay in Mulegé.

There are 10 back-in sites here suitable for RVs to about 35 feet, several are available for short-term use. These are full hookup sites with 15, 30 and 50-amp outlets. Parking is on good gravel. A hotel room with hot shower is set aside for the RV guests and there's a restaurant (summer only), a laundry room, and internet access. There's also a swimming pool. Since this is a small park it is important that you park on the pull-off at the entrance and walk down to see if there is room for you. If you don't you may have to back out – and that's not easy! The monthly rate is $300.

The entrance road is 1.1 miles (1.8 km) southeast of the Mulegé bridge off Mex 1.

VILLA MARIA ISABEL RV PARK *(Open All Year)*

Address: Apdo. 5, CP 23900 Mulegé, B.C.S., México
Telephone: (615) 153-0246 or (615) 104-1247 (Cell)
Email: mariveldemulege@gmail.com
Website: www.mulegetoday.com.mx

GPS Location: 26.89591 N, 111.96390 W, Near Sea Level

This is a place to stay if you are looking for an easily accessible RV park in Mulegé. Like the other Mulegé campgrounds it sits near the south shore of the Mulegé River.

The campground has about 40 sites. There are tent sites, partial hookup RV sites, and full hookup RV sites including 18 pull-thrus. Parking is on dirt and many sites will accommodate larger RVs although they're narrow and if the park is full it is difficult

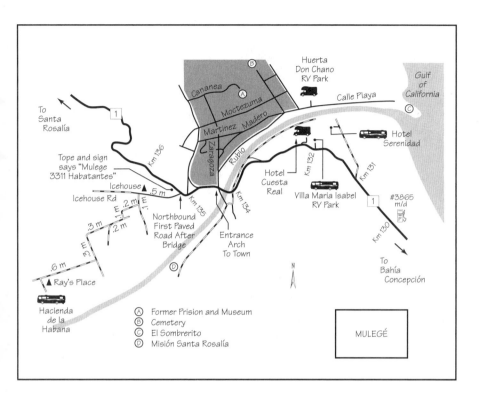

to find room to extend an awning. There is also an area for tent campers with a shared palapa. The restrooms have hot water showers. There's an unheated swimming pool above the campground at the owner's residence, nice in the summer. Wi-Fi is from the residence near the pool and does not reach the campground. The monthly rate here is the daily rate of $20 with one free day per week.

The campground is 1.3 miles (2.1 km) south of the Mulegé bridge off Mex 1.

HOTEL SERENIDAD *(Open All Year)*

Address: Apdo. 9, CP 23900 Mulegé, B.C.S., México
Telephone: (615) 153-0530, (615) 153-0311, (615) 153-0111
Email: hotelserenidad@prodigy.net.mx
Website: www.hotelserenidad.com

GPS Location: 26.89755 N, 111.95827 W, Near Sea Level

The Serenidad is a hotel located on the south bank of the Mulegé River near the mouth. It has its own airstrip and was a popular fly-in fishing destination even before the Transpeninsular Highway was built.

The hotel has 7 available RV spaces along a wall at the back of the property, they'll take RVs to 40 feet. The location is hot and unappealing considering the nearby alternatives, but there are full hookups with 15-amp outlets. Restrooms are available with hot showers. The hotel has nice facilities, there is a swimming pool and restaurant

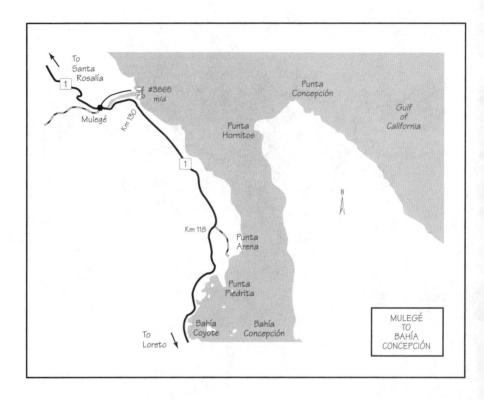

(closed during the month of Sept.). A pig roast, Mexican buffet, and mariachi performance draws people from around the area on Saturday night.

The entrance to the Serenidad is the farthest south along Mex 1 of all the Mulegé campgrounds. If you zero your odometer at the bridge you'll see the entrance road at 2.2 miles (3.5 km). There's a half-mile gravel entrance road leading along the side of the airstrip to the hotel.

MULEGÉ TO BAHÍA CONCEPCIÓN
12 Miles (19 Km), .25 Hour

This is only a short drive to the northernmost beaches on Bahía Concepción from Mulegé. Of course it's a lot farther to the southernmost beaches on the bay. An important stop along the road is the Pemex station 3 miles (5 km) south of the Mulegé bridge. It has excellent access for big RVs.

BAHÍA CONCEPCIÓN (BAH-HEE-AH KOHN-SEP-SEE-OHN)

For many people, especially RVers, Bahía Concepción is the ultimate Baja destination. This huge shallow bay offers many beaches where you can park your camping vehicle just feet from the water and spend the winter months soaking in the sunshine. Mex 1 parallels the western shore of the bay for about 20 miles (33 km), you'll see many very attractive spots and undoubtedly decide to stop. The many beaches offer different levels of services. Full hookups are seldom available, but many have toilets, showers, water, and restaurants. Information about the most popular beaches is offered below. While many of these places seem to have no formal organization do not be surprised if someone comes by in the evening to collect a small fee. This usually covers keeping the area picked up, trash removal and pit toilets. Ask one of your fellow campers about arrangements if you have questions. During the winter season you'll seldom be alone on these beaches. The closest place to get supplies is Mulegé.

It is important to be concerned about sanitation, particularly about disposal of both black and gray water at all of the beaches along here. A lot of RVers winter here and some people feel that in recent years there's been a noticeable increase in the growth of vegetation offshore at some beaches. If the trend continues it's possible that camping along these beaches might be restricted, something no one wants to happen. You should assure yourself that waste is being properly handled before using any of the dump stations on these beaches.

Bahía Concepción Campgrounds

PLAYA SANTISPAC *(Open All Year)*

GPS Location: 26.76637 N, 111.88988 W, Near Sea Level

The most northerly beach on sheltered Bahía Coyote is very popular, partly because the entrance road is so short and easy.

The long beach offers beachside parking for many rigs. There are pit toilets and two restaurants: Ana's and Armando's.

The entrance to Playa Santispac is just south of the Km 114 marker. The beach is visible from the road, it's hard to miss since it's the first of Bahía Concepción's great beach campgrounds that you'll see from the road as you head south. While short and in good shape the entrance road is at the bottom of a hill if you're coming from the north, exercise care when leaving the highway. There is an entrance station where the fee is collected, it's usually manned but not always. It's the only one on any beach along here, that should give you some idea of the popularity of this beach. If there's no one at the station just continue on in and park, someone will come around to collect later. Vendors often visit this beach selling fruit and vegetables, water, fish, and crafts.

PUNTA PIEDRITA *(Open All Year)*

GPS Location: 26.76138 N, 111.87851 W, Near Sea Level

This camping area is hidden behind Santispac but much the same. It's small with a more open beach. To enter you drive into the Santispac entrance, then to the left through Santispac to follow the water for about a quarter mile. You'll see the gate and rigs parked along the water. You can stay or go back to Santispac, your choice.

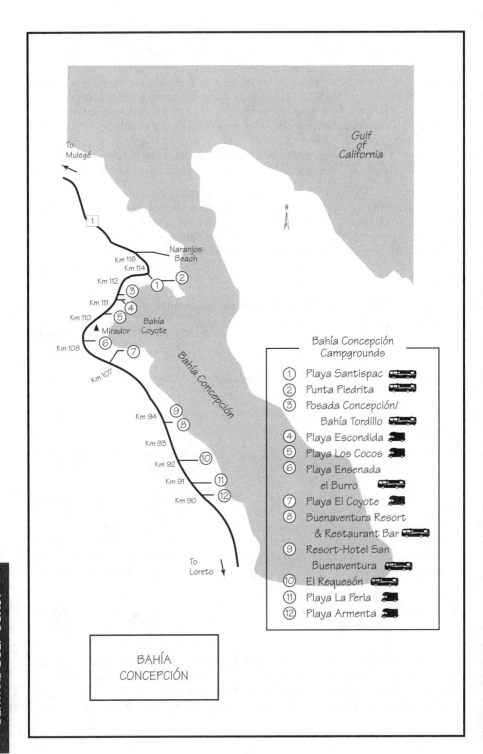

Gulf
of
California

To
Mulegé

Km 118
Km 114
Km 112
Km 111
Km 110
Km 108
Km 107

Naranjos
Beach

Mirador

Bahía
Coyote

Bahía Concepción

Km 94
Km 93
Km 92
Km 91
Km 90

To
Loreto

Bahía Concepción
Campgrounds

① Playa Santispac
② Punta Piedrita
③ Posada Concepción/
   Bahía Tordillo
④ Playa Escondida
⑤ Playa Los Cocos
⑥ Playa Ensenada
   el Burro
⑦ Playa El Coyote
⑧ Buenaventura Resort
   & Restaurant Bar
⑨ Resort-Hotel San
   Buenaventura
⑩ El Requesón
⑪ Playa La Perla
⑫ Playa Armenta

BAHÍA
CONCEPCIÓN

POSADA CONCEPCIÓN/BAHÍA TORDILLO *(Open All Year)*
Address: Apdo. 14, Mulegé, B.C.S., México

   GPS Location: 26.75422 N, 111.89844 W, Near Sea Level

Posada Concepción is really more subdivision than beachfront camping area, most of the people here live in houses or permanently installed trailers. There are a few spaces for travelers, they are nowhere near the water but they do have hookups.

There are three slots here with full hookups, electricity is from 15-amp outlets. Power is from a generator here, it runs from 10 am to 10 pm. The spaces are fine for large RVs. Restrooms have flush toilets and hot showers. This beach is well-protected, at low tide the water is very shallow and there are a few hot-water seeps in shallow water. There is also a tennis court. Just ask around when you arrive, you'll eventually find the people in charge of the rental RV sites.

The entrance to Posada Concepción is 0.2 mile (0.3 km) south of Km 112.

PLAYA ESCONDIDA *(Open All Year)*

   GPS Location: 26.74560 N, 111.89574 W, Near Sea Level

This small isolated beach is picture-perfect. There is a row of palapas along the water. Outhouses are on the hillside behind.

The road in to this beach is much better than in prior years, but still not good for larger RVs Take a look before you try it. The entrance road is just south of Posada Concepción, 0.4 mile (0.6 km) south of the Km 112 marker. At first glance you'll think the road leads to the south side of the same bay occupied by Posada Concepción, but instead it leads 0.5 miles (0.8 km) up over a low saddle to an unexpected beach, hence the name which means hidden beach.

PLAYA LOS COCOS *(Open All Year)*

   GPS Location: 26.74246 N, 111.90155 W, Near Sea Level

Playa los Cocos is another beautiful beach with minimal facilities. There are palapas and pit toilets. Mangroves are at the rear.

The entrance is midway between Km 110 and 111 markers. There is no sign and the entrance road is about 0.3 miles (0.5 km) long. It's in poor condition but short, take a look, you might make it in a big rig. The campground can easily be seen from the highway because it runs very nearby.

PLAYA ENSENADA EL BURRO *(Open All Year)*

   GPS Location: 26.72944 N, 111.90750 W, Near Sea Level

This beach offers the standard pit toilets and also has a restaurant. It's less desirable than the other beaches because there are permanent structures along the water. Visiting rigs park at the south end of the lot.

The entrance to Playa el Burro is midway between Km 108 and Km 109. You can easily see the beach from the highway.

CENTRAL GULF COAST

PLAYA EL COYOTE *(Open All Year)*

GPS Location: 26.72078 N, 111.91010 W (At Entrance), Near Sea Level

Playa El Coyote is another good beach with few facilities. A tree or two provide some shade. Parking is in two locations. Near the entrance off the highway there are about six sites with palapas, most will take larger rigs and they have easy access. Then, on the south end of the long entrance road described below, there is a large open beach with lots of places to park and also some palapa shelters along the beach. Pit toilets are provided. There is a hot spring along the rocks to the east. Many books about the Baja have a picture on the cover of RVs parked on this beach. A few palm trees right next to the water, often with RVs parked beneath, make an enticing shot.

The entrance road to El Coyote is just north of the Km 107 marker. After leaving the highway and driving down to the water turn right. You'll pass about six sites to the left of the road and then the road runs 0.5 miles (0.8 km) along the water below the cliff to the second camping area. Big RVs usually use the first camping area but occasionally use the second one, if you have a large RV it would be best to scout the route in a tow car or on foot before trying it. The entrance road is a long stretch right along the water with no wide places for vehicles to pass, possible soft spots, and some years it's eroded by the ocean.

BUENAVENTURA RESORT & RESTAURANT BAR
  (Open All Year)

  Telephone: (858) 206-4104
  Email: bajabuenaventura@gmail.com

GPS Location: 26.64306 N, 111.84417 W, Near Sea Level

This restaurant and bar has a small area for no-hookup parking for RVs and camping for tents along the water. In addition to the restaurant there are flush toilets and solar showers. You'll note that there are also rustic beach cabañas for rent, also a beach house.

This campground is on the same cove as the similarly named Resort Hotel San Buenaventura (a motel). It is closed but there are plans to renovate it as an Eco-hotel since it has no electricity. Until that happens there are some nice RV parking spots along the bay and you may be able to arrange parking there.

The entrance is near Km 94 on Mex 1. The main road is almost at beach level here. There's quite a bit of room out front making this a good turn-around spot if you have missed a turn-off to the north or south..

EL REQUESÓN *(Open All Year)*

GPS Location: 26.63525 N, 111.83395 W (At Entrance), Near Sea Level

This is the most picturesque of the Bahía Concepción beaches. The beach is a short sand spit which connects a small island to the mainland at low tide. Small, shallow bays border both sides of the spit. There are pit toilets but no other amenities. You can hike along the water to the south beyond Playa La Perla. Someone will come by to collect a fee each evening.

EL REQUESÓN IS THE MOST PICTURESQUE OF THE BAHÍA CONCEPCIÓN BEACHES

The entrance to El Requesón is just north of the Km 92 marker. The entrance road is paved with cobblestones and should present no problems for most RVs, it is about 0.2 miles (0.3 km) long. When you reach the beach go left for El Requesón, right for Playa La Perla (see below). Large RVs, the Green Tortoise tourist bus, and even caravans drive in here and there's lots of maneuvering room for big RVs once they're in. You will find that it is easier to enter the road if you are approaching from the north so northbound travelers may drive on less than a mile and turn around in front of Playa Buenaventura.

PLAYA LA PERLA *(Open All Year)* $$ ⛺ ⚓

 GPS Location: 26.63500 N, 111.82500 W, Near Sea Level

This beachside camping area offers pit toilets and six palapas. It is a small sandy cove with a lot of additional camping locations to the north and south of the cove. The cove itself is probably better for tent campers while RVs may prefer the adjoining areas.

The best entrance is the same one that accesses El Requesón (see above). Turn right as you reach the beach, and trundle slowly along the shoreline south to Playa La Perla. There are other entrances but they can be narrow and bushes will scratch the sides of your vehicle.

PLAYA ARMENTA *(Open All Year)* $$ ⛺ ⚓

 GPS Location: 26.62528 N, 111.81028 W, Near Sea Level

CENTRAL GULF COAST

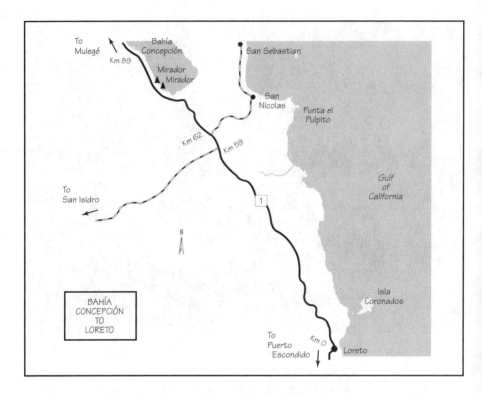

The most southerly of the Bahía Concepción campgrounds has an exposed location but a decent beach in a north-facing cove. There are pit toilets.

The entrance road is at the 90 km marker. The entrance road is 0.5 miles long (0.9 km) and somewhat difficult for RVs. We think it's only suitable for smaller ones. Take a look before you try it. Entering off the highway is also difficult for some RVs because of a sharp drop-off from the paved surface.

BAHÍA CONCEPCIÓN TO LORETO
71 Miles (115 Km), 2 Hours (from the northern end of the bay)

From Bahía Concepción to Loreto the kilometer markers continue to count down with zero at Loreto. After winding alongside Bahía Concepción for about 26 miles (42 km) the road climbs over a low saddle and then runs along a wide inland valley all the way south to Loreto. In some areas where water is available you'll see scattered ranchos in the valley. Off to the right are the Sierra de la Giganta. Prepare yourself, you'll soon be crossing them.

LORETO (LOH-RAY-TOE)
Population 15,000

Loreto is considered the oldest continuously occupied town on the Baja having been founded in 1697. This is theoretically true, however the town was virtually abandoned from the time of a major hurricane in 1829 until resettlement in the 1850s. The **Museo de los Misiones** has exhibits explaining the history of the area and also of the missions throughout the Baja. It is located next to the **Misión Nuestra Señora de Loreto**.

Today the town is part of a FONATUR development scheme like those in Cancún, Huatulco, Ixtapa, and Los Cabos (Cabo San Lucas and San José del Cabo). Most of the infrastructure was put in Nopoló, about 5 miles (8.2 km) south of Loreto. There you'll find an uncrowded but very nice golf course, a tennis center, the Loreto Inn, and a convention center. Even Bahía Escondido is part of the scheme, it is now supposed to be called Puerto Loreto. See the *Puerto Escondido* section below for more information.

Fishing and boating are popular activities in Loreto. The **Parque Marítimo Nacional Bahía de Loreto**, with several islands, is just offshore. You can arrange a trip in a panga or larger fishing cruiser. Kayak and diving tours are available.

Loreto Campgrounds

🚐 **RIVERA DEL MAR TRAILER RV PARK**

   (Open All Year)

Address:	Francisco I. Madero Norte No. 100, Loreto, B.C.S., México
Telephone:	(613) 135-2248 or (613) 135-2248 (Cell)
Email:	riverasticeent@gmail.com

GPS Location: 26.01760 N, 111.34557 W, Near Sea Level

This campground is in a residential area and sits behind the house of the very friendly and accommodating owners. It is well-supervised and security is excellent. By staying here you're within walking distance of the beach and the center of town.

The park has 23 back-in RV spaces with full hook-ups (15-amp outlets) and also a nice tent-camping area with shade. These sites vary in length but the longest is really only about 35 feet although longer units fit by projecting out into the driveway. That's the rub here, there's just not enough room, particularly if the guest rigs have tow cars. The spaces are narrow without room for wide slide-outs or awnings. As a practical matter large RVs have been staying here, but it's a struggle if the park is full. The restrooms are very clean and well-maintained, they are individual rooms with showers, toilets, and sinks. There's also a laundry area with washer and dryer and a barbeque area. Wi-Fi is provided and can be received in the RV parking area.

The campground is in a residential area about a kilometer north of the business district. Access is a little convoluted but not difficult in any size RV. There are many routes, the owners think the following is the easiest. Enter Loreto at the main entrance to town on Paseo Pedro de Ugarte which is just north of Km 119. After .5 mile (.8 km) you'll come to a large traffic circle. Go about 210 degrees around the circle and turn into Juarez St. Follow Juarez for ten blocks, .7 mile (1.1 km), and turn left onto Francisco I. Madero St. Follow Madero for 5 blocks, a distance of .4 mile (.6 km). You'll see the entrance on the left.

LORETO IS CONSIDERED THE OLDEST OCCUPIED TOWN ON THE BAJA

🚐 LORETO SHORES VILLAS AND RV PARK
(Open All Year)

Address:	Colonia Zaragoza (Apdo. 219), CP 23880
	Loreto, B.C.S., México
Telephone:	(613) 135-1513 or (613) 104-7577 (Cell)
Fax:	(613) 135-0711
Email:	loretoshores@yahoo.com
Website:	www.loretoshoresvillasandrvpark.com

GPS Location: 25.99889 N, 111.33861 W, Near Sea Level

This is the big rig RV park in Loreto and a good place to stop for the night if you're traveling. It has plenty of room on entry roads and inside the park. The spaces look a lot like those in the government parks, perhaps this was one of them. If so it has an unusually good waterfront location. Unfortunately the waterfront is now blocked by permanent structures.

There are 14 pull-thru spaces remaining here, some with 30-amp outlets, sewer, and water. The restrooms are new and have hot water showers. There's also a laundry and best of all, a swimming pool. Wi-Fi is free is you're paying for hookups, $2 if you're dry camping.

Zero your odometer as you turn from Mex 1 at the main entrance to town on Paseo Pedro de Ugarte which is just north of Km 119. This will take you toward the ocean through a traffic circle and then a stop light. Take the turn to the right at 1.4 miles

(2.3 km) onto Francisco Madero at another light. In another .3 miles (.5 km) you'll cross a dry arroyo. When you are 0.8 miles (1.3 km) from the turn make a left turn onto Ildefonso Green, the RV park is directly ahead.

CASA PALMAS ALTAS CAMP *(Open All Year)*

Telephone: (613) 135-0897
Email: palmasaltascamp@gmail.com
Website: www.palmasaltascamp.com and
www.palmasaltascamp.wordpress.com

GPS Location: 26.00640 N, 111.34040 W, Near Sea Level

This is a small fenced camping area near the center of Loreto. Thanks to those palmas altas (tall palms) there's lots of shade. It's a quiet place best for tent campers. The occasional small van does visit, but that's unusual. There are no hookups and space is limited. Facilities include a central barbeque and seating area, restrooms with flush toilets but not showers, a swimming pool, outlets for charging electronics, and clothes washing sinks and lines. It's has a very relaxed atmosphere and often hosts local cultural events.

From the center of town on Avenida Miguel Hidalgo go south on Francisco Madera for one block. Jog left one block on Calle Fernando Jorden to Nicholas Bravo. Now follow Nicholas Bravo south for three blocks and a little more, there's a signed gate on the left.

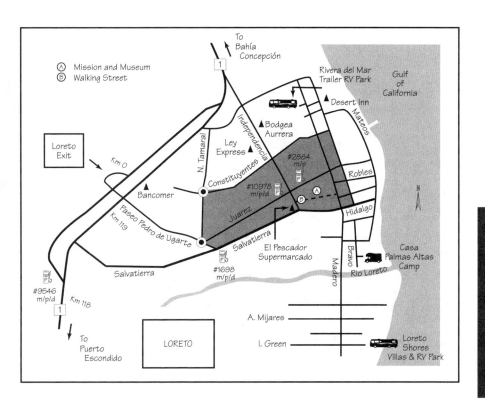

LORETO TO PUERTO ESCONDIDO
16 Miles (26 Km), .5 Hour

Just south of the entrance road to Loreto is a road leading westward into the mountains to the **Misión San Francisco Javier**. This is the only mission on the Baja still standing that has not been rebuilt. The distance to the mission is 22 miles (35 km). See the *Backroad Adventures* section of this chapter for more information.

Five miles (8 km) south of the Loreto junction a road leads east to the **Nopoló resort area**. There's a hotel, a golf course, and tennis courts open to the public for reasonable fees.

South of the Nopoló junction you'll see the golf course along the road, as well as two bridges used to cross water hazards.

Near Km 97 you'll see a road to the left which leads to the camping beach called Juncalito. See the listing below for more information.

You'll reach the junction for the short stub road eastward to Puerto Escondido 15 miles (24 km) south of the Loreto junction.

Loreto to Puerto Escondido Campground

JUNCALITO BEACH *(Open All Year)*

GPS Location: 25.83246 N, 111.33025 W, Near Sea Level

A SCENIC BEACH CAMPING SPOT AT JUNCALITO BEACH

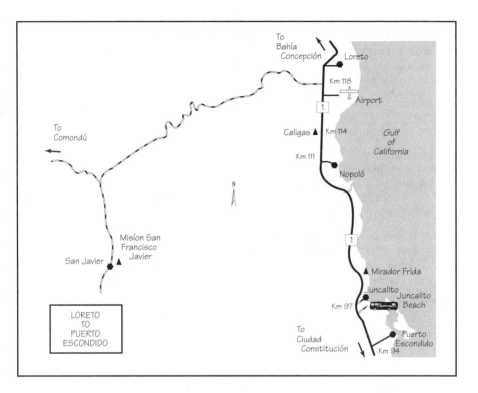

This little beach has nothing in the way of amenities except a few garbage cans. However, it is a nice beach, close to the road, and excellent for self-contained campers. The road in follows a short arroyo and is poor, but it's only 0.7 mile (1.1 km) long and large rigs make it OK. Owners of large RVs will probably want to walk it or drive it in a tow car before committing.

The unmarked road to the beach is .3 mile (.5 km) south of the Km 97 marker, that's 1.7 miles (2.7 km) north of the road out to Puerto Escondido.

PUERTO ESCONDIDO (PWER-TOE ESS-KOHN-DEE-DOE)
Population 100

Long popular as a camping and yachting destination, Puerto Escondido is now again part of the FONATUR plan to turn the Loreto area into a world-class resort. Recently construction has forged ahead, there's now a yachting center, a boatyard, and equipment for lifting pretty good-sized boats. Since there's now a fee for anchoring in the bay you'll find many visitors anchored outside it. There's a boat ramp here so fishermen like to use Puerto Escondido as a base for accessing the offshore waters and long stretch of coast to the south toward La Paz which has little road access. Kayakers put in here for the trips out to Isla Danzante and down the coast to La Paz.

Puerto Escondido Campgrounds

HOTEL TRIPUI *(Open All Year)*

Address:	Lote 1, Manzana 1, Puerto Escondito, Loreto, B.C.S., México
Telephone:	(613) 133-0814 or (613) 133-0818
Email:	reservations@hoteltripui.com.mex
Website:	tripuihotel.com.mx

GPS Location: 25.81944 N, 111.31639 W, Near Sea Level

The long-established Hotel Tripui offers a variety of RV parking choices. The resort is located on the entrance road to Puerto Escondido. You'll pass a relatively grim looking fenced RV park and then come to the entrance to the Hotel Tripui offices. There is a restaurant and hotel behind the offices. This is also the entrance to the Tripui RV Park. There are three types of RV sites available as follows.

Behind the office is a large RV park that has been there for years. Most of these residential sites are occupied by nice casitas of people who spend much of the year living here. There are several sites with full hookups for any sized rig that are available in this area. The rate is $25 daily or $500 per month for these sites.

Next to the office and near the swimming pool are three back-in sites with electricity and water. These sites are near the pool and restaurant, but really in the parking area.

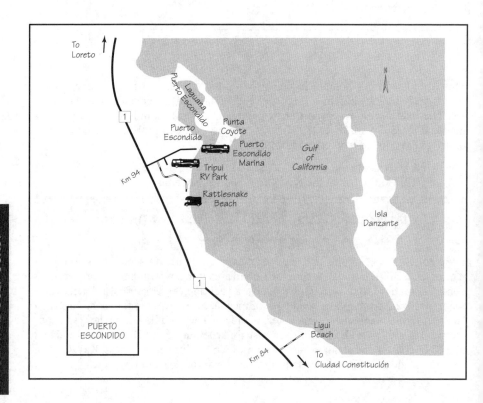

They cost $20 daily or $350 a month. The advantage is that they may have free Wi-Fi from the office area and are near the pool and restaurant.

Finally, there are the sites in the RV area you passed as you approached the park. Here there are 31 spaces in a fenced gravel lot with 20, 30 and 50-amp outlets, sewer, and water. Cement curbs separate the sites. These sites can take large rigs. Dedicated restrooms nearby have hot showers and flush toilets. Spaces here are also $20 daily or $350 per month.

If you are staying in any of these sites you have access to the swimming pool and restrooms with flush toilets and showers near the pool and office. Wi-Fi is available in this area and there's also a nice restaurant.

Take the Puerto Escondido cutoff from Mex 1 near Km 94 about 16 miles (26 km) south of Loreto. Drive 0.6 miles (1 km) on the paved road and you'll see the resort on the right.

PUERTO ESCONDIDO MARINA *(Open All Year)*

GPS: 25.81389 N, 111.31174, Near Sea Level

Puerto Escondido has a very nice marina that was built to be part of the now abandoned Escalera Maritima. It was a plan to truck boats from the west coast of the peninsula to the east side. The marina remains and is popular with boaters. There is a gated gravel parking lot and lately RVers have been allowed to park there overnight and use the marina facilities. These include a restaurant, laundry, pay Wi-Fi, restrooms with toilets and hot showers.

Take the Puerto Escondido cutoff from Mex 1 near Km 94 about 16 miles (26 km) south of Loreto. Drive 0.6 miles (1 km) on the paved road and you'll see the parking entrance on the left. Go to the gate and ask about parking overnight, it seems to be a case-by-case situation and the price may vary, but maybe you'll get lucky – if you ask nicely!

PLAYA EL QUEMADO, AKA RATTLESNAKE BEACH
(Open All Year)

GPS Location: 25.79723 N, 111.31204 W, Near Sea Level

Rattlesnake Beach is located on the coast just south of Puerto Escondido. Campers park just back from the beach and there are no facilities other than trash barrels although water is available from a public well on the far side of the highway. A large community spends the winter on this beach.

The access road to the beach is very poor. It's unmarked and starts about 100 yards west of the west fence of the Hotel Tripui RV park. The road is 1 mile (1.6 km) long and is narrow and difficult for large rig. Drive it in something small so you can judge whether to bring your RV out.

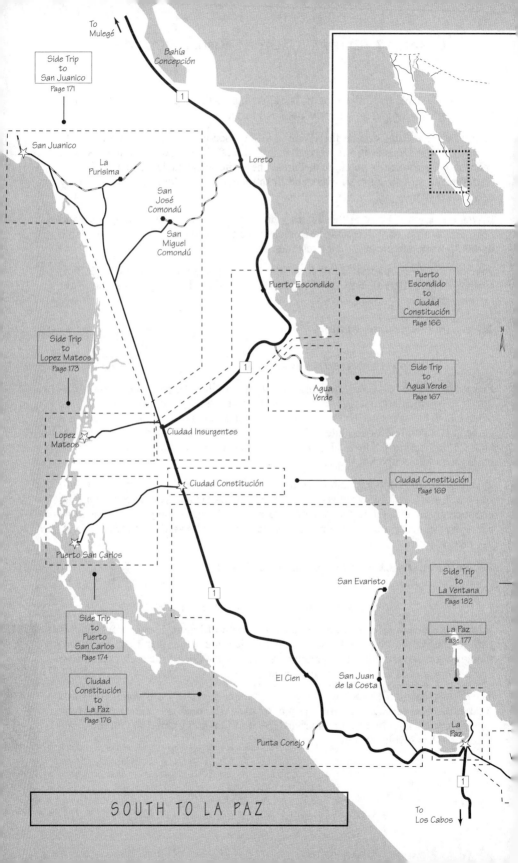

To
Mulegé

Bahía
Concepción

Side Trip
to
San Juanico
Page 171

San Juanico

La
Purisima

San
José
Comondú

San
Miguel
Comondú

Loreto

Puerto Escondido

Puerto
Escondido
to
Ciudad
Constitución
Page 166

Side Trip
to
Lopez Mateos
Page 173

Side Trip
to
Agua Verde
Page 167

Agua
Verde

Lopez
Mateos

Ciudad Insurgentes

Ciudad Constitución

Ciudad Constitución
Page 169

Puerto San Carlos

San Evaristo

Side Trip
to
La Ventana
Page 182

La Paz
Page 177

Side Trip
to
Puerto
San Carlos
Page 174

El Cien

San Juan
de la Costa

Ciudad
Constitución
to
La Paz
Page 176

Punta Conejo

La
Paz

N

SOUTH TO LA PAZ

To
Los Cabos

Chapter 8
South to La Paz

INTRODUCTION

This chapter of the book covers the peninsula from the point where the highway turns inland south of Loreto to the point where it again reaches the Gulf at Baja Sur's largest town, La Paz. Between the two is a huge farming area centered around Ciudad Constitución. Many folks just hurry through this section bound for points farther south, but if you want to slow down there are several side trips offering fishing, whale watching, and sightseeing possibilities

Highlights

La Paz is the largest city in Baja Sur and the one that feels the most like a mainland Mexican city. It is the best place to buy supplies south of Ensenada and north of Los Cabos. Many Norteamericanos live here and there are two formal RV parks serving the town. La Paz celebrates Carnival, it's a fun time to be here.

Roads and Fuel Availability

South of Loreto the road climbs to cross the Sierra la Giganta. On the far side you'll find a long and very gradual descent to the town of Ciudad Insurgentes. After a 90-degree left turn you'll drive for almost 50 miles (81 km) on an arrow-straight road through Ciudad Constitución and irrigated farming country. After that the road crosses dry rolling hills for another 90 miles (145 km) until it again reaches the east coast on the Gulf of California at the town of La Paz.

Kilometer markers on this section of the Baja count down from Loreto to Ciudad Insurgentes, a distance of 119 kilometers. Then they again count down until you reach La Paz, a distance of 239 kilometers.

Fuel is readily available in this section. Here are the locations, with types and distances between stations: **Loreto**, gas and diesel; **Ciudad Insurgentes**, gas and diesel, 72 miles (116 km); **Ciudad Constitución**, gas and diesel, 14 miles (23 km); **San Juan de la Costa Cutoff**, gas and diesel, 118 miles (190 km); **La Paz**, gas and diesel, 6 miles (10 km).

Sightseeing

During the months of January to March it is possible to visit the **gray whales** in Bahía Magdalena. Pangas go out to visit the whales from two different towns: San Carlos and Puerto Lopez Mateos. Both of them have places to park an RV overnight and are described below.

You can visit the remote and scenic villages of **San José Comondú** and **San Miguel Comondú**, see *Backroad Adventures* below.

Also easily accessible now with recently completed paved roads is the remote surfing village of San Juanico. See the *Side Trip to San Juanico* section below.

Beaches and Water Sports

Access to beaches in this section, except in the La Paz vicinity, requires taking side roads since the Transpeninsular does not run along the coast.

Bahía Magdalena is one of the three places on the Baja where gray whales can easily be seen in their nursery lagoons. The others, of course, are near Guerrero Negro and San Ignacio. Access to the bay is easiest at Puerto Adolfo Lopez Mateos and at Puerto San Carlos, paved roads lead to both of them. The northern part of the bay is also an excellent kayaking and fishing location during months when access is not restricted due to the presence of the whales.

South of Bahía Magdalena are miles of Pacific Ocean beaches. A side roads lead from the highway to **Punta Conejo**, see *Backroad Adventures* below.

Ensenada de Aripes, La Paz's bay, doesn't have great beaches inside the protecting Peninsula el Mogote, but there are several good ones off the paved road that runs to the ferry terminal at Pichilingue and beyond. They include Playas **Palmira**, **El Coromuel**, **Caimancito**, **El Tesoro**, **Pichilingue**, **Balandra** and **Tecolote**. Tecolote is suitable for camping and is described in the *La Paz Campgrounds* section.

Southeast of La Paz Highway BCS 286 leads to **Bahía La Ventana**. There's a long sandy beach bordering the bay, this is a very popular kiteboarding location. There are also campgrounds. See *Side Trip to La Ventana* from La Paz below.

Fishing

The waters of the northern half of **Magdalena Bay**, north of Puerto San Carlos, are good small-boat fishing waters when the whales are not present. Small car-top aluminum boats and kayaks work well. These are mangrove waters and offer bass, pargo, and corvina. Waters outside Bahía Magdalena are difficult to reach and hazardous because of strong surf and sand bars at the bay entrances.

SCENERY ALONG THE REMOTE DRIVE TO LA PURÍSIMA

La Paz has fishing too. At one time this was a top destination for big game fish and it continues to be pretty good although not as good as farther south. Charter cruisers and pangas are readily available in La Paz, the best season for billfish is May through October.

Small aluminum boat fishermen around La Paz will find few fish, there is just too much fishing pressure near town. Try heading north on the **coastal road toward San Evaristo** or southeast to **Ensenada de Los Sueños**, both are described in the *Backroad Adventures* section of this chapter.

Backroad Adventures

See the ***Backroad Driving*** section of ***Chapter 2 - Details, Details, Details*** for essential information about driving off the main highway on the Baja and for a definition of road types used below.

🚙 **From Km 63 Between Loreto and Ciudad Constitución** - For a last visit to the Gulf of California before heading east you might try the road to **Agua Verde**. This small and isolated village sits on the shore of a bay and is a popular yachting destination. There are spots for primitive camping and the location is good for kayaking and sailboarding. The distance is 26 miles (42 km) on what is normally a Type 2 road. Be prepared for a narrow road along cliffs as it descends to the coast. See *Side Trip to Agua Verde* below for more information about camping there.

🚙 **From Km 0 at the Ciudad Insurgentes Junction** - At the 90-degree turn of Mex 1 in Ciudad Insurgentes turn right and head north. Follow the paved road for 78 miles (126 km) to the oasis villages of **La Purísima** and **San Isidro**. Also interesting, and now accessible on paved roads, are **San José and San Miguel Comondú**. These are two small villages in verdant valleys. The 20 mile (33 km) access road is now paved and leaves the highway north of Ciudad Insurgents at Km 64 some 41 miles (66 km) north of where Mex 1 makes its 90-degree turn.

🚐 **From Km 194 Between Ciudad Constitución and La Paz -** From Mex 1 about 8 miles (13 km) south of Ciudad Constitución a 23 mile (37 km) Type 1 road leads to San Luis Gonzega, an isolated farming town with its **Misión San Luis Gonzega**. It makes a nice drive through the desert. Last time we drove it we saw a number of raptors perched on cactus along the way including Crested Caracara, Red-tailed Hawk, Harris's Hawk, Osprey, Kestral, and of course, Turkey Vultures. Also Loggerhead Shrike and Vermillion Flycatcher. We've known RVers to boondock in town near the mission.

🚐 **From Km 80 Between Ciudad Constitución and La Paz -** A 10-mile (16 km) Type 2 road leads to the windswept coast at **Punta Conejo**. Punta Conejo is popular with surfers, it can also be good for experienced wind surfers and for surf fishing. See the *Rancho El Conejo* description in the *Ciudad Constitución to La Paz Campgrounds* section of this chapter.

🚐 **From Km 17 Between Ciudad Constitución and La Paz -** This road leads up the coast from near La Paz. For the first 24 miles (39 km) to the mining town of **San Juan de la Costa** the road is paved. Just before reaching San Juan a fork leads right and a Type 2 road begins which leads another 34 miles (55 km) north to where the road becomes a rugged Type 3 road and continues another 16 miles (26 km) to **San Evaristo**. This is a very scenic road, there are a few places along it that are suitable for boondocking and the fishing offshore can be good.

🚐 **From the Road to La Ventana -** Follow the route described below from La Paz for the side trip to La Ventana. At mile 23 (km 37) do not take the left turn, continue instead straight on through San Juan de los Planes and then follow the highway as it takes a 90-degree left turn. The paved road leads on now almost all the way to **Ensenada los Muertos** at mile 30 (km 48), site of a real estate development and two good restaurants. This bay has been renamed from Bay of the Dead to the more salable Bay of Dreams or Bahía de los Sueños. From Bahía de los Sueños pangas can take you fishing in winter and early spring out to Isla Cerralvo, about 8 miles out. If, instead of making the 90-degree turn east of Los Planes, you had continued straight for .7 mile (1.1 km) and then angled to the right, you would have been on the back road to Los Barriles. See *Backroad Adventures* in Chapter 9 for a description of this route. It's a Type 3 road for a great deal of the distance.

THE ROUTES, TOWNS, AND CAMPGROUNDS

PUERTO ESCONDIDO TO CIUDAD CONSTITUCIÓN
72 Miles (116 Km), 2 Hours

Five miles south of the junction for Puerto Escondido the highway begins to climb up into the Sierra Giganta.

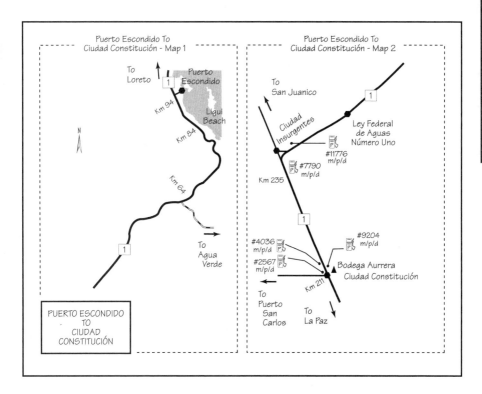

At about Km 63 the road to Bahía Agua Verde goes left. See *Backroad Adventures* in this chapter for more information about this road.

Once the climb is over the road enters Arroyo Huatamote which leads out onto the gently sloping Magdalena Plain. The road is relatively straight and easy to drive as it gradually descends into irrigated farming country. You'll pass the closed gas station at Ley Federal de Aguas Número Uno and come to the Ciudad Insurgentes intersection where the highway turns 90 degrees left to head for Ciudad Constitución, La Paz, and Cabo. If you turn right here you have access to Puerto Lopez Mateos, La Purísima, San José Comondú, and San Miguel Comondú. See the *Backroad Adventures* section of this chapter for more information about these destinations. This is also the cutoff for San Juanico, see *Side Trip to San Juanico* for information about that drive and campground.

About 15 miles (24 km) after making the left turn you'll enter Ciudad Constitución and see a Pemex station on the right side of the highway.

SIDE TRIP TO AGUA VERDE

If you're looking for a remote bay on the Sea of Cortez with just a small village nearby, this is the place. The road in is poor enough to keep the place from being overcrowded. Particularly challenging is a narrow cliff-side descent from high in the mountains to the coast. See the individual campground descriptions for more about the road.

▄ RANCHO SAN COSME *(Open All Year)*

GPS Location: 25.57829 N, 110.16953 W, Near Sea Level

This is a small rancho right at the foot of the descent to the beach. As you enter you'll see a small restaurant on the left. Van tours from Loreto often stop here. Stop and check in, then continue on a few hundred yards to a large open lot next to a rocky beach. The lot has a nice solid surface. The amenities are limited to two palapas and bucket-flush toilets.

Leave Mex 1 near Km 63, that's about 37 miles (53 km) south of Loreto. The road in is paved for the first six miles (10 km), then turns to dirt. You must navigate a challenging winding road including a descent of about 1,250 feet on an narrow road along the edge of a cliff to reach the ranch, a distance of 14.5 miles (23.4 km) from the highway. We recommend the campground only for smaller vehicles because of the steep and narrow road. Two wheel-drive tourist vans drive it frequently. There should be no problem with soft sand at this campground.

▄ AGUA VERDE VILLAGE BEACH CAMPING
(Open All Year)

GPS Location; 25.51385 N, 111.07066 W, Near Sea Level

DRIVING ALONG THE CLIFF-SIDE DESCENT TO THE COAST AT AGUA VERDE

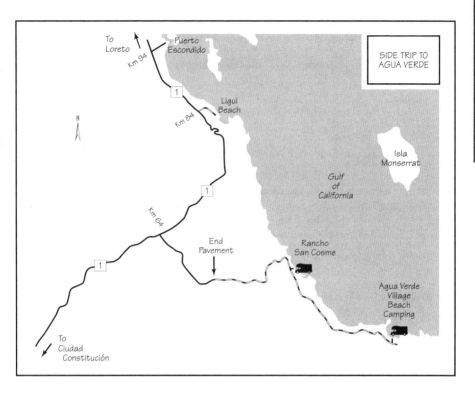

Many yachts anchor off Agua Verde each season. The little town is equally hospitable to vehicle campers, at least the ones able to get there.

The village sits slightly back from a beautiful sandy beach. Several access tracks lead down to the sand, and for a small fee campers are welcome to set up camp. The only facilities are a few palapa shelters and outhouses. However, there's a small store and at least one simple restaurant in the nearby village.

Leave Mex 1 near Km 63, that's about 37 miles (53 km) south of Loreto. The road in is paved for the first six miles (10 km), then turns to dirt. You must navigate a challenging winding road including a descent of about 1,250 feet on an narrow road along the edge of a cliff to reach the village, a distance of 26 miles (42 km) from the highway. We recommend the campground only for high clearance cars, vans and pickup campers, mostly due to the access road but also the soft sand surface of the camping area. Exercise caution to avoid getting stuck in the sand.

CIUDAD CONSTITUCIÓN (SEE-OOH-DAHD KOHN-STIH-TOO-SEE-OHN)
Population 45,000

This burgeoning farm town isn't found in most tourist guides. It has little to offer tourists but RV travelers will find services they can use. It has RV parks, supermarkets and automobile dealerships. Ciudad Constitución's location makes it a handy stop if you're headed north from beyond La Paz (only 130 easy miles (212 km) southeast) or need a base for whale watching in Bahía Magdalena to the west.

Ciudad Constitución Campgrounds

MISIONES TRAILER PARK *(Open All Year)*

Address:	Km 213, Colonia Vargas, Cd.
	Constitución, B.C.S., México
Telephone:	(613) 132-1103 or (613) 108--0468
Email:	npso@hotmail.com

GPS Location: 25.04858 N, 111.68057 W, 200 Ft.

There are about 25 sites here including eight long pull-thrus with 15-amp outlets, sewer, and water. Two older restrooms in poor condition usually have hot showers. There is a small unheated swimming pool. Internet access is available in the office or using Wi-Fi from some sites. This campground also offers rental rooms. The owner lives on site and is an English teacher.

The campground is very near the northwestern border of Ciudad Constitución and right on the east side of Mex 1 at about Km 212.

PALAPA 206 RV PARK AND MOTEL *(Open All Year)*

Address:	PO Box 186, Km 206, Ciudad Constitución, B.C.S.,
	México
Telephone:	(613) 109-4867
Email:	palapa206@prodigy.net.mx

GPS Location: 24.99972 N, 111.65917 W, 200 Ft.

This campground just outside Ciudad Constitución to the south is a very popular stop for big RVs and caravans.

The campground has 11 pull-thru and 6 back-in full-hookup sites, suitable for any size RV. There's lots of maneuvering room. Power is 20 amps. Restrooms have hot showers and English is spoken, although with a British accent. The owner is very helpful and knows the area well. There are also motel rooms.

The campground is on the west side of the highway near Km 206, that's about 1.4 miles (2.3 km) south of Ciudad Constitución.

CAMPESTRE LA PILA BALNEARIO AND TRAILER PARK
(Open All Year)

Address:	Apdo. 261, Ciudad Constitución, B.C.S., México
Telephone:	(613) 132-0582

GPS Location: 25.01778 N, 111.67750 W, 100 Ft.

The La Pila is a balneario trailer park, in summer the pool area is very popular but in winter the pools are unheated so the area is nice and quiet. It's a pleasant place to relax with a covered palapa area.

There are 9 pull-thru spaces with 15-amp outlets and water. Sites are situated in a sandy lot surrounded by palm trees. There is quite a bit more room for tent and no-hookup camping. The nicely landscaped pool area next to the camping area has the bathrooms and there are hot showers. There is also a dump station.

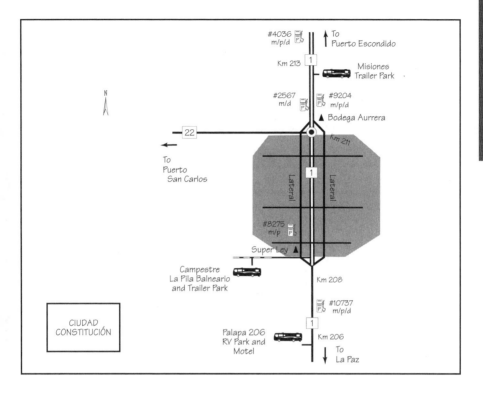

The turn-off from Mex 1 to the campground is the street south of the Ley supermarket in Ciudad Constitución. Turn here on Franco Palayo Lopez and drive two blocks. Continue straight onto the gravel under the power lines and in .4 mile (.6 km) from where the gravel started turn left at the sign for the campground. As you enter the yard look ahead and to the left for the camping area. The campground is around to the left near the pools. The office is in the pool area.

SIDE TRIP TO SAN JUANICO
111 Miles (179 Km), 3 Hours

From Ciudad Constitución you can drive north on paved roads to the remote surfing and fishing village of San Juanico, known to surfers as Scorpion Bay. First, drive north on Mex 1 for 14 miles (22.6 kilometers) to the intersection where Mex 1 goes 90 degrees right toward Loreto. Instead of turning go straight. You'll immediately pass through the town of Ciudad Insurgentes and continue north on a paved road, formally called BCS 53. This paved road goes all the way to La Purísima, a distance of about 71 miles (114 km). Instead of going all the way you only want to drive to the cutoff for Las Barrancas which is near unmarked Km 82. That's 55 miles (89 km) north of the 90 degree turn near Ciudad Insurgentes. Turn left and head for the coast. As you approach Las Barrancas the road branches right and then points north. Eventually, 35 miles (56 km) from where you left BCS 53 you'll reach San Juanico.

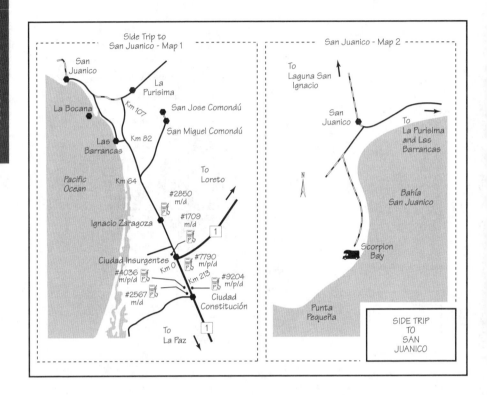

SAN JUANICO
Population 500

San Juanico is an isolated little fishing village that is growing as Norteamericanos buy land and build houses. It's particularly popular with surfers. There's not much here in the way of tourist facilities other than a couple of restaurants and a camping area. Of course there is the beach and the surf.

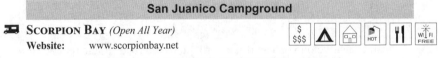

San Juanico Campground

SCORPION BAY *(Open All Year)*
Website: www.scorpionbay.net

GPS Location: 26.24389 N, 112.47667 W, Near Sea Level

The camping area here is simple but very convenient for surfers, you can park on the bluff and watch the action right out front.

Campers park pretty much where they like along several hundred yards of bluff area above a nice sandy beach and rocky headland. It can be tough to find a level spot and the area is mostly unprotected from the wind. There are no hookups but there is a cantina behind a house that serves meals as well as a toilet and shower building. Hot showers are included in the camping price and there is slow, limited, satellite Wi-Fi at the cantina. A few apartments, rooms and palapas are available for rent.

To reach the campground after reaching San Juanico from the south just stay on the road through town. The entrance road is .8 mile (1.3 km) north of he end of the pavement. It's signed and leads left to the campground. Access is also possible on a road along he cliff from town. Both roads are dirt and uneven, only smaller rigs can easily reach the campground.

SIDE TRIP TO LOPEZ MATEOS
36.6 Miles (59 Km), 1 Hour

From Ciudad Constitución drive north on Mex 1 for 14 miles (22.6 kilometers) to the intersection where Mex 1 goes 90 degrees right toward Loreto. Drive straight on through Ciudad Insurgents for another 1.6 miles (2.6 km) to the cutoff where the paved road to Lopez Mateos goes left. Turn here and you'll arrive in Lopez Mateos in another 21 miles (34 km).

LOPEZ MATEOS
Population 2,000

This small but easy to reach fishing village has become one of the best places on the Baja to see gray whales. The whale-watching area is fairly restricted so there's a good concentration of whales and they're easy to find. The village has a nice embarcadero area where the pangas dock with lots of parking, a new restroom building, and several restaurants. To find it just follow the embarcadero signs through town. It's a little convoluted but this is a small town, the map will help.

PETTING THE WHALES ON AN OUTING FROM LOPEZ MATEOS

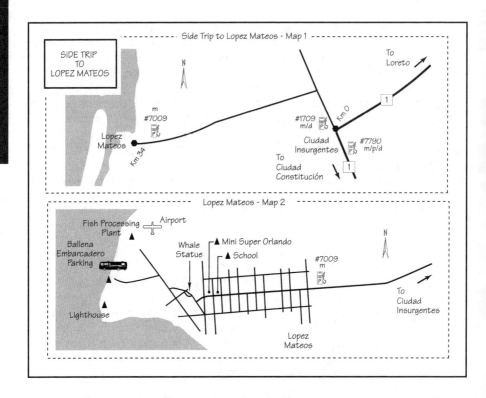

Lopez Mateos Campgrounds

 **BALLENA EMBARCADERO PARKING** *(Open All Year)* $ | | | | | | BIG RIGS

GPS Location: 25.19377 N, 112.12318 W, Near Sea Level

It is possible to overnight in the parking lot of the whale-watching dock area. There are restrooms, restaurants during the day, and overnight security during the whale-watching season.

SIDE TRIP TO PUERTO SAN CARLOS
34 Miles (55 Km), .75 Hour

The road out to San Carlos heads west from the middle of Ciudad Constitución. This is a fine two-lane paved highway running across the very flat coastal plain. You'll know you're getting close when you spot the big electrical generation plant.

PUERTO SAN CARLOS (PWER-tow sahn KAR-lohs)
Population 5,000

This little town serves as one of the only two deep-water ports on the west coast of the Baja, the other is Ensenada far to the north. Puerto San Carlos' port is primarily

SOUTH TO LA PAZ

used for exporting the farm products of the plain to the east, and also for offloading fuel for the big electrical plant that is located there. Puerto San Carlos also provides access to Bahía Magdalena, one of the three gray-whale watching locations on the Baja. A cannery is the largest building in town, the smell of fish processing tends to be noticeable almost everywhere.

Bahía Magdalena's protected waters are a good place to use your small boat, the fishing is excellent. It's also good kayaking and windsurfing water. There is a concrete launch ramp in town. Gray whales are present from January to March and during this season boating is limited to certain areas and boating permits are required. Puerto San Carlos has only small stores but does have several restaurants. During whale-watching season there are actually quite a few tourists in town since this is the closest location to La Paz and Cabo San Lucas. Check at hotels in town for information about whale-watching tours. Camping options are limited here, but it's only 34 miles (55 km) to Ciudad Constitución.

Puerto San Carlos Campground

MAR Y ARENA RESTAURANT, HOTEL, AND ECO TOURS *(Open All Year)* $$

Telephone: (613) 136-0076 or (613) 136-0599
Email: info@villasmaryarena.com
Website: www.villasmaryarena.com

GPS Location: 24.79657 N, 112.11565 W, Near Sea Level

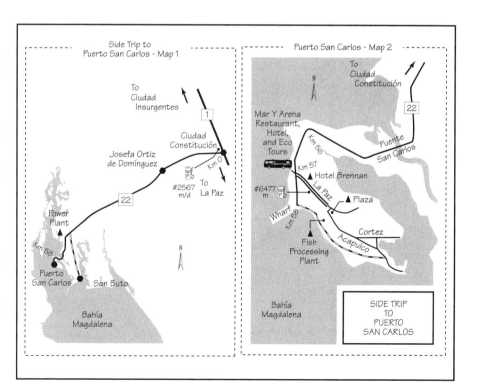

This waterfront restaurant and hotel is one of the first businesses you'll see as you arrive in town. It's not a formal campsite, but it has some space for parking RVs next to the restaurant. Restaurant guests and whale tour customers are welcome to park their RVs and spend the night. It's a good place to leave your RV while watching whales or fishing. The restaurant offers restrooms and Wi-Fi. There are also waterfront rooms for rent.

The restaurant and hotel are on the right near Km 57 as you enter town, right next to the highway.

CIUDAD CONSTITUCIÓN TO LA PAZ
130 Miles (210 Km), 3.75 Hours

The road south from Ciudad Constitución is flat and pretty much straight for 50 miles (82 km). You'll soon pass through the roadside town of El Cien, so named because it is 100 kilometers from La Paz.

Fourteen miles (23 km) south of El Cien a road goes west for **Punta Conejo** which offers access to the coast. See this chapter's *Backroad Adventures* for more information about this road. There is a camping area at the beach called Rancho El Conejo.

From El Cien the road crosses a region of hills and the highway is slower going, just exercise a little patience and soon you'll be in La Paz. As you finally begin to

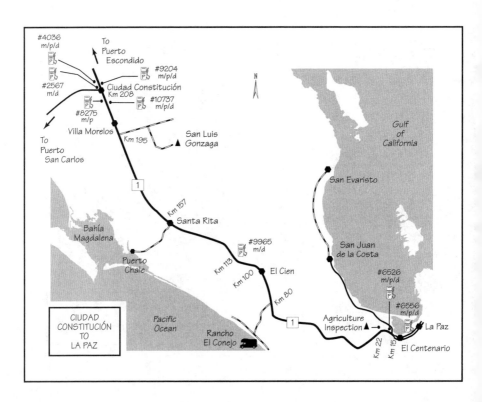

descend toward the coast you'll see La Paz ahead. Just before you reach the outlying town of El Centenario the road to **San Evaristo** goes left, this road is described in this chapter's *Backroad Adventures*.

Ciudad Constitución to La Paz Campground

🚐 **RANCHO EL CONEJO** *(Open All Year)* $ 🏕 ❄ 🚿 ⚡

GPS Location: 24.07106 N, 111.00369 W, Near Sea Level

Punta Conejo is a popular camping location for surfers and other beach fans. It's an isolated place but really pretty easy to reach with vans, pickups, and other smaller vehicles. The sites here are in low vegetation back from the beach, some are protected from the wind. Sites are pretty well separated and some have fire pits. There are outhouses and very poor cold showers are sometimes available. There's $5 fee for camping here.

The road out to Punta Conejo leaves Mex 1 very near Km 80, there's a sign. The road is a Type 2, OK for small RVs and other vehicles with good ground clearance. Larger rigs sometimes travel this road but if you have one you should drive it in something smaller first to make your decision. Also, the road varies from year to year. It's 10 miles (16 km) to the beach. The favorite sites are across an arroyo to the south, access to this area often requires high clearance or even four wheel drive. Watch the weather during the storm season, camping in the arroyo could be dangerous.

LA PAZ (LAW PAHS)
Population 220,000

A favorite city on the Baja Peninsula, La Paz has lots of stores for supplies and has always had a few campgrounds. There are two formal RV parks in town and a commonly used beach boondocking location. This is not really just a tourist town although it does have tourist amenities like hotels, good restaurants, beaches, and tour operators.

La Paz has been continuously occupied by Europeans only since 1811. Earlier settlement attempts, including one by Cortez in person, were not successful. The local Indians were not cooperative.

The city feels more like a larger mainland city than any other on the Baja. The waterfront **malecón** is good for strolling and you'll enjoy exploring the older part of town a few blocks back from the water. La Paz's best **beaches** are outside town toward and past Pichilingue and are virtually empty except on weekends. There's a simple museum, the **Museum of Anthropology**, covering the area's early inhabitants. Carnival is celebrated here. It is the week before Ash Wednesday, some time in late February or March. La Paz now has quite a few big-box stores including Mega, Soriana, Liverpool, Walmart, Sam's Club, Home Depot, and a Costco promised soon. **Ferries** to the mainland cities of Topolobampo and Mazatlán dock at Pichilingue, see the *Ferries* section in the *Details, Details, Details* chapter. Note that there is now a good bypass route around town to Pichilingue, it's shown on the La Paz Area Map No. 1 and the route is described in the Playa Tecolote campground description.

CARNIVAL IS A FUN TIME TO BE IN LA PAZ

Route to Pass Through La Paz Heading Farther South

The route that you follow to continue south past La Paz is usually missing important signs and always seems to confuse people. It's really an easy route, it's just that folks miss an unmarked turn.

When you arrive at the dove statue (whale's tail) at the entrance to La Paz (at about Km 7) take the right fork and zero your odometer. It's usually marked for La Paz Libramiento. In just .7 mile (1.1 km) at the stop sign take the right turn. Don't miss this turn, it's usually **not** marked! In another 2.0 miles (3.2 km) you'll reach a T with a stoplight at Mex 1 south of town. Turn right here and you're on the highway to Cabo San Lucas.

La Paz Campgrounds

CAMPESTRE MARANATHA *(Open All Year)*

    Address: Carr. Al Norte, Km 11, La Paz, B.C.S, México
    Telephone
    and Fax: (612) 124-6275

    GPS Location: 24.09667 N, 110.38694 W, Near Sea Level

Campestre Maranatha has been in La Paz for many years. It's a camp with facilities to host groups including rooms, a kitchen, restrooms with hot showers, a laundry, and a swimming pool. There are also RV sites, these are built for individual RV travelers and are available on a daily or monthly basis.

There are thirty-seven full-hookup RV sites large enough for 40 footers. Each has

SOUTH TO LA PAZ

20 and 30 amp outlets, water, and sewer hookups .They are in two locations on the property: 25 sites in a new lot out front and 12 along the west wall of the property. There are also a few scattered no-hookup sites. There's also Wi-Fi at the sites and telephone service to the US in the office. The monthly rate here is $420. It is possible to dump or take on water here even if you are not camping. The fee is $6 for a dump and also $6 for water. There's a handy coffee shop on the road out front.

The campground is located just east of El Centenario. As you leave El Centenario headed east on Mex 1 watch for the El Exquisito coffee shop on your right, it's at about Km 11.3, turn south on the road to the west of the coffee shop, the camping area entrance is on the left in about 100 yards.

AQUAMARINA RV PARK *(Open All Year)*

Address:	Calle Nayarit #10 y Playa, La Paz, BCS, Mexico 23060
Telephone:	(612 122-3761 or (612) 125-9612

GPS Location: 24.14997 N, 110.33497 W, Near Sea Level

The Aquamarina is the only RV park actually in central La Paz. It's been closed for a few years but is now open again. It's changed a bit. It's a little smaller and no longer has a swimming pool, but it's quiet and has great facilities.

The campground has 15 back in sites with full hookups. They'll take large rigs and

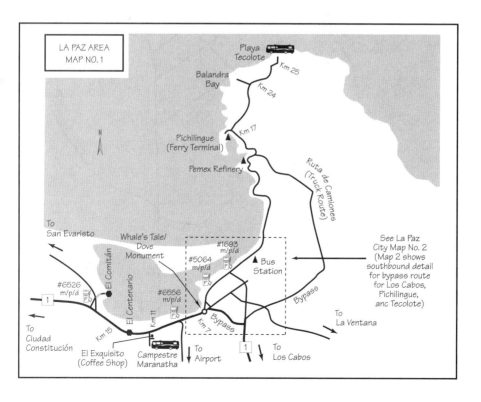

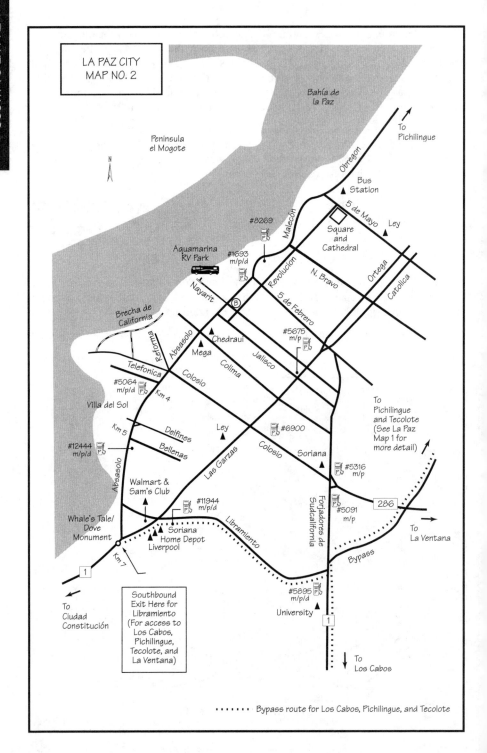

are paved off paved drives with patios. Palm trees provide a nice tropical ambiance. The owner lives on site and it is fully fenced with an electric gate. Restrooms are very clean and have hot showers. There is a rooftop lounge area with excellent views. There are also rooms for rent.

The RV park is located on the ocean end of Av. Nayarit, which is a paved street off Absolo as it comes in to La Paz. If you zero your odometer at the dove statue Nayarit goes to the left at 2.5 miles (4 km). If you watch for the Chedraui Supermarket on the right Nayarit it is the third street after that. Turn left and follow Nayarit almost to the end, the distance is about 0.4 miles (0.6 km), watch for the paved entryway and gate on the right. Honk your horn to get the gate opened, you'll probably be issued your own key fob to open it when you sign in.

PLAYA TECOLOTE *(Open All Year)*

GPS Location: 24.33583 N, 110.31528 W, Near Sea Level

This large open beach is a popular camping location for RVers. This can be an unpleasant windy location when a north wind is blowing as it often does in the winter but when it's not the camping is great. There is no security but normally there are many campers here, for most folks the main concern is theft of things left outside the RV overnight or while they're gone.

As you arrive at the beach you'll see that there are several restaurants ahead and to the left. They have primitive restrooms with cold showers. During the winter they're

FERRIES TO THE MAINLAND LEAVE THE BAJA AT PICHILINGUE

pretty quiet, only during Easter week and the summer do a lot of people visit the beach. Most campers park along the beach to the right, there is normally no fee. Watch for soft spots. We recommend that you walk the route first to make sure it's OK. Lots of people get stuck out here. To the left there's a large open area, so large you might think it's a runway. Caravans often park in this area and tell us that they pay a fee to do so.

There is a new bypass that makes it easy to reach the beaches east of La Paz without driving through town. When you arrive at the dove statue (whale's tail) at the entrance to La Paz (at about Km 7) take the right fork and zero your odometer. It's marked for La Paz Libramiento. In just .7 mile (1.1 km) take the right turn at the stop sign. This turn is usually unmarked but don't miss it. In another 2.0 miles (3.2 km) you'll reach a T with a stoplight at Mex 1 south of town. If you went right here you'd be heading for Cabo, instead turn left. In .3 mile (.5 km) take the right turn signed for Pichilingue or Ruta de Camiones. After 16.2 miles (26.1 km) you'll reach the ferry terminal. Continue past the terminal, you have to take a right at the small intersection outside the terminal. In another 4.1 mile (6.6 km) the road forks, left is Balandra Bay, right is Tecolote, turn right. You'll reach Tecolote in another 0.9 miles (1.5 km).

SIDE TRIP TO LA VENTANA
28 Miles (45 Km), .75 Hour

From La Paz you can follow a paved highway (BCS 286) southeast to the farming country in the vicinity of San Juan de los Planes. Just to the north along the coast of Bahía La Ventana is the town of La Ventana, a popular kiteboarding destination. Five basic campgrounds located in La Ventana are discussed below.

There is a new bypass that makes it easy to reach the road to La Ventana on the far side of La Paz. Coming from the north, when you arrive at the dove statue (whale's tail) at the entrance to La Paz (at about Km 7) take the right fork and zero your odometer. It's marked for La Paz Libramiento. In just .7 mile (1.1 km) take the right turn at the stop sign. This turn is usually unmarked but don't miss it. In another 2.0 miles (3.2 km) you'll reach a T with a stoplight at Mex 1 south of town. If you went right here you'd be heading for Cabo, instead turn left. In .3 mile (.5 km) take the right turn signed for Pichilingue or Ruta de Camiones. After 1.2 miles (2 km) this bypass road intersects BCS 286 to Los Planes. Turn right here.

The two-lane paved highway climbs as it leaves town, it reaches a summit at 15 miles (24 km). Twenty-two miles (37 km) from the intersection you'll reach another intersection, turn left. This road is marked for La Ventana and El Sargento. You'll reach La Ventana in 5 miles (8 kilometers).

La Ventana (lah vehn-TAH-nah)

This is a very small village stretched along the west shore of the bay. Actually, the towns of El Teso and El Sargento, both to the north, tend to merge together with La Ventana to form one town. Facilities in the towns are limited to a small store or two and a few restaurants. The villages are growing rapidly as this area becomes more well known in the kiteboarding community.

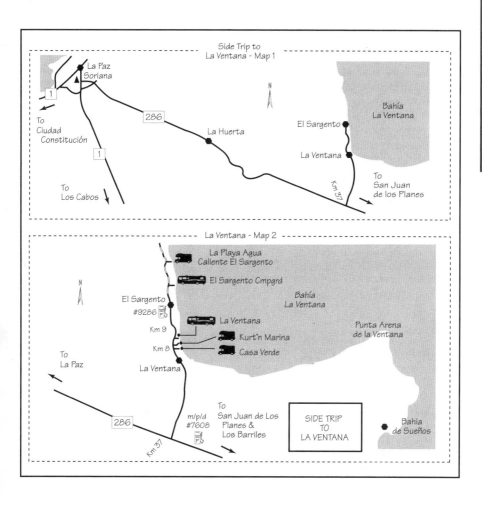

La Ventana Campgrounds

🚐 **CASA VERDE** *(Open All Year)*

Address: Calle Salome Lucero S/N, 23232, La Ventana,
                  B.C.S., Mexico
Telephone: (509) 843-7549
Email: info@bajacasaverde.com
Website: www.bajacasaverde.com

GPS Location: 24.04905 N, 109.98964 W, Near Sea Level

The Casa Verde is a very nice little hotel on the water in La Ventana. Behind the hotel off the main highway there it has a walled RV camping area. There are about eight sites here with full hookups as well as restrooms with hot showers and a cooking area with seating. Sites are suitable for RVs to about 30 feet. This is a popular camping area so staying here during the kiteboarding season generally requires a stay of 30 days. There are a few nice campground-owned RVs there too that are rented out. The hotel also has a restaurant. Reservations are essential at this campground during the winter kiteboarding season.

From the intersection on Highway 286 22 miles (35 km) from La Paz that is marked for La Ventana and El Sargento drive north for about 4.7 miles (7.6 km). You'll see the campground gate on the right.

KURT'N MARINA *(Open All Year)*
Telephone: (612) 114-0010
Website: www.kurtnmarina.com/

GPS Location: 24.05005 N, 109.98931 W, Near Sea Level

Kurt'n Marina is a small beach-front hotel with 10 RV slots, five of them overlooking the beach. These are full hookup sites, some for rigs to 35 feet. There are restrooms with hot showers and an outdoor cooking and lounge area also overlooking the beach. The hotel also has a restaurant.

From the intersection on Highway 286 22 miles (35 km) from La Paz that is marked for La Ventana and El Sargento drive north for about 4.8 miles (7.7 km). You'll see the campground gate on the right leading through the green fence.

LA VENTANA
        (Open All Year)
    Telephone: (612) 114-0375

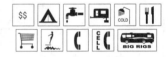

GPS Location: 24.05500 N, 109.99000 W, Near Sea Level

This campground is very popular with kiteboarders, in fact, that's why it is here. It's the largest and most popular camping location in the area. Winter is the season with reliable winds from the north. Expect to find lots of RVs, tents and vans.

The campground is a very large flat sandy area directly adjoining the beach. You can park not twenty feet from the water. If you watched for soft spots you can park pretty large RVs here since it's just a flat piece of ground. Facilities consist of a couple of toilet blocks with flush toilets and cold water showers. There are a few water faucets, a dump station, and also some scattered trees providing some shade. The entire area is fenced. There's a mini-super and a restaurant nearby the street.

From the intersection on Highway 286 22 miles (35 km) from La Paz that is marked for La Ventana and El Sargento drive north for 5.1 miles (8.2 km). You'll see the camping area and its chain-link fence on the right next to the beach.

EL SARGENTO CAMPGROUND *(Open All Year)*
    Telephone: (612) 198-4829
    Email: campgroundelsargento@gmail.com

GPS Location: 24.08829 N, 105.99509 W, Near Sea Level

Located north of most of the kiteboarding action and crowds this new campground has full hookups and a bluff location overlooking the ocean. There are 20 back-in sites and a tent area. Restrooms have flush toilets and hot showers and there's Wi-Fi.

LA VENTANA IS A POPULAR KITEBOARDING DESTINATION

From the intersection on Highway 286 22 miles (35 km) from La Paz that is marked for La Ventana and El Sargento drive north for about 7.5 miles (12.1 km). You'll see the entry road on the right. This is about .4 mile (.6 km) beyond the end of the pavement.

LA PLAYA AGUA CALIENTE EL SARGENTO *(Open All Year)*   FREE

GPS Location: 24.11145 N, 109.99693 W, Near Sea Level

This is a long sandy beach located north of La Ventana and El Sargento. It's popular with kiteboarders. There is a row of palapas, a garbage bin, and nothing else.

From the intersection on Highway 286 some 22 miles (35 km) from La Paz that is marked for La Ventana and El Sargento drive north for about 11 miles (17.5 km). You'll pass through La Ventana and El Sargento and the road will turn to dirt and sand but is usually firm. However, there's a very steep descent into an arroyo and it's very possible that larger rigs would need a tow to get out so take a look before descending. We would prefer 4-wheel drive to access this campground because of that hill and its loose sand surface.

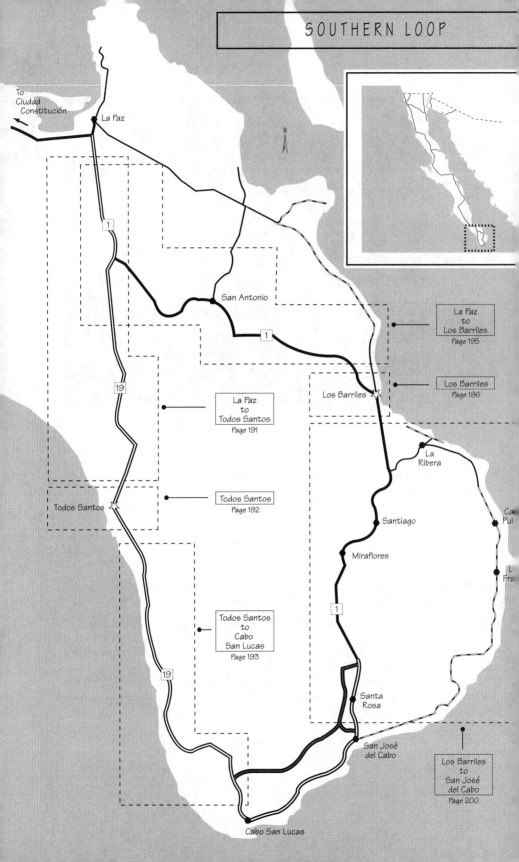

To
Ciudad
Constitución

La Paz

N

San Antonio

1

1

19

Los Barriles

La Paz
to
Los Barriles
Page 195

Los Barriles
Page 196

La
Ribera

La Paz
to
Todos Santos
Page 191

Todos Santos
Page 192

Todos Santos

Ca
Pul

Santiago

Miraflores

L
Fra

1

Todos Santos
to
Cabo
San Lucas
Page 193

19

Santa
Rosa

San José
del Cabo

Los Barriles
to
San José
del Cabo
Page 200

Cabo San Lucas

Chapter 9
Southern Loop

INTRODUCTION

This chapter of the book covers the area of the peninsula between La Paz and the Los Cabos area at the tip. The loop drive accesses both the west and east coasts, there are a good selection of destinations and activities.

Highlights

Todos Santos, near the west coast about half way between La Paz and the cape, has become something of an artist colony and day-trip destination for people who have flown in to Los Cabos. You'll find some good shopping and restaurants in the town.

Fishing fanatics congregate at **Los Barriles**. The combination of decent campgrounds and great fishing make this a place to stop or even base yourself for an extended stay. It's also a popular kiteboarding destination during the winter.

Cabo Pulmo and **Los Frailes** offer some of the best diving, beach fishing, and seaside boondocking on the whole peninsula.

Roads and Fuel Availability

South of La Paz there is a Y, you have a choice of traveling the west coast on Mex 19 or the eastern side of the peninsula on Mex 1. Most camping is to the left on Mex 1 but the choice is yours, you'll probably drive the whole circle before you head back north.

The distance from La Paz to Cabo San Lucas via the western route is 99 miles (160 km). The kilometer markers on this highway, unlike all kilometers markers on Mex 1 in Baja Sur, run from north to south. They start with zero at the Y on Mex 1 at Km 185 and end with 124 in Cabo San Lucas. With recently completed improvements it's now four lane highway from La Paz to Cabo San Lucas.

The distance from La Paz to San José del Cabo in the Los Cabos area is 112 miles (180 km) via the eastern Mex 1 route. Mex 1 from La Paz to the Y 16 miles (26 km) south of town is four-lanes. Beyond that it's all two-lane blacktop except the last 6 miles (10 km) of 4-lane after you reach the main airport for the Los Cabos region just north of San José del Cabo. Kilometers on this section begin in Cabo San Lucas, they have reached 30 at San José del Cabo and 185 at the junction with Mex 19 south of La Paz and then 211 at La Paz.

There is a bypass of the built-up area from north of San José del Cabo to north of Cabo San Lucas that runs inland. This is a toll road and as the area grows in population people appreciate it more and more.

Driving south on Mex 19 you'll find gas as follows, with types, and distances between stations: **La Paz**, gas and diesel; **Todos Santos**, gas and diesel, 48 miles (77 km); **Cabo San Lucas**, gas and diesel, 45 miles (72 km).

Driving south on Mex 1 you'll find gas as follows, with types and distances between stations: **La Paz**, gas and diesel; **San Antonio**, gas only, 36 miles (58 km); **Los Barriles**, gas and diesel, 28 miles (45 km); **Miraflores**, gas and diesel, 23 miles (37 km); **Santa Rosa**, gas, 17 miles (27 km); **San José del Cabo**, gas and diesel, 2 miles (3 km).

Sightseeing

Don't miss **Todos Santos** for excellent shopping and restaurants.

As you drive between San José del Cabo and Los Barriles you'll see a monument in the form of a big ball along the side of the road. This marks the **Tropic of Cancer**.

On Mex 1 just south of Los Barriles at Km 85 take the spur road about a mile and a half (2 km) out to **Santiago**. Once the site of a mission the little town now has a zoo that is fun to visit. Follow signs through town to find it.

Beaches and Water Sports

There are excellent beaches for surfing along the west side of the peninsula. Probably the easiest to access is **Playa Los Cerritos**, the beach's access road is near Km 65 about 7 miles (11 km) south of Todos Santos and ends at the big parking lot of the **Los Cerritos Surf Colony**.

The east coast of the peninsula north of Los Cabos is accessible by dirt road, see the *Backroad Adventures* section below. **Cabo Pulmo** is home to one of the very few coral reefs on the whole west coast of the Americas and an excellent diving spot. There's camping there as well as at nearby Los Frailes.

LOS BARRILES IS AN EXCELLENT LOCATION FOR KITEBOARDING

Fishing

Some of the best billfish fishing in the world is along the east coast of the peninsula. The reason is that deep water comes right close to shore. The fishing seasons are spring, summer and fall with May to July and October and November the best periods.

The area lacks formal ramps, La Paz and Cabo San Lucas are the closest. Boats are launched over the beach, there is a fairly sophisticated setup for launching boats at Los Barriles using trucks and trailers over the beach.

Probably the best charter fishing is available at Los Barriles. There are both pangas and cabin boats available, good fishing waters are nearby, and campgrounds are handy.

If you are restricted to fishing from the beach you might want to try Los Frailes. An underwater canyon comes so close to shore here that billfish have actually been caught from the beach!

Backroad Adventures

See the ***Backroad Driving*** section of ***Chapter 2 - Details, Details, Details*** for essential information about driving off the main highway on the Baja and for a definition of road type classifications used below.

From Los Barriles - A road goes north along the coast. If you zero your odometer at Martin Verdugo's RV Park and drive north you will reach the small community

THE BEACH AT CABO PULMO

of **Punta Pescadero** after 9 miles (15 km) and **El Cardonal** after 14 miles (23 km). This is normally a Type 2 road as far as the resort. The road continues north from El Cardonal to connect with the back road to La Paz at San Juan de los Planes, but the road north of El Cardonal is normally a Type 3 road and has some steep hillside sections. Note that there is now a paved road running inland from Los Barriles directly to El Cardonal.

From Km 93 Between San José del Cabo and Los Barriles - This is one of the more interesting back roads on the whole peninsula. Also one of the most heavily traveled, at least at the northern and southern ends. It follows the **eastern coastline of the peninsula** near the cape from San José del Cabo all the way north to La Ribera near Los Barriles. Here's a description from north to south. On Mex 1 at Km 93 a paved road goes east toward La Ribera. Seven miles (11 km) from the junction another paved road goes south. Zero your odometer here at the turn. Pavement last only 11 miles (18 km) from the turn. The road continues to **Cabo Pulmo** (17 miles (27 km) from the turn), **Los Frailes** (22 miles (35 km) from the turn), and south all the way to San José del Cabo (55 miles (89 km) from the turn). The northern part of the road to Cabo Pulmo is usually Type 1, then it becomes Type 2 in the middle section then improves to a Type 1 again near San José del Cabo where it provides access for many impressive homes for miles along the coast. The condition of the central part of this road varies dramatically depending upon how much damage was done by erosion during the last rainy season and how much repair has been done.

From Km 84 Between San José del Cabo and Los Barriles - In the hills behind Santiago there are a number of interesting destinations. Much of this area is designated as a national park and destinations charge small entrance fees and additional for overnight camping. Four of the campgrounds below are in this area and are at places that make good day trips as well as overnight destinations. See the *Los Barriles to San José del Cabo Campgrounds* section for descriptions of *El Chorro Agua Caliente Hot Springs Campground*, *Rancho Santa Rita Hot Springs*, *Rancho Ecologico Sol de Mayo* (at Cañon de la Zorra) and *Rancho La Acacia*. Each of these campground descriptions includes detailed driving instructions.

THE ROUTES, TOWNS, AND CAMPGROUNDS

LA PAZ TO TODOS SANTOS
45 Miles (72 Km), 1.50 Hours

Head out of town toward the south on Mex 1. In 16 miles (26 km) you'll come to a Y. Mex 1 continues straight, Mex 19 cuts off to the right. To get to Todos Santos we'll go right. This is a four-lane road.

The green vegetation that appears as you approach Todos Santos is welcome after crossing miles of dry country. There's now a bypass route around Todos Santos. It splits from Mex 19 at Km 46 and rejoins it at Km 56 to the south of Todos Santos. Unless you are in a hurry you'll probably want to go through town, not around it.

SOUTHERN LOOP

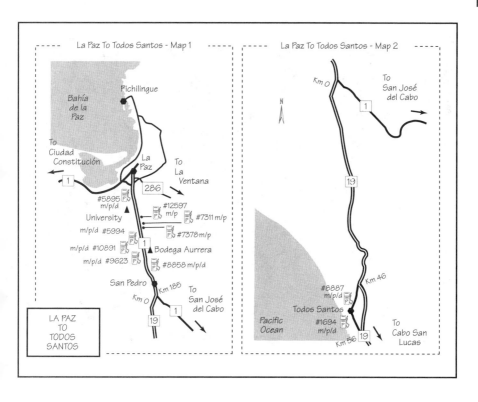

Assuming you do, you'll enter the outskirts of town 29 miles (47 km) after turning right at the Y.

TODOS SANTOS (TOE-DOES SAHN-TOES)
Population 5,000

Todos Santos is the Baja's art colony. This is an old mission and sugar cane town but today it is better known for the many Norteamericanos who have arrived in search of a simple small-town ambiance. There are galleries, crafts stores, and restaurants, as well as a bookstore called El Tecolote. The town is only a mile or so from the coast, there are decent beaches near town but the one at Los Cerritos is one of the best in the area, the access road is at Km 65, about 7 miles (11 km) south of town. The Tropic of Cancer runs just south of Todos Santos, you're in the tropics once you pass through town southbound.

Todos Santos Campground

■ EL LITRO *(Open All Year)*
Telephone: (612) 152-2367

GPS Location: 23.44101 N, 110.22683 W, 100 Ft.

This is a small campground on a dusty back road in the village of Todos Santos. There's a definite small village Mexican ambiance to this campground. The entrance

TODOS SANTOS IS BAJA'S ART COLONY

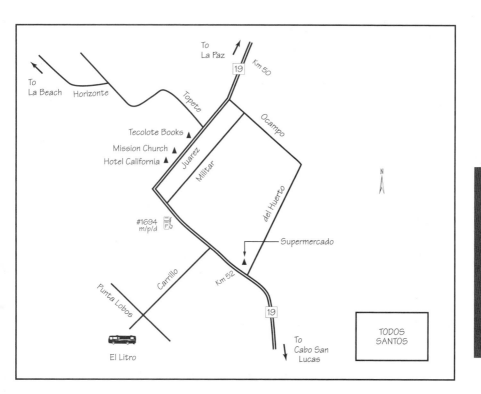

road is a little tight but passable. It is best to park outside the gate and walk in to check for availability, there's little room to turn around.

The campground has 11 back-in spaces with 15-amp outlets, sewer, and water hook-ups. Space is limited but we've seen 40-footers in here. There are also a few small sites with no hookups that make decent tent sites. Several of the spaces have patios, some are even shaded by palapas. A restroom building has flush toilets and hot water showers. There's also an on-site English-speaking manager.

To find the campground turn west on Carrillo near the southern entrance to Todos Santos. The turn is marked by a campground sign. The campground is directly ahead 0.2 miles (0.3 km) from the turn.

TODOS SANTOS TO CABO SAN LUCAS
45 Miles (72 Km), 1.25 Hours

Five miles (8 km) south of Todos Santos is the small farming town of El Pescadero. There are two campgrounds in this town, and probably more to come. Many small roads lead west to the beach. One that you'll see leads to Los Cerritos, formerly a camping area, now primarily a destination beach for tourists from Cabo complete with a bar, the Los Cerritos Beach Club. It's near the Km 65 marker, about 7 miles (11 km) south of Todos Santos.

As you get closer to Cabo the road turns inland. Before long you'll find yourself descending the last hill in to town. The main road doglegs to the left letting you bypass the chaotic streets of this fast-growing town with your RV.

Todos Santos to Cabo San Lucas Campgrounds

BAJA SERENA *(Open All Year)*

Address:	Carretera Transpeninsular S/N KM 62 El
	Pescadero, Baja California Sur, México
Telephone:	(612) 131-7564
Email:	info@bajaserena.com
Website:	www.bajaserena.com

GPS Location: 23.36806 N, 110.17389 W, 100 Ft.

This small campground is away from the beach but one of the few in this area. It's located in the small town of Pescadero, south of Todos Santos.

There are 5 back-in sites. They are suitable for RVs to about 40 feet. Parking is on sand and small plants separate the sites. There are electricity, water and sewer hookups. Bathrooms are provided, they're nice with hot water showers. There is a two day minimum stay in this campground.

Watch for Pemex #7513 in Pescadero near Km 62. The campground is on the far side of the highway along a small lane that leaves the highway just a hundred feet or so to

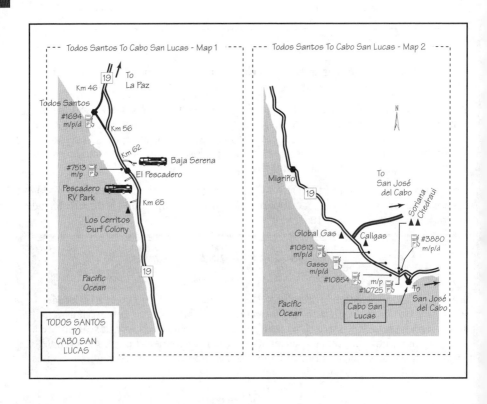

the north of the Pemex. The gated camping area is right beyond a building that now serves and is signed as a Yoga studio.

PESCADERO RV PARK

Telephone:	(604) 628-9532, (619) 780-8048, or
	(612) 139-2713 (Mexico Cell)
Email:	pescaderorv@gmail.com
Website:	www.pescaderorv.com

GPS Location: 23.35489 N, 110.18159 W, 100 Ft.

The Pescadero RV is an extremely nice but small Pescadero park. Most of the 22 sites are occupied by permanently situated RVs, but there are six sites that are kept available for others.

These are long back-in sites suitable for RVs to 45 feet, large rigs aren't a problem here. The full hookups are modern and in excellent shape. There's a modern restroom building with flush toilets and hot showers as well as a swimming pool. Wi-Fi is provided. This is an adult park and children under 14 cannot be residents. Note also that large dogs are not allowed and there's a three-day minimum stay.

It's important to call or email ahead at this small park to determine that a site is available and that the gate is open. To reach the RV park turn toward the beach on the dirt road that is .3 miles (.5 km) south of Pemex 7513 in Pescadero. This turn is near the Km 63 marker, if there were one. In .8 miles (1.3 km) turn left. You'll see the campground entrance on the left in .3 mile (.5 km).

SOUTHERN LOOP

LA PAZ TO LOS BARRILES
61 Miles (98 Km), 2 Hours

Heading south from La Paz you'll come to a Y in the road after 16 miles (26 km). The left fork is Mex 1, that's the one we'll take. Soon the road begins climbing into the northern reaches of the Sierra de la Laguna.

Two towns soon appear. **El Triunfo**, 13 miles (21 km) from the Y is an old gold and silver mining town. The tall smokestack marks the smelter. A few miles farther on is **San Antonio**, a farming town that fills a valley. There is a recently paved road that connects this town with San Juan de los Planes and La Ventana to the north. Some folks from Los Barriles now use this as an alternative route to La Paz.

Near Km 110 there is a paved cutoff to the left that leads to a coastal road and central Los Barriles.

La Paz to Los Barriles Campground

RANCHO VERDE RV HAVEN *(Open All Year)*

Address:	PO Box 1050, Eureka, Montana 59917
	(Reservations)
Location:	Hwy 1, Km 142.5, San Bartolo, B.C.S., México
Telephone:	(406) 889-3030 (U.S.)
Email:	bill@landstore.com (Reservations)
Website:	www.rancho-verde.com

GPS Location: 23.76278 N, 109.97944 W, 1,700 Ft.

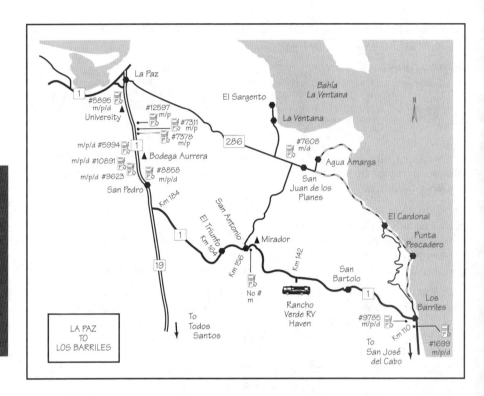

This is a campground located in the mountains west of Los Barriles. The green high wooded country is a nice change from flat desert and sandy seashore.

There are 29 widely separated back-in spaces. Each one has water and sewer hook-ups, there is no electricity. Most sites are large and can take big rigs, the entry road is not tight but turning around might be difficult so take a look, it's easy to walk the road from the highway where there's a pull-off. The restrooms are in a simple palapa roof building but are extremely clean and have hot water for showers. There's also limited slow satellite Wi-Fi in the office and it can be used from your rig if you're parked in a site nearby. This is ranch country and there are miles of trails for hiking and bird-watching. Lots are for sale but you need not fear high pressure sales tactics.

Rancho Verde is located in the mountains about 20 miles (32 km) west of Los Bar-riles near San Bartolo. The entrance road is off Mex 1 near Km 142.

LOS BARRILES (LOES BAR-EEL-ACE)
Population 5,000

Los Barriles and nearby La Ribera are enjoying a surge of RVer popularity as devel-opment overtakes the campgrounds farther south near Cabo. This is an excellent area for kiteboarding. You'll find a number of restaurants, some small hotels, trailer parks, and a few shops in Los Barriles. Fishing is quite good because deep water is just off-shore, campers keep their car-top boats on the beach. Trucks are used for launching larger boats, there is no ramp. If you're looking for a place to spend the winter on the lower Baja with nice hookup campgrounds this is it.

Los Barriles Campgrounds

BAJA SUNRISE RV PARK *(Open All Year)*

Address:	Km 108 Carretera Transpeninsular Los Cabos-La Paz, Los Barriles, BC, Sur, Mex CP 23501
Telephone:	(624) 141-0065, (624) 145-5769, or (612) 143-5382
Email:	jbremer@bajasunriservpark.com
Website:	bajasunriservpark.com

GPS Location: 23.67029 N, 109.69903 W, Near Sea Level

Los Barriles' newest RV park is also its easiest to find. Rather then being located in the town itself, it's just off the highway to the south. It's also right on the beach.

There are pull up beach-front sites as well as pull-thrus farther back. Sites have full hookups and are suitable for large rigs. This is a large open lot with little landscaping yet. There are restrooms with flush toilets and hot showers, a washer for laundry, Wi-Fi, and a dump station.

The campground is located right on Mex 1 just .9 mile (1.5 km) south of the Los Barriles turn-off, across from the Pemex station.

A FISHING DAY TRIP FROM LOS BARRILES IS AWESOME

SOUTHERN LOOP

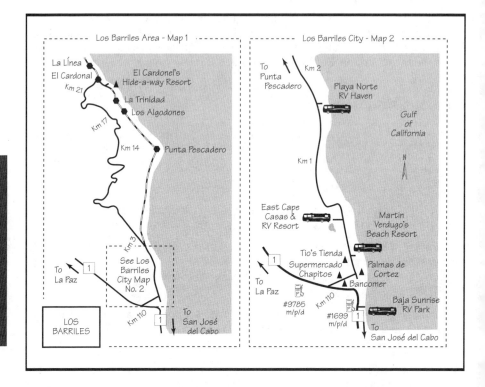

 **MARTIN VERDUGO'S BEACH RESORT** *(Open All Year)*

Address:	Apdo 17, CP 23501 Los Barriles, B.C.S., México
Telephone:	(624) 141-0054, (949) 226-7168 (U.S.), (888) 567-8552
Email:	martinverdugo@prodigy.net.mx
Website:	www.verdugosbeachresort.com

GPS Location: 23.68231 N, 109.69857 W, Near Sea Level

This old-timer is a popular place. The property is located on a wide beach although there are two large hotel buildings between the camping area and the water. There is a swimming pool and a palapa bar overlooking the beach. The resort offers fishing expeditions on its own cruisers and room to keep your own small boat on the beach.

The campground has 65 older RV spaces with 15 and 30-amp outlets, sewer, and water. You'll see RVs to 45 feet in here. There are also 25 tent spaces with water and electric hookups. Restrooms are clean and in decent repair, they have hot water showers. There is a coin-operated laundry, a library in the office, a restaurant (breakfast only) in one of the two hotel buildings, and of course the pool and palapa bar overlooking the beach. English is spoken and reservations are recommended. The monthly rate here is $460 for RVs and $310 for tents.

Take the Los Barriles exit from Mex 1 between La Paz and Cabo San Lucas near the

Km 110 marker. You'll reach a T in .3 miles (.5 km). Turn left and you'll see the RV park on the right in .2 miles (.3 km).

EAST CAPE CASAS & RV RESORT *(Open All Year)*

Address:	185 Calle 20 de Noviembre, Los Barriles, B.C.S., México
Telephone:	(624) 141-0231, (909) 266-9707 (USA-Vonage)
Email:	res@eastcaperv.com
Website:	www.eastcaperv.com

GPS Location: 23.68639 N, 109.69889 W, Near Sea Level

This campground is one of the most popular on the peninsula. It's the place to stay if you have a big rig since there's plenty of room and good hookups and amenities.

This is a large campground with both back-in and pull-thru sites. There are about 60 sites. Palm trees provide shade and there are lots of shrubs and flowers. In fact, there are so many different kinds of plants here that a pamphlet has been written to help you identify them. The palapa-style restroom building has some of the nicest and cleanest facilities on the Baja and there are coin-operated washers and dryers. Wi-Fi is available throughout the park. There's a spa and a nice swimming pool and they're kept at a proper temperature, even in the winter. This is a well-managed park with lots of information provided about things to do in the area. From the park it's just a short walk for groceries and restaurants. It's also a short walk to the beach. The campground owners/managers operate two popular sport-fishing boats, it's easy to make arrangements for a fishing trip or a day trip up the coast for marine wild-

SOUTHERN LOOP

SPA AND SWIMMING POOL AT THE EAST CAPE RV RESORT

life watching and snorkeling. Recently horseback (horses are off-site) riding on the beach and back into the arroyos has been added. Many folks lease lots here long-term, build a casita, and come back every year.

Take the Los Barriles exit from Mex 1 between La Paz and Cabo San Lucas near the Km 110 marker. You'll reach a T in .3 miles (.5 km). Turn left and you'll see the RV park on the left in 0.4 miles (0.6 km).

PLAYA NORTE RV HAVEN *(Open All Year)*

Telephone:	(425) 252-5952 (U.S.)
Fax:	(425) 252-6171
Email:	harneckerw@gmail.com
Website:	www.playanortervpark.com

GPS Location: 23.70139 N, 109.70111 W, Near Sea Level

This campground occupies a large piece of land north of Los Barriles on a good beach. It's been a popular wind-surfing campground. There are long pull-thru sites with full hookups and others with electricity and water only. If you want to park with no hookups or pitch a tent there's plenty of room for that too. Restrooms have flush toilets and hot showers. Wi-Fi is at a hot spot. There's also a dump station.

Take the Los Barriles exit from Mex 1 between La Paz and Cabo San Lucas near the Km 110 marker. You'll reach a T in .3 miles (.5 km). Turn left and drive 1.8 miles (2.9 km), the campground entrance is on the right. There's a manager on-site during the busy winter season.

LOS BARRILES TO SAN JOSÉ DEL CABO
48 Miles (77 Km), 1.5 Hours

Heading south from Los Barriles you'll spot a road going east at Km 93. This is the highway to La Ribera, and it provides access to the rough coastal road described in *Backroad Adventures* above, and three campgrounds described in the *Los Barriles to San José del Cabo Campgrounds* section below.

Continuing south on Mex 1 you'll soon see a cutoff to the right near Km 85 for **Santiago**. It's a little over a mile off the road and has a Pemex, as well as a zoo. This was once a mission town but the mission is gone, now it's a ranching and farming town with a town square. We describe four no-hookup camping areas in the foothills behind Santiago below in the *Los Barriles to San José del Cabo Campgrounds* section.

When you cross the **Tropic of Cancer** at latitude N 23° 26' near Km 81 you have entered the tropics. There's a monument in the shape of a globe, stop for a picture.

Miraflores, right from near Km 71, is known for its leather crafts. There's a Pemex on the highway and a 1.5 mile (2.4 km) paved road leads to the village. Watch for **leather tannery and shop** before you reach town.

The road turns to four lanes near the international airport at Km 44, about 6 miles (10 km) north of San José del Cabo. You're about to enter Baja's tourist zone. See the next chapter for details.

Los Barriles to San José del Cabo Campgrounds

CABO PULMO CAMPING AREA *(Open All Year)*

GPS Location: 23.44083 N, 109.42750 W, Near Sea Level

The Cabo Pulmo area is known for its diving. The coral reef here is one of the few on the west coast of the Americas. Note that summer is the best time to dive here. There are several dive shops in town, a couple of basic restaurants, and this very simple campground.

The is a large fenced area next to the beach to the north of town. In the rear near the road is sand, but parking for RVs overlooks the beach from a mound of gravel with some shrubs near the south end. Other than the mound of gravel the surface is flat, large RVs can maneuver and park but watch for soft spots. The beach here is mostly gravel but there is some sand near the water. Showers are available at dive shops in town. Management of this area varies from year to year. Some years it is supervised and a fee charged, at other times it's ignored by the locals and camping is free. Occasionally it's even gated and no camping allowed.

To reach Cabo Pulmo turn east on the paved road near Km 93 south of Los Barriles. Follow the road for 6.8 miles (10.9 km) until just before La Ribera another paved

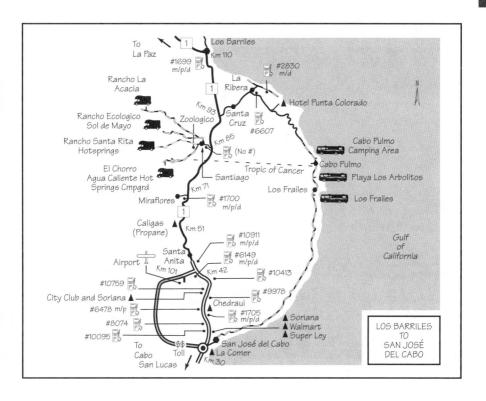

road goes right. Turn to the right, you'll soon see a sign saying that Cabo Pulmo is 30 km. The road remains paved for only 10.7 miles (17.2 km) then turns to gravel. It's a road that's passable in any vehicle as far as Cabo Pulmo (and also Los Frailes, see below) but it's like driving on a washboard, very unpleasant in an RV. You'll see the campground on your left 5.9 miles (9.5 km) after the road turns to gravel.

PLAYA LOS ARBOLITOS *(Open All Year)*

GPS Location 23.40401 N, 109.42531 W, Near Sea Level

Here's a fall-back if the camping area up at Cabo Pulmo is closed. This beach has an access road and limited facilities. You can tent camp on the beach at one of the palapas or park your RV in their small parking area. Facilities are limited to a bucket-flush bathroom with cold shower.

From Cabo Pulmo drive south 2.6 miles (4.2 km). You'll spot the entrance road on the left.

LOS FRAILES *(Open All Year)*

GPS Location: 23.38240 N, 109.42983 W, Near Sea Level

This remote campground is very popular with folks from the north, even in big RVs. Winter finds dozens of RVs parked in areas of a gravel arroyo outwash near the beach. You'll find even the largest RVs here, care must be taken to avoid soft spots,

LAS FRAILES IS POPULAR WITH FOLKS FROM THE NORTH

there are lots of them. The only amenity is a well where water can be drawn by bucket, don't drink it without treating it first. This would be a poor place to camp during storm season, you could get washed away.

Reaching the campground is a bit of a trial due to 10.9 miles (17.5 km) of gravel road which often has a washboard surface. From Mex 1 south of Los Barriles turn east on the paved road near Km 93. Follow the road for 6.8 miles (10.9 km) until just before La Ribera another paved road goes right. Turn to the right, you'll soon see a sign saying that Cabo Pulmo is 30 km. The road remains paved for only 10.7 miles (17.2 km) then turns to gravel. It's a road that's passable in any vehicle as far as Los Frailes. You'll reach the small community of Cabo Pulmo 5.9 miles (9.5 km) after the road turns to gravel, continue on through town. After another 5.0 miles (8.1 km) you'll come to the arroyo and see the RVs parked off to your left and right.

EL CHORRO AGUA CALIENTE HOT SPRINGS CAMPGROUND *(Open All Year)*

GPS Location: 23.44078 N, 109.80581 W, 700 Ft.

This is a small backwoods campground just inside the border of the Sierra de la Laguna park. The attraction is the small hot spring nearby. There is rooms for perhaps 10 small RVs or tents in small pull-offs in the trees. Outhouses are provided. The hot spring seeps from the rocks at the edge of a lake behind a concrete dam. Rocks have been used to form a pool that stays warmer than the lake. Small sites and a marginal access road make this a campground for tents and RVs to about 25 feet.

There are several routes to this campground, including quite a few ways to drive through Santiago. Here's an interesting one. From Mex 1 near Km 84 take the paved road west toward Santiago and zero your odometer. You'll reach Santiago and its central plaza at 1.5 miles (2.4 km). Turn left on the far side of the square and then go straight ahead and down the hill until at 2 miles (3.2 km) you'll reach a T. Turn right and at 2.4 miles (3.9 km) you'll reach another T. Turn left and at 2.6 miles (4.2 km) you'll see the zoo on your right and soon after that the road turns to dirt. Continue straight on the road and at 6.3 miles (10.1 km) you'll reach the village of Agua Caliente. Continue straight on through the town and at 7.7 miles (12.4 km) you'll turn and cross the arroyo you've been paralleling. Cross the (hopefully) dry riverbed and at 8.5 miles (13.7 km) you'll enter a small village and see a gate where the access or camping fee will be collected. Then continue to the camping area at mile 9.2 (14.8 km). High clearance is not usually required but drive carefully.

RANCHO SANTA RITA HOTSPRINGS *(Open All Year)*

GPS Location: 23.47175 N, 109.80738

This is a remote parking lot with a nice area for tent camping that includes a palapa and pit toilet. The real attraction is a stream flowing over rocks that form several pools, some of them pretty warm. Due to the rough road in only vehicles with high clearance are suitable, we wouldn't want to come in with anything larger than a high-clearance van. Tent camping is best here because it's a fenced area. The vehicle parking isn't too charming, you can tell that there are often a lot of cows wandering around the area.

SOUTHERN LOOP

ENJOYING THE RANCHO SANTA RITA HOTSPRINGS

The first part of this driving route is the same as that for El Chorro, described above. Then, in Santiago, just before reaching the zoo, you turn right onto a dirt road and follow that along a large arroyo and through a village to the hotsprings. From Mex 1 near Km 84 take the paved road west toward Santiago after you zero your odometer. You'll reach Santiago and its central plaza at 1.5 miles (2.4 km). Turn left on the far side of the square and then go straight ahead and down the hill until at 2 miles (3.2 km) you'll reach a T. Turn right and at 2.4 miles (3.9 km) you'll reach another T. Turn left and at 2.5 miles (4.0 km) (which is on the near side of the zoo) turn right. Now follow the sandy dirt road along a large wash, left along the hills (don't take the good road to the right up the hill) and though several arroyos, always following the main track. You'll reach the small village of San Jorge at 7.5 miles (12.1 km). At the square the route goes left, soon climbs a steep hill with a sharp switchback, and arrives at the parking area at 8.8 miles (14.2 km).

RANCHO ECOLOGICO SOL DE MAYO *(Open All Year)*

Address:	Calle Guadalupa Victoria, No 410B, Col Loma Sur., CP 23500, Santiago, Baja California Sur, México
Telephone:	(624) 130-2055 or (624) 191-8024
Website:	www.ranchoecologicosoldemano.com

GPS Location: 23.49929 N, 109.79031 W, 800 Ft.

This is a small, well-kept resort located well back into the Sierra Laguna. The prime attraction here is the Cascada Sol de Mayo, a beautiful little waterfall and pool a short hike from the resort in the Cañon de la Zorra.

The resort has a number of rental casitas. RVs and tent campers can overnight in a flat dirt area near the trail to the waterfall. There is a small restaurant, but it's not always open. The waterfall is a quarter-mile hike from the resort. Swimming in the pool below it is excellent! There is a fee for access to the waterfall, it's included in the camping price above. Limited maneuvering room at the campground and the marginal access road make this campground best for tents and rigs to about 25 feet.

While the route described here is fairly complex most turns are signed for Sol de Mayo. From Mex 1 near Km 84 take the paved road west toward Santiago and zero your odometer. At 1.5 miles (2.4 km) after crossing a big wash and just as you reach town turn right on Francisco J Mujca, a paved road heading north. At 1.9 miles (3.1 km) the paved road goes left, continue straight on a the dirt road. At 2.3 miles (3.7 km) at a Y (a driveway on the right makes it seem to be almost a crossroads) go left. At 2.6 mile (4.2 km) take a right. From here the road has several turns, always take the most trafficked route. You'll cross two cattle guards and just after the second, at 4.5 miles (7.2 km) take a right. Now just follow the road as it zigzags generally westward to the resort at 7.7 miles (12.4 km). High clearance is not usually required but drive carefully.

RANCHO LA ACACIA *(Open All Year)*
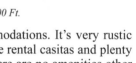
Telephone: (612) 139-4843 or (612) 117-1967
Email: ranchoacacia@hotmail.com

GPS Location: 23.55203 N, 109.85110 W, 1400 Ft.

Rancho Acacia is an orchard with simple tourist accommodations. It's very rustic and pretty remote, and that's the attraction. There are some rental casitas and plenty of space on the property to pitch a tent or park an RV. There are no amenities other than an outhouse. A rocky arroyo is next to the property and at times there's a swimming hole there. The manager lives near the entrance but you'll probably find him out working on the property somewhere when you arrive. The marginal access road makes this campground best for tents and rigs to 25 feet.

From Mex 1 near Km 84 take the paved road west toward Santiago and zero your odometer. At 1.5 miles (2.4 km) after crossing a big wash and just as you reach town turn right on Francisco J Mujca, a paved road heading north. At 1.9 miles (3.1 km) the paved road goes left, continue straight on a the dirt road. At 2.3 miles (3.7 km) at a Y (a driveway on the right makes it seem to be almost a crossroads) go straight. From here continue to follow the main track, you'll find the entrance on the right at odometer 13.7 miles (22 km). High clearance is not required, but drive carefully.

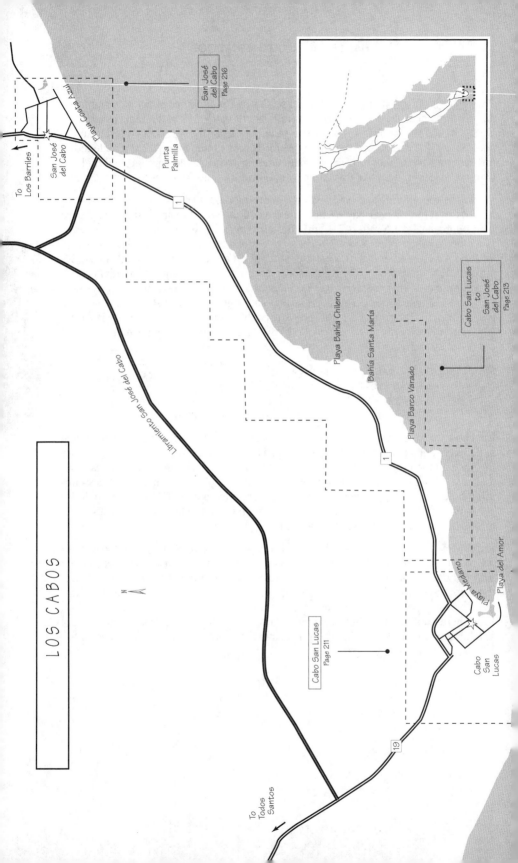

LOS CABOS

To
Los Barriles

San José
del Cabo

Playa Costa Azul

Punta
Palmilla

1

Libramiento San José del Cabo

San José
del Cabo
Page 216

Playa Bahía Chileno

Bahía Santa María

Playa Barco Varado

1

Cabo San Lucas
to
San José
del Cabo
Page 213

Playa Médano

Playa del Amor

Cabo San Lucas
Page 211

Cabo
San
Lucas

19

To
Todos
Santos

N

Chapter 10
Los Cabos

INTRODUCTION

For many campers headed down the peninsula for the first time Los Cabos (The Capes) is the end of the rainbow, the ultimate destination. While Los Cabos is a world-class resort and very popular destination for tourists flying out from the U.S. and Canada you may find that you've seen a fine selection of much more desirable stops during your trip south. The truth is that Los Cabos is hectic and oriented toward folks looking for a few days of fun in the sun.

Campers and RVers have limited options in this area. As land prices have increased a number of campgrounds and RV parks have closed their doors. The center of RV camping has moved from Cabo to Los Barriles. It's only 48 miles (77 km) from Los Barriles to San José del Cabo. That said, there are still a few options for staying in the Cabo area. We'll cover them below.

The Los Cabos area really includes two major towns: Cabo San Lucas and San José del Cabo which is located about 20 miles (33 km) east. San José del Cabo is the older town and is more relaxed and comfortable. Cabo San Lucas, on the other hand, is chock full of hotels, restaurants, shops, and activity. The area between the two is known as the Cabo Corridor. All of the campgrounds described below are located in the Cabo Corridor just to the east of Cabo San Lucas.

Highlights

Los Cabos is probably best known for its **deep-sea fishing**. This is one of the world's premier fly-in resort areas as well as a cruise ship port so it also offers lots of excellent **restaurants**, **shopping**, and **golf**. It's much different than the much quieter country to the north, if you judiciously indulge in the entertainment offerings you'll find the area to be a lot of fun.

Roads and Fuel Availability

The primary road on this section of the peninsula is the four-lane free highway between Cabo San Lucas and the Los Cabos International Airport which is located about six miles (10 km) north of San José del Cabo. The distance between Cabo San Lucas and San José del Cabo is 18 miles (29 km). The road is marked with kilometer posts, they start in Cabo San Lucas and have reached 30 by the time you reach San José del Cabo.

For quickly getting from Cabo San Lucas to San Jose del Cabo, or for bypassing the whole area, there is now a toll road running through the back country to the north. It runs from Km 17 on Mex 19 north of Cabo San Lucas to Km 42 on Mex 1 north of San Jose Del Cabo near the airport. There are also direct access roads from both Cabo San Lucas and San José del Cabo.

Sightseeing

Probably the most popular excursion from Cabo San Lucas is a boat ride out to see **Los Arcos** at **Finisterra** (Land's End), perhaps with a stop at **Playa del Amor** (Lover's Beach). This trip really does offer the chance for some spectacular photos. You'll probably see sea lions on the rocks and at the entrance to the boat harbor.

San José del Cabo's **Boulevard Mijares** is a good place to do some shopping for Mexican folk art and souvenirs. It's much quieter than similar places in Cabo San Lucas, and just as good.

There are some spectacular **hotels** in Los Cabos and they can be fun to visit. There are also lots of time share sales. If you want to do that we suggest that you don't tell them you're in an RV. Even though the sales people don't think RVers are good prospects we know from our friends that that isn't always true. Attending one of the sales presentations can be an experience, and you might buy one yourself. That would give you a good reason to drive down the peninsula on a frequent basis!

Like La Paz to the north the Cabo area now has lots of big box stores including Walmart, Sam's Club, Soriana, Mega, Home Depot, and Costco.

Golf

Los Cabos now has at least ten golf courses. Most of these are world-class, with prices to match. If you're looking for a deal (and you will be since normal green fees are extremely high) always ask about twilight rates.

Beaches and Water Sports

The best known beach in Los Cabos must be **Playa del Amor** (Lover's Beach). It is a small beach out on the Lands End cape that is hemmed in by rocks. Snorkeling is decent here on the east side. Access is via water taxis and tour boats from the Cabo San Lucas harbor. Just offshore (to the east) is a 3,000-foot un-

THE BEST KNOWN BEACH IN CABO MUST BE PLAYA DEL AMOR (LOVERS BEACH)

derwater canyon that is the most popular scuba location in the area, unique sandfalls down the underwater cliffs are the attraction.

The most populous swimming beach near Cabo San Lucas is called **Playa Medano**. It stretches east from the harbor mouth. The beach on the western side of Land's End is called **Playa Solmar**, the water is considered dangerous and access is difficult so the beach doesn't get much use.

Between Cabo San Lucas and San José del Cabo, along the Cabo Corridor, there are quite a few beaches although many are difficult to access because hotels, condos, and housing developments overlook them. Access routes of one kind or another are usually available since, in theory, under the law access cannot be cut off. The ones with decent access have small signs along the road, usually in the form of a blue sign with a snorkeling mask. The two most popular, good for sunning, swimming, and snorkeling, are **Bahía Santa María** near Km 12, and **Playa Bahía Chileno** near Km 14.

The **Playa Costa Azul** is a long beautiful beach stretching from the lagoon at San José del Cabo westward for several miles. You might note that water temperatures tend to be higher here than on the beaches farther west.

Fishing

Fishing for large game fish is the thing to do in Los Cabos. The possible catch includes marlin, sailfish, dorado, and tuna. The months for the best fishing are May to July and October to December. Catch-and-release fishing is popular here, no one wants to see the fishing decline as it inevitably would if everyone

FISHING FOR LARGE FISH IS THE THING TO DO IN CABO

kept all the fish caught. It is easy to arrange charter fishing trips in cruisers or pangas.

Backroad Adventures

See the *Backroad Driving* section of *Chapter 2 - Details, Details, Details* for essential information about driving off the main highway on the Baja and for a definition of road types used below.

From very near the central shopping district in San José del Cabo - A dirt road goes east and leads all the way up the coast to **Los Frailes**, **Cabo Pulmo**, and **La Ribera**. It is described in more detail in the previous chapter under *Backroad Adventures*. This is usually a Type 1 road at both ends but can be Type 2 in the middle section.

From Km 54.5 North of San José del Cabo - North of the airport and the village of Santa Anita on the road to Los Barriles (Mex 1) a gravel and dirt road runs all the way across the peninsula to meet the Cabo San Lucas to Todos Santos Highway

(Mex 19) near Km 72.5. It's called Camino Las Naranjas and is 31 miles (50 km) in length. Neither end is marked. This is usually a Type 2 road and gives you the chance to see some pretty desert and mountain scenery as well as extensive views to the west from some pull-offs near the crest of the route.

THE ROUTES, TOWNS, AND CAMPGROUNDS

CABO SAN LUCAS (KAH-BOW SAHN LOO-KAHS)
Population 80,000

Cabo San Lucas is the major resort town in the Los Cabos area. It is filled with fly-in visitors and often also with cruise ship passengers wandering the streets during their short visits.

The town is centered around the **marina**. The marina itself is surrounded by modern shopping malls and restaurants, they almost cut it off from the streets of town which stretch off to the north. These streets become less touristy and more Mexican, also less flashy and more interesting, as you progress northward. There is a large Mexican population here attracted in recent years by the employment offered by the tourism industry.

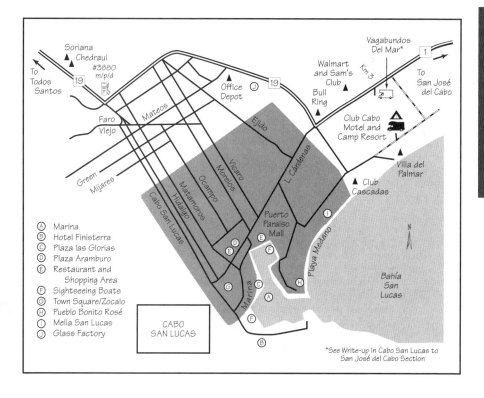

THE ARCH AT FINISTERRA (LANDS END)

In the marina area you can arrange for a boat trip. Many people come to Los Cabos primarily for the fishing and this is where most of the charter boats are based. You can also find water taxis or tour boats to take you out to see **Finisterra (Lands End)** or visit **Playa Amor (Lover's Beach)**. There's always a lot of activity in the harbor and you can stroll along taking it in. Note that the guys trying to sell you something generally stay on the far side of the line scribed near the edge of the water.

In the streets immediately north of the marina you'll find most of the **restaurants and tourist-oriented shops** in town. This is actually a pretty good place to shop for Mexican gifts and art.

The closest beach to Cabo San Lucas is **Playa Medano**. It is on the east side of the harbor entrance. Driving access is actually best from Mex 1 near the point where Mex 19 joins it just east of town.

Cabo San Lucas Campground

🚐 **CLUB CABO MOTEL AND CAMP RESORT** *(Open All Year)*

Telephone	
and Fax:	(624) 143-3348
Email:	clubcaboinn@hotmail.com or info@clubcabo.com
Website	www.clubcaboinn.com

GPS Location: 22.90000 N, 109.89475 W, Near Sea Level

Club Cabo is a small motel and tent and RV campground a bit off the beaten track. It's the European owners' long-time home with a variety of guest facilities.

This is a walled compound located off the main routes. There are 10 RV sites, most have 15-amp outlets, sewer, and water. These are all back-in sites. They'll take any size rig but large rigs limit the maneuvering space in the compound so only a few will fit comfortably. This is also the best tent campground in the area. The bathroom and shower building has a flush toilet and good hot shower. There is also a pool. Laundry service is available. A shaded outdoor lounge area has a TV, barbecue, and kitchen clean-up station. It takes about 7 minutes to walk to the beach from here, or about a minute by bus from the front gate. English is spoken and reservations are highly recommended, particularly for rigs larger than 30 feet.

The Club Cabo is located almost right behind the Vagabundos campground. To get to it you must take a roundabout route. Start from Mex 1 east of downtown Cabo San Lucas where Mex 19 and Mex 1 intersect. Go south from this intersection for 0.3 miles (0.5 km) until the boulevard dead-ends. Turn left and drive 0.2 miles (0.3 km). The road appears to end in a parking lot but to the left you'll see a small dirt road. Follow it and, in 0.6 mile (1 km) you'll see the Club Cabo on the left.

CABO SAN LUCAS TO SAN JOSÉ DEL CABO
20 Miles (32 Km), 0.5 Hour

Mex 1 starts in Cabo San Lucas so kilometer markers count up as you drive eastward and then turn north in San José del Cabo. The area between the two towns is known as the "Cabo Corridor" or simply as "The Corridor". From Cabo San Lucas all the way to the Los Cabos International Airport north of San José del Cabo the highway is four lanes wide and heavily traveled.

The campgrounds in this section are located near the western end of the Cabo Corridor.

As the highway approaches San José del Cabo near Km 30 it turns north to pass just west of central San José del Cabo. There are several stop lights along this section of the highway. You can turn right along Paseo San José if you are in a tow car or small RV to reach the shopping district south of the central plaza.

Frequent busses run both ways along the Cabo Corridor. They are inexpensive and convenient, and they are the best way to visit the central area of either Cabo San Lucas or San José del Cabo. During the high season it can be difficult to find convenient parking in either of these towns.

Cabo San Lucas to San José del Cabo Campgrounds

TRAILER PARK VAGABUNDOS DEL MAR
(Open All Year)

Address:	Apdo. 197, Cabo San Lucas, B.C.S., México
Telephone:	(624) 143-0290 (Mex)
Email:	xe2iir@hotmail.com
Website:	www.vagabundosrv.com

GPS Location: 22.90083 N, 109.89611 W, Near Sea Level

In the past the Vagabundos park was a large park with traveler's spaces up front and long term leased spaces in back, almost all with casitas built by the leaseholders. This has changed.

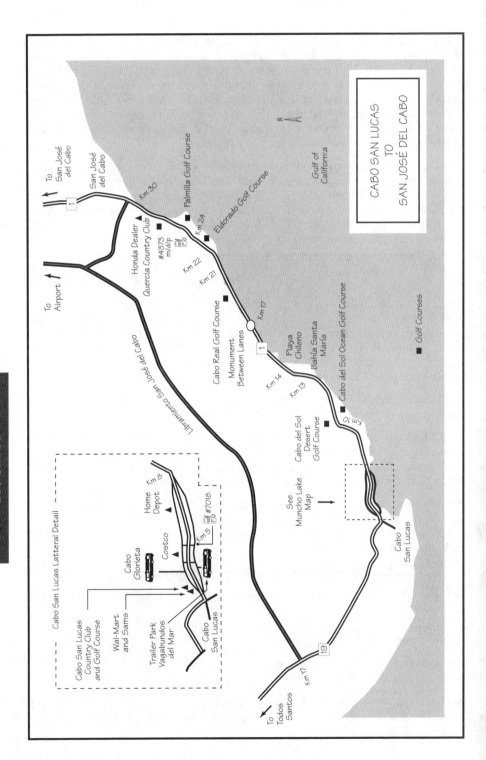

CABO IS CHOCK FULL OF ACTIVITIES TO KEEP TOURIST OCCUPIED

LOS CABOS

All of the traveler spaces are gone. That area is now occupied by an automobile dealer. The leased spaces, most with casitas, remain. A few of these spaces are available to travelers if they are not rented long-term. If you want to stay in this park it is essential that you call ahead as soon as you know that you will be visiting Cabo to reserve one of these spaces. All other facilities remain. The office at the entrance is open. The restrooms are clean and modern and have hot water showers. There's a swimming pool with a palapa bar and good restaurant, a laundry, a computer for internet access, and free Wi-Fi that can be received in the office area. The bus running from Cabo San Lucas to San José del Cabo stops right out front. Again, early reservations are essential.

The campground is right at the Km 3 marker on Mex 1 east of Cabo San Lucas. It is on the south side of the road. Access is from a lateral in this section so be sure to get into the lateral as soon as possible eastbound. Westbound traffic can pass the park, take the exit marked Retorno and San José del Cabo, make a 180 at the traffic circle at the Walmart parking lot entrance, and then return over the overpass to the eastbound lateral to enter the campground.

CABO GLORIETA *(Open All Year)*
   Telephone: (624) 155-4671
   Email: caboglorieta@yahoo.com.mx
   GPS Location: 22.90707 N, 109.89347 W, Near Sea Level

This is a unique RV based housing area just outside Cabo San Lucas. Thirty casitas, most enclosing RVs, are arranged in a circle or glorieta around a central pool area. It's an upscale place.

There are six rental sites on the outside of the glorieta but inside the surrounding security-gated fence. These are large sites with 50-amp full hookup connections. In addition to the pool there is a laundry room and library. There is no daily rate, the rate shown above is for a month. It might be possible to arrange a stay of as little as two weeks if things are slow. Reservations are required, there are no arrangements for dealing with those arriving with no reservations.

To reach the Glorieta you must be westbound on the coastal highway. Take the exit to the lateral near Km 4, the lateral actually descends below the level of the main highway. In .3 mile (.5 km) you'll see a small shopping center on the right. Take the paved road just beyond to the right and in .2 mile (.3 km) you'll see the road over to the entrance gate on your right.

SAN JOSÉ DEL CABO (SAHN HO-SAY DELL KAH-BOH)
Population 70,000

San José is the older of the two Los Cabos towns. A Jesuit mission was founded here in 1730 but the estuary to the east had been used by ships as a watering stop far before that. Today San José is the center of business and government for the cape area.

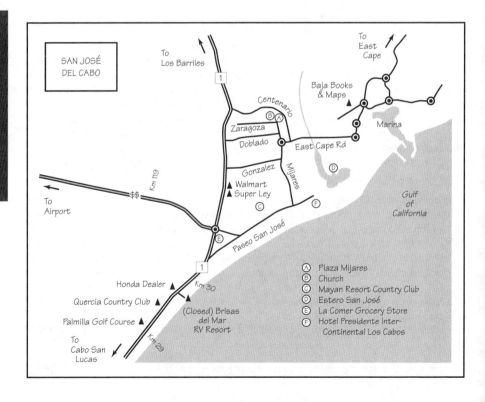

We find the streets of San José much more pleasant to wander than those of Cabo San Lucas. Boulevard Mijares running south from the plaza is the center of the action for Norteamericanos, there are many restaurants and shops along it. If you walk westward on the streets between the plaza and Mex 1 you'll find a much more authentic Mexican town, and it has been around longer than Cabo San Lucas so it has more character. Saturday nights during the busy winter tourist season there's usually a fiesta in the plaza. The biggest holiday in San José is March 19, the feast day of the town's patron saint.

South of the downtown area and beyond the **Mayan Resort Country Club** are the hotels along the ocean. East of town is the **Estero San José**, a swampy lagoon with a walking path along the western border, it's a very good birding location. You can follow a road across the northern border of the estero to Puerto Los Cabos Marina, Mexico's largest. It has restaurants, shops, hotels, and tours.

San José has a huge modern La Comer supermarket, you can't miss it as you drive through town. A little farther north on Mex 1 there are also a Soriana and a Walmart. San José also has a traditional Mercado Municipal on Calle Coronado in the neighborhood between the Av. Mijares and Mex 1.

It's always tough to get RV supplies or to have RV systems work done on RVs in Mexico. San José has a place: **Wahoo R.V. Center** (Calle Misión de Mulegé #166, Col. Chula Vista, San José del Cabo. BCS, (624) 142-3792; 1wahoorv@prodigy.net.mx). They specialize in gas refrigeration problems, gas heaters and toilets. They also carry an inventory of RV supplies. Give them a call for detailed driving instructions, they speak English.

It can be hard to find travel books and maps specific to the Baja. San José has the best source anywhere for these. It's **Baja Books and Maps**, a bookstore located to the east of town in the La Choya neighborhood ((624) 142-5596; info@bajabooksand-maps.com). It's shown on the map above.

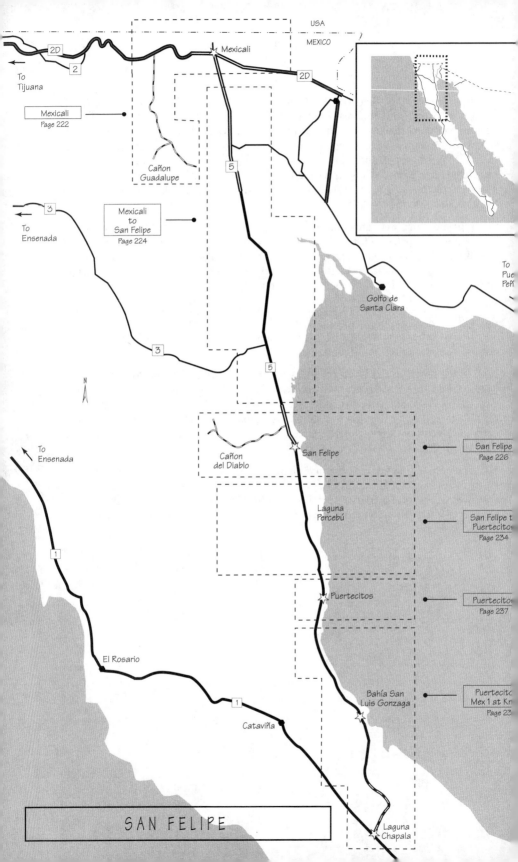

USA
MEXICO

To
Tijuana

2D
2

Mexicali

2D

Cañon
Guadalupe

5

To
Ensenada

3

3

To
Pue
Peñ

Golfo de
Santa Clara

5

N

To
Ensenada

Cañon
del Diablo

San Felipe

Laguna
Percebú

1

Puertecitos

El Rosario

1

Cataviña

Bahía San
Luis Gonzaga

Laguna
Chapala

SAN FELIPE

Chapter 11
San Felipe

INTRODUCTION

Many folks think San Felipe offers a better combination of easily accessible sand, sun, and laid-back Mexican ambiance than any destination close to the border. It's an excellent choice for your first camping trip into Mexico. A word or warning though. The big-rig RV parks in San Felipe have been closing and new big-rig parks haven't appeared yet so if good hookups and big spaces are what you are looking for, you'll probably like Puerto Peñasco better.

San Felipe may soon get a lot more visitors. Within a few years it will be on what many will consider the best route south to central Baja and Baja California Sur. This chapter covers campgrounds extending far down the coast from San Felipe. Work is being completed on a good paved road that follows the coast south from San Felipe and then west to connect with Mex 1 not far south of Cataviña at Km 233 of Mex 1. Only about 23 miles (37 km) remain unpaved at the time of publication of this book and the road is actually already open to and passable for any size rig. The gravel portion is a slow slog and at least one flat is almost guaranteed, but it's being used.

When finished this route will let travelers avoid the whole section of Mex 1 along the northern Pacific Coast. Distance from the border to the southern Baja will only be about 70 miles (113 km) shorter but it will be a quicker and easier drive. You'll be driving across remote country on quiet roads from the time you leave Mexicali.

Highlights

The **drive south to San Felipe** and then south across the driest of Baja's deserts is an experience itself. If you've not been in to Mexico before you'll probably have the chance to experience your first **army checkpoint**, there's usually at least one along this road.

Once you reach **San Felipe** the prime attraction is beautiful sandy beaches, lots of good places to park your RV, and a friendly little town to enjoy.

Little **Puertecitos** is famous for it's hot spring. Stop and soak a while.

Bahía San Luis Gonzaga has miles of beautiful remote beach. Access has never been this easy before.

Roads and Fuel Availability

The road south from Mexicali to San Felipe is paved all the way. Kilometer markers count up as you drive south. The highway starts as four lanes and then, about 24 miles (39 km) south of Mexicali, narrows to two. It is generally in fine condition and you can easily maintain the speeds shown on the speed-limit signs, usually 80 kph. At Km 150, as you reach the northern outskirts of San Felipe, the road becomes four lane, and you'll reach the town itself after 122 miles (196 km).

San Felipe to Puertecitos is 54 miles (87 km). It's all paved road but not as good as that farther north.

South of Puertecitos for 56 miles (91 km) there's a good paved road. Then there's 23 miles (37 km) of rough gravel that is under construction. See *Puertecitos to Mex 1 at Km 233 Near Laguna Chapala* below for more about that road.

There are lots of Pemex stations in Mexicali offering both gas and diesel. Between Mexicali and San Felipe, at least once you pass Km 31, there are no Pemexes until you reach San Felipe. In San Felipe there are five Pemexes, not all sell diesel. Farther south there's one Pemex in Puertecitos, it sells only gas. Then there's another between Puertecitos and the Mex 1 junction, it sells both gas and diesel.

Golf

San Felipe now has a golf course. It's part of the El Dorado development, now called La Ventana del Mar. This is an 18-hole course overlooking the Sea of Cortez called Las Caras de Mexico. You'll spot it on your left at Km 174 as you approach town. The clubhouse also has a restaurant. Call (686) 576-0517 for information and reservations.

Beaches and Water Sports

San Felipe's malecón (waterfront promenade) borders **Playa San Felipe**. Like other beaches in the north end of the Gulf of California when the tide goes out here it *really* goes out. Locals use pickups and special trailers to launch and retrieve their pangas across the wide hard-packed sand flats. When the tide is in, however, this is a nice beach.

North of San Felipe is **Playa Las Almejas** (Clam Beach). It's eight miles long and starts about 5 miles (8 km) north of town. Several no-hookup campgrounds are on this beach.

PLAYA SAN FELIPE IN FRONT OF SAN FELIPE'S MALECÓN

For many miles south of San Felipe there is a wide sandy beach. Many of the camp-grounds and camps listed here are along this beach.

Another beach south of San Felipe is near **Laguna Percebu**. The lagoon is great for swimming and kayaking and there's a beach good for collecting sand dollars.

Bahía San Luis Gonzaga (Gonzaga Bay), south of Puertecitos, has miles of virgin beaches.

Fishing

Fishing in San Felipe is not nearly as good as it once was. Over fishing, much of it by big commercial boats, decimated fishing in the northern gulf during the late sixties. Things have recovered somewhat, charter pangas and long-range overnight boats are available.

Puertecitos has a boat ramp and decent fishing.

Gonzaga Bay, farther south, is another famous fishing destination. There's a ramp at Punta Willard Campground which is described below.

Backroad Adventures

See the ***Backroad Driving*** section of ***Chapter 2 - Details, Details, Details*** for essential information about driving off the main highways on the Baja and for a definition of road type classifications used below.

SAN FELIPE

The back country around San Felipe is extremely popular with folks who have dune buggies and other vehicles capable of traveling across soft sand. If you have a high-flotation vehicle you'll have a great time following the many tracks in the area. It is best to stay on established tracks to minimize damage to the desert and your tires.

🚐 **From Km 178 Between San Felipe and Mexicali** - One possibility is the road to the **Cañon del Diablo**. Access is via the road that heads for the Sierra de San Pedro Mártir from near Pemex #9207 to the north of San Felipe. This road goes out past the El Dorado home sites and then continues across the dry lakebed of the Laguna Diablo and then right up to the mountains. It is possible to park and hike up into the Sierra from here. This is real backroad exploration on a Type 3 road, take all the precautions we recommend in the *Backroad Driving* section of *Details, Details, Details* and discuss your plans with someone with good local knowledge before attempting this drive.

🚐 **From Km 28 on Mex 2D West of Mexicali** - While not strictly in the San Felipe area **Cañon Guadalupe** is a popular camping destination also near Mexicali. Access to the canyon and the campground there requires driving a Type 2 road with soft sandy spots 35 miles (56 km) south across the desert to the campground. Once there you will find no hookups but campsites have tubs with hot water fed by springs. You should make reservations, get directions, and check road conditions by calling (619) 937-1546 or sending an email to contact@guadalupecanyonoasis.com. There is also a website: www.guadalupecanyonoasis.com.

THE ROUTES, TOWNS, AND CAMPGROUNDS

MEXICALI (MECK-SEE-KAL-EE)
Population 800,000

This large border city is the capital of Baja California. The big business here is farming, the Colorado river irrigates thousands of surrounding acres where produce is grown, primarily for markets north of the border. Mexicali is a sprawling low-rise town. There are two border crossings, one at the center of town and another about 7 miles to the east. Neither crossing is usually particularly busy but the one east of town is much easier.

Most RVers probably think of Mexicali as a barrier to get around rather than as a place to stop. On the outskirts of town you'll find some of the large Mexican supermarkets, if you didn't stock up north of the border these offer a much better selection than anything in San Felipe. There's even a Costco. There are also lots of Pemex stations. See our route log from the east border crossing outlined below, it passes near several of these stores.

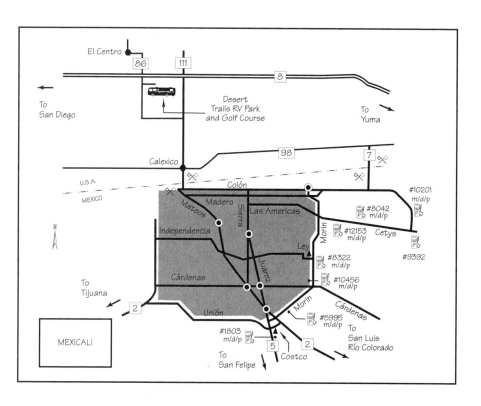

Mexicali Campground

🚐 **DESERT TRAILS RV PARK AND GOLF COURSE**
   (Open All Year)

Address:	225 Wake Avenue, El Centro, CA 92243
Telephone:	(760) 352-7275
Fax:	(760) 352-7474
Email:	deserttrails@hotmail.com
Website:	www.deserttrailsrv.com

GPS Location: 32.77028 N, 115.54722 W, Near Sea Level

This campground is really in the U.S. In fact, it's a good 10 miles north of the border on the southern edge of El Centro. Still, it's a great place to park the night before heading south.

This is a big campground, and in the winter it's full of snowbird RVers. It's built around a nine-hole golf course and has amenities which include a good pool and a spa. While there are hundreds of nice sites, if you're only staying for a night or two you are most likely to be parked in their gravel lot near the swimming pool. It's very handy with good access to restrooms and the pool area. There are 30-amp electrical and water hookups and a dump station.

You'll find the Desert Trails just south of Interstate 8 on Highway 86. From Interstate

SAN FELIPE

8 take the exit for Highway 86, go south one block, then turn left and you'll soon see the campground entrance on your right.

MEXICALI TO SAN FELIPE
126 Miles (203.2 Km) along route detailed below, 4 Hours
(including border crossing)

Most RVers cross at the eastern border crossing because it's less congested and easier. Here are the directions you'll need to head south on Mex 5.

The crossing is about 7 miles east of Calexico, Mexicali's alter ego on the north side of the border. If you are approaching from the north on Highway 111 you'll want to head east on the northern outskirts of Calexico on Highway 98. The way to the border crossing is well signed, the turn to the south from Highway 98 is 7.2 miles (11.6 km) east of Highway 111. You turn south on Highway 7. Follow the signs for the car crossing, not the truck crossing. In 1.6 mile (2.6 km) you'll pass the U.S. border station and a short distance later arrive at the Mexican station.

Zero your odometer as you pass through the Mexican crossing. In 0.3 mile (0.5 km) the road comes to a T. Turn right here and you will be on a four-lane divided highway. At 2.2 miles (3.5 km) you'll reach a traffic circle or glorieta with an artistic monument in the middle, turn left here onto Morin. At 2.9 miles (4.7 km) you'll pass Pemex #5595, it will be on the right and you'll know you're on the right road. At 4.5 miles (7.3 km) you'll see a large Ley supermarket on the right, continue straight or stop for groceries. At 6.6 miles (10.6 km) you'll see Pemex #5995 on the left. At 7.2 miles (11.6 km) a sign tells you to go left for Mex 2 and San Louis Colorado, don't do it. Finally, at 7.3 miles (11.8 km) turn left for San Felipe. Almost immediately you'll see a Costco off to your left, and Pemex #1803 also on the left. You're on Mex 5, straight ahead to San Felipe.

For the first 24 miles (39 km) the road has four lanes and is bordered by scattered homes and business. There are several Pemex gas stations along here. Watch the speed limit signs, they require you to drive much slower than the speed you will feel is safe.

After the 4-lane ends the highway skirts the western edge of the Rio Hardy, a small river that drains into the Colorado to the east. Soon the highway makes a 12-mile (19 km) crossing of the dry Laguna Salada, at one time this area flooded with Colorado River water.

Once south of the Laguna the highway runs through very dry desert country. Mex 3 from Ensenada joins the highway at a crossroads known as El Crucero at Km 140. Often there are army checkpoints along the highway near El Crucero where soldiers may search your rig. See the *Drugs, Guns, and Roadblocks* section of the *Details, Details, Details* chapter. Just south of El Crucero, near Km 150, the road widens to 4 lanes.

Finally, near Km 175 the highway nears the ocean although you really can't see it from the highway. Many small roads lead eastward to campos along the water. Many offer camping, usually little more than boondocking sites. You'll have a selection of these almost all the way in to San Felipe which the road reaches at about Km 189.

Mexicali to San Felipe Campgrounds

CAMPO MOSQUEDA *(Open All Year)*

Address:	Carretera San Felipe, Km 53 ½, Mexicali, B.C.S.	
Telephone:	(686) 566-1520	
Email:	campo_mosqueda@yahoo.com	
Website:	www.campomosqueda.com.mx	

GPS Location: 32.15626 N, 115.27888 W, Near Sea Level

This is the most popular of the Rio Hardy campgrounds. It's a going concern, a resort area for folks from Mexicali. There is a grassy camping area for tents and RVs of any size with no electricity. The restrooms have flush toilets and hot showers. There is a restaurant. The campground is on the river, the big attraction here for both fishing and watersports.

The road to the campground leaves Mex 3 to the east at about Km 54. The rough gravel road leads 2 kilometers to the campground.

EL MAYOR TRAILER PARK *(Open All Year)*

Location:	Km 55 of Mex 3

GPS Location: 32.13163 N, 115.28124 W, Near Sea Level

El Mayor is the second Rio Hardy campground. It's right along the highway near

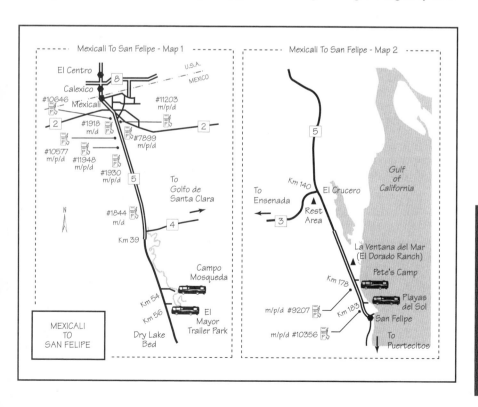

Km 55, about one mile south of the Campo Mosqueda. There are 15 no-hookup sites and basic restrooms.

PETE'S CAMP *(Open All Year)*

Address:	PO Box 516, Temecula, CA 92593
Telephone:	(951) 694-6704 (US)
Email:	renel@petescamp.com
Website:	www.petescamp.com

GPS Location: 31.13444 N, 114.88925 W, Near Sea Level

This is an older campground, actually more of a community, located along the beach north of San Felipe. There are many permanently located trailers here but also a large camping area below overlooking the excellent beach.

The camping area has about 80 sites with thatched-roof ramadas (shade shelters) with room for small RVs to squeeze between them. Large RVs park behind the ramadas, and if they're over 15 feet long are required to rent two sites, that's the price reflected in the icons above. There are no hookups but a dump station is available as is drinking water. There are restrooms with flush toilets and hot showers (extra charge) as well as a restaurant.

The campground access road is at about Km 177.5. This is about 7.5 miles (12.1 km) north of the San Felipe entrance monument. There's a 1.1 mile (1.8 km) good oiled road east to the camp.

PLAYAS DEL SOL *(Open All Year)*

Location:	Km 182.5, Carretera Fed #5, San Felipe, BC 21850
Address:	PO Box 3635, Calexico, CA 92232
Telephone:	(686) 123-6452
Email:	playasdelsol@live.com.mex
Website:	www.playasdelsol.com.mx

GPS Location: 31.08961 N, 114.87013 W, Near Sea Level

This is a large camping area on the beautiful beach north of San Felipe. Similar to Pete's but it has some sites with electricity. There are about 65 ramadas near the beach with parking for smaller RVs beside them or larger ones behind if things aren't too crowded. Flush toilets are provided, hot showers and water are available for an extra charge. There's also a dump station. The restaurant is only open in winter.

The campground entrance is near Km 183, about 4 miles (6 km) north of the San Felipe entrance monument. Follow the somewhat grand divided entrance road east a mile to the beach.

SAN FELIPE (SAHN FAY-LEE-PAY)
Population 17,000

Although San Felipe is a Baja town, its location in the far northeast portion of the peninsula means that it is not normally part of a visit to the peninsula's destinations farther south. That doesn't mean that this isn't a popular place. Like Puerto Peñasco this town is full of Americans looking for easily accessible sun and sand. The majority of them seem to be RVers.

ARRIVING AT THE ENTRY MONUMENT TO SAN FELIPE

In many ways San Felipe and Puerto Peñasco are very similar. Both are small towns at the north end of the Gulf of California pretty much devoted to RV tourism. Both are probably on the cusp of a development boom, both have recently opened golf courses although those struggle with limited fresh water for watering the grass.

Most of the action in San Felipe is found along its **malecón** (waterfront promenade) and the street one block inland - Mar de Cortez. Overlooking the malecón and the strip of sandy beach that fronts it is Cerro El Machorro, a tall rock with a shrine to the Virgin de Guadalupe at its top. This is a great place for photos. The bay in front of town goes dry at low tide, the panga fishermen who use the beach launch and retrieve their boats by driving pickups out on the solid sand. Several of the campgrounds are located along the southern extension of Mar de Cortez so strolling in to central San Felipe is very easy. The town has a selection of decent restaurants and small shops as well as four Pemex stations.

Most of the important streets in town are paved and the rest present no driving problems. Watch for stop signs, however. They are in unexpected places. Sometimes the smallest dusty side street has priority over a main arterial.

At this time San Felipe does not have a large supermarket but there are two medium-sized ones. Long term residents sometimes drive north to Mexicali for supplies.

It seems like San Felipe always has some kind of celebration in the works. The **San Felipe 250** is a big off-road race at the end of March. Just before the off-road race is the **Mid-Winter West Hobie Cat Regatta**. Like many Mexican ports San Fe-

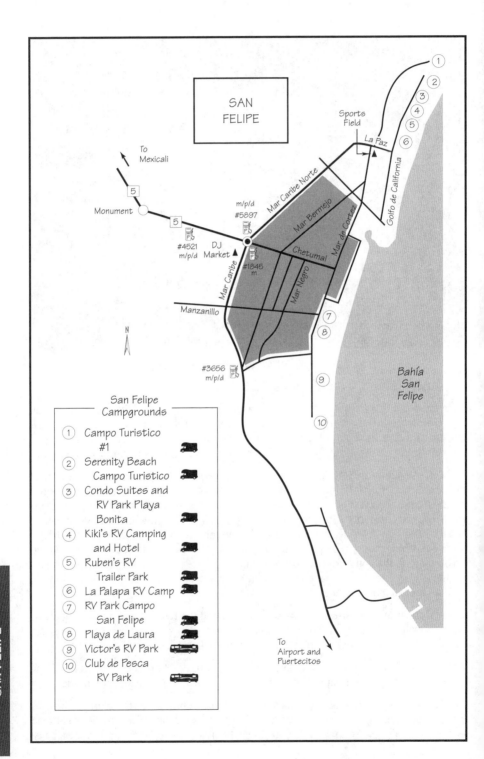

lipe celebrates **Carnival** (Mardi Gras) at the appropriate time in the spring. **Spring Break** is big here, just as on the rest of the peninsula, it happens during the third and fourth weeks of March. **Semana Santa**, the week up to and including Easter, is a big Mexican beach holiday and San Felipe is very popular as it hosts a number of sporting events. During the summer the town celebrates **Día de la Marina** on June 1. And in November there's the **Shrimp Festival**, one of the biggest celebrations of the year in San Felipe.

In addition to all of the above San Felipe gets lots of visitors from Mexicali and California on weekends and any excuse for a holiday in either the States or Mexico. Many of the campgrounds are really set up for tent campers with ramadas for shade. Expect lots of noise and activity when these visitors are in town.

San Felipe Campgrounds

In the last few years the campsite situation has changed considerably in San Felipe. Virtually every campground with large sites and decent hookups has closed. Recently closed big-RV campgrounds include the San Felipe Marina Resort RV Park and both the main El Dorado Ranch RV park and the El Cachanilla. These parks haven't closed because they weren't doing well, the land was just needed for other projects. Looking at Puerto Peñasco it is apparent that there is an opportunity for several good big-rig parks in San Felipe and it's probably just a matter of time before one is built. Until then you'll find that there are still a few parks in the San Felipe area that can take large RVs, but most are either non-hookup parks or they squeeze big RVs into sites that are really built for smaller rigs.

SAN FELIPE IS KNOWN FOR ITS UNIQUE TWO STORY CAMPING SITES

SAN FELIPE

The prices we have given for the parks in San Felipe are the normal winter rates for slots back from the water. Expect to pay a bit more for waterfront sites at the campgrounds that offer them and also expect rates to be from $5 to $10 higher on holiday weekends or during special events. Summer rates are about $5 higher in most parks.

CAMPO TURISTICO #1 *(Open all Year)*
Telephone: (686) 112-2106, (686) 577-1390 or (686) 216-1034
Email: camposfbc@gmail.com

GPS Location: 31.03910 N, 114.82575 W, Near Sea Level

Located at the far north end of town, this campground is alone on the north side of an arroyo and above a quiet beach.

The campground is really designed for tent campers with a row of about 30 palapas but there is rooms for smaller RVs to park behind without being in the way. Sites have electricity and there is water and a dump station. Restrooms have cold showers and flush toilets and there is a restaurant with Wi-Fi.

From the traffic circle at the entrance to town take the road that leads northeast. This is Mar Caribe Norte and is the road to the left as you come from Mexicali. It will curve to the right at .8 miles (1.3 km) and you turn left on Mar de Cortez at .9 miles (1.5 km). Follow this road for .5 mile (.8 km) and you will see the campground on your right.

SERENITY BEACH CAMPO TURISTICO *(Open all Year)*
Address: Golfo de California #800, San Felipe, BC, México
Telephone: (686) 577-2280 (US) or (686) 211-3040
Email: noracio@hotmail.com

GPS Location: 31.03523 N, 114.82802 W, Near Sea Level

The Serenity Beach is the farthest north of a string of five small-rig RV and tent campgrounds along the beach. It's a basic camping area, nothing fancy. There are 25 back-in sites with full-hookups, ramadas, and picnic tables. It's a narrow lot and limited space here means the campground is best for rigs to about 30 feet. Restrooms have hot showers in winter, cold in summer.

From the traffic circle at the entrance to town take the road that leads northeast. This is Mar Caribe Norte and is the road to the left as you come from Mexicali. It will curve to the right at 0.8 miles (1.3 km) and come to a T at 1 mile (1.6 km). Turn left and you'll see the entrance to the campground on the right just past the Playa Bonita.

CONDO SUITES AND RV PARK PLAYA BONITA
(Open All Year)

Address: 475 E. Badillo Street, Covina, CA 91723
   USA (Reservations)
Telephone: (686) 577-1215 (Mex), (626) 967-8977 (USA)
Email: playabonita@aol.com
Website: www.sanfelipebeachcondos.com

GPS Location: 31.03503 N, 114.82793 W, Near Sea Level

This is a beachfront campground at the north end of town. There is a building with condo suites in front of some of the RV sites.

The spaces are suitable only for vans, tents or small trailers. Most of these smaller spaces have 15-amp electricity, sewer, and water. All spaces have paved patios with ramada-style roofs and picnic tables. The restrooms are older and rustic, the showers are often barely warm. Wi-Fi is usable near the office. There's a nice beach out front.

From the traffic circle at the entrance to town take the road that leads northeast. This is Mar Caribe Norte and is the road to the left as you come from Mexicali. It will curve to the right at 0.8 miles (1.3 km) and come to a T at 1 mile (1.6 km). Turn left and you'll soon see the entrance to the campground on the right.

KIKI'S RV CAMPING AND HOTEL *(Open All Year)*

Address:	Golfo de California No 80, San Felipe, B.C., México
Telephone:	(686) 577-2021
Email:	kikimr.baja@hotmail.com
Website:	www.kiki.com.mx

GPS Location: 31.03418 N, 114.82822 W, Near Sea Level

This is the northern half of the old Ruben's RV Trailer Park, there are 27 spaces. Now there's a fence between the north and south halves and motel rooms have been added. Like Ruben's it has some platforms for tents but Kiki's also has some sites for RVs to 30 feet. Kiki's is also cleaner, in better condition, and has more attentive management. Sites have 30-amp outlets, sewer, and water. Access is tight for RVs so exercise caution. People also tent camp on the beach out front.

From the traffic circle at the entrance to town take the road that leads northeast. This is Mar Caribe Norte and is the road to the left as you come from Mexicali. It will curve to the right at 0.8 miles (1.3 km) and come to a T at 1 mile (1.6 km). Turn left and you'll almost immediately see the entrance to Kiki's on the right.

RUBEN'S RV TRAILER PARK *(Open All Year)*

Address:	Apdo. 59, CP 21850 San Felipe, B.C., México
Telephone:	(686) 114-3634 (Cell)
Email:	rubenscamp.sf@hotmail.com
Website:	www.rubenscamp.blogspot.com

GPS Location: 31.03390 N, 114.82848 W, Near Sea Level

Ruben's is well known in San Felipe for its two-story patios. These are very popular with tenters during the Mexican holidays, it is easy to enclose the patio below and use the roof for added room. Some people think the two-story patios give the crowded campground the atmosphere of a parking garage but Ruben's remains a popular beach-front campground. There's always a lot of activity at this place, maybe too much.

There are about 30 camping spaces, all with 15 or 30-amp outlets, sewer and water. Most spaces are small and maneuvering room is scarce. This campground is really for tent campers and perhaps very small RVs. The restrooms are adequate and have hot water showers.

From the traffic circle at the entrance to town take the road that leads northeast. This is Mar Caribe Norte and is the road to the left as you come from Mexicali. It will curve to the right at 0.8 miles (1.3 km) and come to a T at 1 mile (1.6 km). Turn left and you'll almost immediately see the entrance to Ruben's on the right.

LA PALAPA RV CAMP *(Open All Year)*

GPS Location: 31.03356 N, 114.82855 W, Near Sea Level

This little trailer park is located right next to the much better known Ruben's. At first glance it even looks like Ruben's, it has some of the same two-story ramadas. It's much quieter, however.

There are 12 spaces in this park. Six are along the front next to the beach. Most spaces are really van-size or short-trailer-size but a few will take RVs to about 30 feet. The camping slots have 15 or 30-amp outlets, sewer, water, and paved patios with a roof serviced by a ladder. You can use them for the view or pitch a tent up there. The bathrooms are old and need maintenance, they have hot water showers in winter, cold in summer. The router for the Wi-Fi is in the office/house near the entrance so it works better in the back of the park.

From the traffic circle at the entrance to town take the road that leads northeast. This is Mar Caribe Norte and is the road to the left as you come from Mexicali. It will curve to the right at 0.8 miles (1.3 km) and come to a T at 1 mile (1.6 km). Turn left and the campground will be on the right almost immediately, the sign is very small.

RV PARK CAMPO SAN FELIPE *(Open All Year)*

Address:	Ave. Mar de Cortez #301, San Felipe, B.C., México
Telephone:	(686) 577-1012
Website:	www.camposanfelipe.com

GPS Location: 31.01944 N, 114.83472 W, Near Sea Level

This campground is undergoing major upgrades They've recently added a swimming pool next to the beach and plan a bar and restaurant on the beach in front of that. New restrooms are under construction and also a laundry room. It's a lot to squeeze in to a small space. The campground has the distinction of being the closest to central San Felipe.

There are now 29 sites but a few more are planned, the closer to the beach you are the more you pay. They have 50 or 30-amp outlets, sewer, water, and covered patios with tables. RVs to 35 feet can use some of the sites but maneuvering is difficult. Restrooms have hot water showers.

As you enter town zero your odometer at the glorieta (traffic circle). Turn right toward the airport and drive 0.7 miles (1.1 km) to Pemex #3556. Turn left here and drive down the hill toward the beach. You'll come to a T at 1.1 miles (1.8 km). Turn left and you'll see the Campo San Felipe on the right in 0.25 miles (0.4 km).

PLAYA DE LAURA *(Open All Year)*

Address:	Ave. Mar de Cortez Sur #333, San Felipe, Baja California Sur, México
Telephone:	(686) 577-1128 or (686) 554-4712
Email:	playadelaura@yahoo.com
Website:	www.playadelaura.com

GPS Location: 31.01848 N, 114.83531 W, Near Sea Level

This older RV park is in need of maintenance. Still, it has a good location and is quite popular.

Forty-five campsites are arranged in rows running parallel to the beach. The front row is really packed and limits beach access by campers in the rows farther from the beach. Pricing varies with beach slots more expensive than those farther back. Each camping space has electricity, some are 30-amp outlets, water and a covered patio with table and barbecue. Many have sewer hookups. Most of the spaces are pull-thrus but maneuvering space is limited, some sites are good for RVs to about 35 feet. Restrooms are older and need maintenance, they have hot water showers. Monthly rates here are 15,000 pesos per month.

As you enter town zero your odometer at the glorieta (traffic circle). Turn right toward the airport and drive 0.7 miles (1.1 km) to Pemex #3656. Turn left here and drive down the hill toward the beach. You'll come to a T at 1.1 miles (1.8 km). Turn left and you'll see the Playa de Laura on the right in 0.2 miles (0.3 km).

VICTOR'S RV PARK *(Open All Year)*

Address:	PMB #419, PO Box 9019, Calexico, CA 92232
Telephone:	(686) 577-2817 or (686) 577-1383
Email:	victors-rvpark11@hotmail.com

GPS Location: 31.01335 N, 114.83566 W, Near Sea Level

This 40-space campground is older with some permanently located or long-term RVs. About 30 slots are available for daily rent.

Victor's parking slots have 30-amp outlets, sewer, and water. Traveler sites are back from the water with permanents up front. Some sites are large enough for RVs to 40 feet. The restrooms have hot showers. Last time we visited the restrooms were recently renovated, the site hookups desperately needed maintenance. The campground has a lounge area near the front next to the beach. The Wi-Fi router is in the office near the gate so reception is best nearby.

As you enter town zero your odometer at the glorieta (traffic circle). Turn right toward the airport and drive 0.7 miles (1.1 km) to Pemex #3656. Turn left here and drive down the hill toward the beach. You'll come to a T at 1.1 miles (1.8 km). Turn right and almost immediately you'll see Victor's on your left.

CLUB DE PESCA RV PARK *(Open All Year)*

Reservations:	PO Box 3090, Calexico, CA 92232
Telephone:	(686) 577-1180
Fax:	(686) 577-1888
Email:	clubdepesca@prodigy.net.mx

GPS Location: 31.01250 N, 114.83611 W, Near Sea Level

This is an old San Felipe favorite. The campground has many permanents, but also some choice slots for tents and smaller RVs along the ocean and others toward the rear of the park.

There are 32 slots along the beach with ramadas and with 50 and 30-amp outlets and water but no sewer hookups. These spaces are paved. We've seen RVs to 34 feet in them but usually only shorter RVs park here. At the rear of the park are 15 slots with 30-amp outlets, sewer, water and patios. Larger RVs fit here better, some will take 40 footers and even a bit larger. Restrooms are neat and clean and have hot water showers in winter, cold in summer. There is a small grocery store and a room with a ping-pong table next to the beach dividing the beachside sites. The Wi-Fi router is in the store, there are tables out front that make a convenient place to sit while using it.

As you enter town zero your odometer at the traffic circle. Turn right toward the airport and drive 0.7 miles (1.1 km) to Pemex #3656. Turn left here and drive down the hill toward the beach. You'll come to a T at 1.1 miles (1.8 km). Turn right and you'll find the Club de Pesca at the end of the road.

SAN FELIPE TO PUERTECITOS
54 Miles (87 Km) , 1.5 Hours

The road to the San Felipe airport goes south from town. Some 7.1 miles (11.5 km) from the glorieta in San Felipe you'll see the road to Puertecitos cutting off to the left. This is where the kilometers posts start counting up for the road to Puertecitos and points south to Mex 1. From here to Puertecitos it's 47 miles (76 km).

South from San Felipe the road is once again two lanes. This road usually has a decent surface but it's not built to as high a standard as the one north of San Felipe or the one south of Puertecitos You'll find yourself rising and falling like a ship at sea as the road follows the contour of the desert.

Near Kilometer 14 an entrance road goes right for the signed **Valle de los Gigantes**. There's an entry fee and a place to park so you can take a look at the huge cardóns. They're much like the saguaro cactus we see in the U.S., but larger and with a lot more arms. There's lots more of these near Cataviña but this is a lot closer to the border.

At about Km 21 a road goes east to Rancho Percebu at the north end of the shallow **Laguna Percebu**. There's a campground there that's described below. It's an excellent place for swimming and kayaking.

For shell collecting there's **Shell Beach** just south of Laguna Percebu. There's a road out to the beach at Km 26.

There's a Pemex in Puertecitos, but it only sells gasoline, no diesel.

San Felipe to Puertecitos Campgrounds

🚐 RESIDENCE *(Open All Year)*

GPS Location: 30.93710 N, 114.72816 W, Near Sea Level

The old El Faro, now called the Residence, is worth a stop for a look even if you decide not to stay. This was once one of the most elaborate RV resorts in Mexico, yet it's been virtually abandoned to the sand. There must be a story here.

The campground occupies a hillside above a beautiful sandy beach. There are many back-in sites as well as a resort complex near the water, all abandoned. A few tenters and smaller RVs occupy some of the sites (with no usable hookups) but a few RVers have rigged their own water tanks and drains and enjoy the solitude. The restrooms have flush toilets and showers (they might light them up if you ask). An attendant guards the gate, drive in and take a look.

The campground is located south of San Felipe. Zero your odometer as you reach the glorieta (traffic circle) at the entrance to town. Turn 90 degrees right toward the airport and head south. At 7.1 miles (11.5 km) the road makes a right angle turn to the left, the airport is straight. Turn left. In another 4.2 miles (6.7 km) you'll see the entrance on your left. The paved entrance road will take you to the park.

VILLA MARINA CAMPO TURISTICO *(Open All Year)*

Address:	Km 8.5 Carret. a Puertecitos, San Felipe, BC
Telephone:	(686) 221-3797
Email:	villamarinabaja@gmail.com
Website:	www.villamarinaresort.com

GPS Location: 30.91618 N, 114.71492 W , Near Sea Level

This is the nicest and most modern campground south of San Felipe. There are 36 full-hookup spaces. They have 15-amp electrical outlets. The camping area is located on a low bluff above a sandy beach. Many sites are covered and have stairways leading to terraces on top with excellent views. Amazingly, sites are long enough, wide enough, and even high enough for most big RVs although you'll have to maneuver

To
Mexicali

#3656
m/p/d

San Felipe

Residence

Airport   Km 6   Villa Marina Campo Turistico
                 Km 9

Km 12

Rancho Punta Estrella

Km 21   Rancho Percebu

N

SAN FELIPE
TO
PUERTECITOS

To
Puertecitos   Km 32   Rancho Nuevo Mazatlán

SAN FELIPE

with care. Modern clean restrooms have flush toilets and hot showers. There's laundry service and this is a gated and attended campground.

The campground is located south of San Felipe. Zero your odometer as you reach the glorieta (traffic circle) at the entrance to town. Turn 90 degrees right toward the airport and head south. At 7.1 miles (11.5 km) the road makes a right angle turn to the left, the airport is straight. Turn left. In another 5.4 miles (8.7 km) you'll see the entrance on your left. The 0.3 mile (0.5 km) gravel road will take you to the park.

RANCHO PUNTA ESTRELLA *(Open All Year)*

Address: Km 13 Carretera San Felipe a Puertecitos
Telephone: (686) 565-2784 or (664) 637-3290

GPS Location: 30.88461 N, 114.71079 W, Near Sea Level

This is a large campground with simple facilities. There are miles of beach and desert behind. The camping sites are a long row of over 100 wood-roofed ramadas stretched along the beach. They are intended for tent camping. The sand between the ramadas is soft, probably too soft for any RV parking. An electrical cord with light bulbs hanging from it has been strung along the front of the camping ramadas. There's water at each site. Behind the row of ramadas the surface is harder so RVs can boondock there. Simple restrooms have flush toilets and hot showers. There's also a dump station. There's also a very small but deep swimming pool built above the sand, and adjacent lounge area.

The campground is located south of San Felipe. Zero your odometer as you reach the glorieta (traffic circle) at the entrance to town. Turn 90 degrees right toward the airport and head south. At 7.1 miles (11.5 km) the road makes a right angle turn to the left, the airport is straight. Turn left. In another 7.7 miles (12.4 km) you'll see the entrance on your left. It's 0.9 mile (1.4 km) to the campground.

RANCHO PERCEBU *(Open All Year)*
Telephone: (686) 946-3873 or (686) 111-0954

GPS Location: 30.81633 N, 114.70381 W, Near Sea Level

The Rancho is located at the north end of Percebu Lagoon. It's an excellent protected place for swimming and kayaking. There's a restaurant and bar as well as about 30 sites, some with metal ramadas, for picnicking or camping. A restroom has flush toilets and showers. There is a day use fee for picknickers.

The campground is located south of San Felipe. Zero your odometer as you reach the glorieta (traffic circle) at the entrance to town. Turn 90 degrees right toward the airport and head south. At 7.1 miles (11.5 km) the road makes a right angle turn to the left, the airport is straight. Turn left. In another 12.8 miles (20.6 km) you'll see the entrance on your left. It's 2.3 mile (3.7 km) to the campground.

RANCHO NUEVO MAZATLÁN *(Open All Year)*
Telephone: (686) 225-0727 or (686) 230-9024

GPS Location: 30.72180 N, 114.70668 W, Near Sea Level

This campground is unique in the San Felipe area. Sites are situated under pines about 100 yards back from a pristine beach. Many sites have picnic tables and there

CAMPING UNDER THE PINES AT THE RANCHO NUEVO MAZATLÁN

are scattered water faucets. There's rooms for perhaps 50 camping rigs or tents, the campground is OK for RVs to about 30 feet. There are outhouses and cold showers.

The campground is located south of San Felipe. Zero your odometer as you reach the traffic circle at the entrance to town. Turn 90 degrees right toward the airport and head south. At 7.1 miles (11.5 km) the road makes a right angle turn to the left, the airport is straight. Turn left. In another 19.7 miles (31.8 km) you'll see the entrance on your left. Follow signs toward the beach and campground.

PUERTECITOS (PWER-TAY-SEE-TOWS)
Population 200

This is a small fishing village. For tourists, its claim to fame is a reliable oceanside hot springs. There is a fee for use and a campground, described below. Puertecitos has a launching ramp usable at high water and fishing is better than in San Felipe. The town also has a small store, motel, and a restaurant. There's a Pemex selling only gasoline.

Puertecitos Campgrounds

🚐 OCTAVIO'S CAMP *(Open All Year)*

GPS Location: 30.36161 N, 114.63917 W, Near Sea Level

Octavio's occupies the sandy beach of an inlet just north of town. A long row of

SAN FELIPE

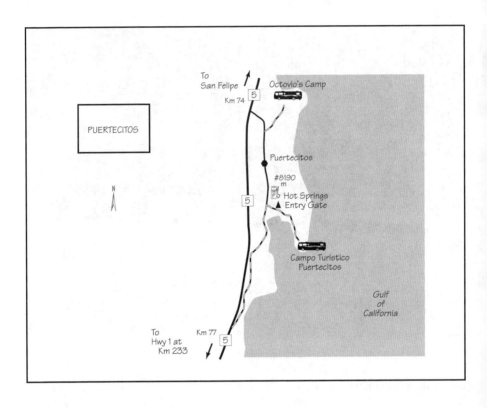

ramadas runs along the beach, each with a picnic table. There are restrooms with toilets and cold showers.

To reach Octavio's take the left fork going into town at Km 74, not the bypass. In .2 mile (.3 km) the road out to the beach goes left..Coming from town this is .6 mile (1 km) north of the Pemex.

CAMPO TURISTICO PUERTECITOS *(Open All Year)*

GPS Location: 30.35058 N, 114.64091 W, Near Sea Level

The main draw here is the hot springs, but there's camping at the sheltered beach nearby.

The camping area here has palapas with low amp electricity overlooking the beach. Parking is OK for big rigs. Water is available and there are now showers and flush toilets. The hot springs aren't right here, you have to take a short hike to reach them. Electricity hours are limited, from 5-10 pm.

The camping area is easy to find, this is a small village. You'll easily spot the Pemex, the campo entrance is a bit south and east. Just follow the main street.

PUERTECITOS TO MEX 1 AT KM 233 NEAR LAGUNA CHAPALA
79 Miles (127 Km), At least 3 Hours until the road is paved

From Puertecitos south to the start of construction the road compares with Mexico's best. Lots of fill, wide shoulders – it's excellent. From Puertecitos it's 56 miles (91 km) to the end of the pavement.

The new road being constructed follows a slightly different route than the old road until you reach the mountains, and you can't drive on it, so the final mileage of this road may be slightly shorter when finished than what it is today. From the end of the pavement it's 23 miles (37 km) of gravel to the intersection with Mex 1.

We drove this road in April 2017. Every kind of vehicle was driving it including two-wheel drive cars with low clearance and full-size RVs. For the big rigs it was a 10 mph or slower drive, and lots of people, including us, stopped to change flats. There was lots of heavy equipment and huge amounts of dirt were being moved, they were really going at it. Coco, of nearby Coco's Corner, guesses that road might be done in three years. That seems about right although the word is that funding for the work is granted year-by-year and work could stop completely at any time.

There's a Pemex south of Puertecitos at Km 147 with Magna and Diesel. That's 44 miles (71 km) south of Puertecitos and 35 miles (56 km) north of the intersection with Mex 1 near Laguna Chapala.

THE NEW HIGHWAY SOUTH OF PUERTECITOS IS ONE OF THE NICEST ON THE BAJA

SAN FELIPE

🚐 PUNTA WILLARD (PAPA FERNANDEZ) CAMPGROUND
AT GONZAGA BAY *(Open All Year)*

Email: lightner@lightner.net
Website: www.papafernandez.com

GPS Location: 29.82902 N, 114.40295 W, Near Sea Level

This campground sits on the water just north of Punta Willard and Bahía San Luis Gonzaga. There's lots of parking and maneuvering room on a good solid surface. There are 10 palapa sun shades with rock fire rings and an outhouse in good condition. On this beach you're just out of site of the restaurant building and permanent structures nearer the road, about 200 yards away. Access to the campground is through a controlled gate. Inland and to the south about 3.5 miles (5.6 km) is Rancho Grande which has a small store and Pemex (M,D – sometimes without fuel). Twenty-three miles beyond that is Coco's Corner, the famous watering hole.

Follow the road south from Puertecitos for 42 miles (67 km). You'll see the entrance sign for Papa Fernandez near Km 143 Turn in and drive 1 mile (1.6 km) to the restaurant and gate.

🚐 SAN LUIS GONZAGA (RANCHO GRANDE) *(Open All Year)*

GPS Location: 29.79341 N, 114.39659 W, Near Sea Level

This is a simple beach camping area with palapas on Ensenada de San Francisquito,

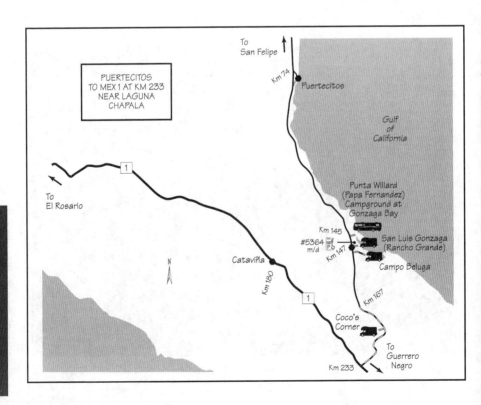

the southern portion of Bahía San Luis Gonzaga. It has palapas on the beach and pit toilets behind. The sand here can be soft and deep, four-wheel-drive is a very good idea.

From the Rancho Grande gas station, store, and market at Km 149 follow the road to the beach, a distance of 1.0 miles (1.6 km)

⊞ **CAMPO BELUGA** *(Open All Year)*

    Website: www.campbeluga.com

GPS Location: 29,77495 N, 114.38405 W, Near Sea Level

This is a another simple beach camping area with palapas on Ensenada de San Francisquito, the southern portion of Bahía San Luis Gonzaga. They have flush toilets and showers. While there's lots of room for big rigs soft sand is a real possibility.

The beach is about .7 mile (1.1 km) from the highway, watch for the sign at Km 147.

⊞ **COCO'S CORNER** *(Open All Year)*

    GPS Location: 29.51707 N, 114.29135 W, 1,500 Ft.

This little bar is a Baja institution. Actually, it's Coco that's the institution. It's a very simple little place with room for a few people to sit around a central table. Coco has a book where he'll insist you enter your name. Buy a beer, talk a bit, and when you ask he'll most likely let you spend the night. Arrive before dark or he'll probably not let you in. There's lots of space in his compound for any rig.

Coco's is on the old road, not the new. He's 10.6 miles (17.1 km) from the Y where the two now separate so it's hard to say exactly what access he'll have once the new road is in. Right now Coco's is 13.1 miles (21 km) from Mex 1 and 67 miles (108 km) from Puertecitos.

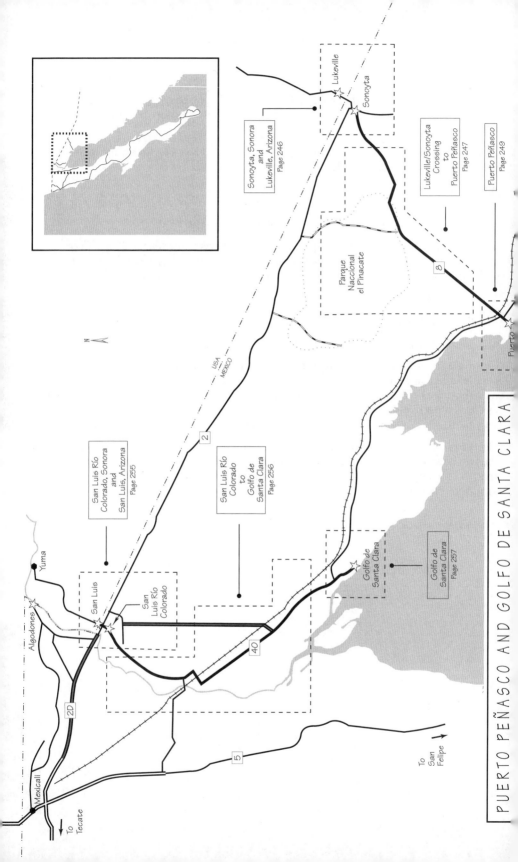

PUERTO PEÑASCO AND GOLFO DE SANTA CLARA

Sonoyta, Sonora
and
Lukeville, Arizona
Page 246

Lukeville/Sonoyta
Crossing
to
Puerto Peñasco
Page 247

Puerto Peñasco
Page 249

San Luis Río
Colorado, Sonora
and
San Luis, Arizona
Page 255

San Luis Río
Colorado to
Golfo de
Santa Clara
Page 256

Golfo de Santa Clara
Page 257

Parque
Nacional
el Pinacate

Lukeville
Sonoyta

Puerto

USA
MEXICO

Yuma
Algodones
San Luis
San
Luis Río
Colorado

Golfo de
Santa Clara

Mexicali
To
Tecate

To
San
Felipe

N

2

8

2D

40

5

Chapter 12
Puerto Peñasco and Golfo de Santa Clara

INTRODUCTION

Two of the easiest places for RVers to visit in Mexico are Puerto Peñasco (Rocky Point) and Golfo de Santa Clara. Both are easy drives from easy border crossings on quiet roads. Of the two, Puerto Peñasco (often called Rocky Point), has the most to offer. There are hundreds of campsites and services designed for folks from north of the border. Golfo de Santa Clara on the other hand has only a handful of camping sites and virtually no services. Golfo is an authentic little Mexican fishing town.

Highlights

The attraction of Puerto Peñasco and Golfo de Santa Clara is that they are beach towns easily available to residents of Arizona. Here you can camp just a few feet from the water. The quality of some of these parks compares favorable with those north of the border. You don't need to worry at all about being able to speak Spanish and dollars are accepted for virtually everything. It's almost like you're still in the U.S.

Roads and Fuel Availability

The road from the Lukeville/Sonoyta crossing leads 62 miles (100 km) south to Puerto Peñasco. The route passes through Sonoyta, but this is a quiet little town and driving through is no problem. You can wait until you reach Puerto Peñasco if you want to change money or shop.

From the junction in Sonoyta where Mex 8 intersects Mex 2 the road is marked with kilometer posts, they count up from 0 at the junction to 95 as you enter Puerto Peñasco.

Gas is available in Lukeville if you wish to gas up before heading south. However, there are two Pemex stations along the road as you drive through Sonoyta. These Sonoyta stations offer both gas and diesel. After Sonoyta there is not another station until you reach Puerto Peñasco.

If you are bound for Golfo de Santa Clara you will want to cross in San Luis Río Colorado. When you cross the border immediately head east on Mex 2 for 6 miles (10 km) to a new ring road, also called a Libramiento. Turn south and follow it for 7.5 miles (12 km) to the beginning of the toll road.

From there a new toll road whisks you south for 35 miles (57). Then you have another 25 miles (40 km) on good two-lane highway to Golfo. Both gas and diesel are available north of the border, in San Luis, and at two Pemex stations in Golfo.

There is a new and very nice paved highway between Golfo de Santa Clara and Puerto Peñasco. It's 82 miles (133 km) from Golfo to Puerto Peñasco. This new road, combined with the new toll road south from San Luis Río Colorado, are the quickest and easiest route for folks bound for Puerto Peñasco from western Arizona and California.

Sightseeing

You will want to visit **Puerto Peñasco's old town on Rocky Point**. You'll find a selection of restaurants and several stores selling Mexican handicrafts.

Another interesting place to visit while visiting Puerto Peñasco is **CEDO**, also known as the **Desert and Ocean Studies Center**. It's located a few miles east of town on the shore in the Las Conchas housing development. It's a learning and research center with the skeleton of a fin whale and other exhibits as well as a gift shop.

Golf

Puerto Peñasco has three golf courses.

There's a course at the Vidanta Puerto Peñasco some 21 miles (34 km) east of town. It's **Vidanta Golf Puerto Peñasco at the Mayan Palace** and was designed by Jack Nicklaus and his son. It's an 18-hole, par 72 course that's over 7,100 yards long. This is a waterfront course. There's also a clubhouse with restaurant and boutique. For reservations call (638) 383-0400 or (866) 231-4423.

There's also a course behind the big condo buildings out on Sandy Beach. It's **The Links at Las Palomas**, an 18-hole par 72 course designed by Forrest Richardson and Arthur Jack Snyder. Call (638) 108-1072 or (866) 286-5053 for reservations.

Finally **The Club at Laguna del Mar Golf** is a Jack Nicklaus signature course located about 15 minutes northwest of town at the Laguna del Mar development. Call for reservations at (638) 383-0032.

PUERTO PEÑASCO'S LONG SANDY BEACH NEAR PLAYA BONITA

Beaches and Water Sports

Puerto Peñasco has beaches both northwest and east of the rocky point that gives the town its name. The sandy beaches are sometimes interrupted by outcrops of the basalt lava rock that makes up the point, in most places at lower tide levels.

East of the point is **Las Conchas**. It is rocky at the western end but sandy to the east. One of the campgrounds is along this beach, and it has a boat ramp.

Northwest of the point is a long sandy beach that begins as **Playa Bonita** and then becomes **Sandy Beach** as it curves westward. There are also campgrounds along this beach. ATV use is popular on Sandy Beach and in the dunes to the north.

In Golfo de Santa Clara the good beach is about a mile south of town. That is where the campgrounds are located. Tides in this section of the Gulf of California can have as much as 25 feet between high and low water. When the tide is in there is a nice sand beach, when the tide is out there are miles of mud flats.

Fishing

While the fishing in the far northern Gulf of California can't compare with the fishing farther south in the gulf, Puerto Peñasco does have a healthy sports fishing fleet. You can easily charter a panga or cruiser for a day of fishing. These aren't really big fish waters but there is something to catch all year long.

 **Backroad Adventures**

See the *Backroad Driving* section of *Chapter 2 - Details, Details, Details* for essential information about driving off the main highways and for a definition of road types used below.

Km 51 Between Sonoyta and Puerto Peñasco - Reserva De La Biosfera De El Pinacate y Gran Desierto De Altar is an infrequently visited but interesting destination located west of the highway. It's an austere desert region filled with volcanic craters, lava fields, and sand dunes. Two craters are accessible by road and have hiking trails along the rim requiring no climb. The last eruption was in 1935. Permits are required to visit the park, you can only get them at the ranger station near the entrance at Km 51. Some of the roads in the park are Type 2, others Type 3. The reserve has two very basic camping areas with no hookup. One of them, Tecolote, is included in the campground section below.

THE ROUTES, TOWNS, AND CAMPGROUNDS

SONOYTA, SONORA AND LUKEVILLE, ARIZONA

These small towns are located on opposite sides of the border about a mile from each other. During the week the crossing here is a pleasant experience because it tends to be very quiet. Sometimes, but not always, weekends are much busier. Lukeville has a gas station and store. Organ Pipe National Monument with a good campground is located just a few miles to the north. The crossing here is open 24 hours. Insurance is available in Lukeville.

After crossing the border the route curves through the edge of quiet Sonoyta and Mex 8 heads southwest toward Puerto Peñasco. Gas and diesel are available at two Pemexes here.

Sonoyta and Lukeville Campground

ORGAN PIPE CACTUS N.M. – TWIN PEAKS CAMPGROUND
  (Open All Year)

  Telephone: (520) 387-6849
  Website: www.nps.gov/orpi/index.htm

  GPS Location: 31.95417 N, 112.80192 W, 1,700 Ft.

This national monument campground is an excellent place to stay on the U.S. side of the border before or after your crossing. It is only a few miles north of the border crossing at Sonoyta, the desert flora here is spectacular. This is the north end of the range for the organ pipe cactus, known as the pithahaya dulce on the Baja.

The campground has over 200 sites. They are all pull-thrus, some as long as 45 feet. There are no hookups. The restrooms have flush toilets and solar showers. There is a dump station and water fill. The entrance road for the campground passes an information center. There are excellent hiking trails from the campground and nearby,

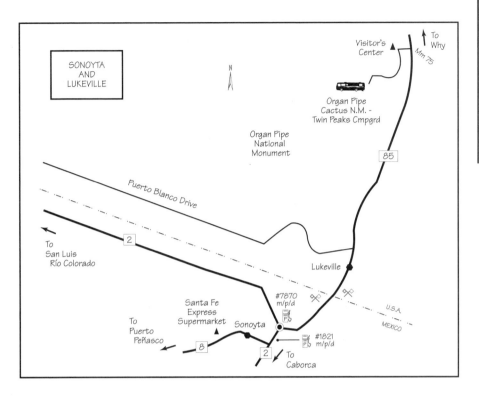

also some interesting drives. There's a $12 per week vehicle fee to enter the park (if you don't have Senior or Access national park pass already) and a $16 fee ($8 with the pass) for the campground. There are no reservations but you can call ahead on the day of your arrival to check availability at (520) 387-6849.

The turn-off for this campground is at Mile 75 of Highway 85, about 6 miles (10 km) north of the crossing at Lukeville/Sonoyta.

LUKEVILLE/SONOYTA CROSSING TO PUERTO PEÑASCO
62 Miles (100 Km), 1.25 Hours

After crossing the border the road leads to an intersection with Mex 2 just 2 miles (3 km) from the crossing. There's a big Pemex on the right at the corner. Turn left, drive past a second Pemex, and turn right in just a quarter-mile to follow Mex 8 southwest toward Puerto Peñasco.

Within a minute or so you'll be driving across the desert. There is little traffic other than folks headed to or returning from Puerto Peñasco.

In about 32 miles (51 km) near the Km 51 marker, you'll reach the entrance to **El Pinacate y Gran Desierto de Altar**. If you have a back-road capable rig you can turn in here, pick up a permit, tour, or camp in the desert at one of two basic camp-

THE CRATER CALLED CONO MAYO IN EL PINACATE NATIONAL PARK

grounds in the park. Access routes and one of the campgrounds are described under *Lukeville/Sonoyta Crossing to Puerto Peñasco Campgrounds* below.

As you approach Puerto Peñasco you'll begin to see a few scattered RV parks. A major new intersection is near Km 90, the road to Caborca is to the left, the new Laguna del Mar land development to the right, Puerto Peñasco is straight ahead.

Lukeville/Sonoyta Crossing to Puerto Peñasco Campgrounds

TECOLOTE CAMPGROUND – EL PINACATE NATIONAL PARK
(Open All Year) $$

GPS Location: 31.89082 N, 113.36682 W, 800 Ft.

Tecolote camping area is well into the park. It's a desert campground with few facilities. The area is starkly beautiful. The campground sits below a crater called Cono Mayo, a 2 km trail with interpretive panels leads from the campground to the top. The surface in the campground is gray volcanic gravel, there are scattered cactus and Palo Verde trees. There are no delineated sites but there are four picnic tables scattered around an area that could easily serve ten camping parties. No restrooms are provided, the sign says to bury your waste. The fee for entering the park is $4 per person each day, you pay for two days when you camp but no other fee.

The roads in the park are fine for high clearance two wheel drive vehicles to about 25 feet. We would classify most of them as a Type 2 road in our *Backroad Adventures* sections. This is desert and it gets hot, be prepared with water, shovel, and tools.

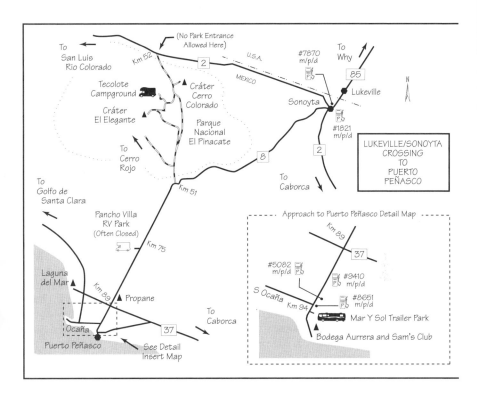

From the entrance station at Km 51 of the Sonoyta-Puerto Peñasco road follow the road 2.5 mile (4 km) to a fork. To the left is another campground called Cerro Rojo as well as the Sierra Colorado. This road was closed when we visited so we have not visited that campground but we are told it is similar to Tecolote. From here it's another 19 miles (31 km) to Tecolote. The road is well marked and there are a number of sights along the way or nearby including Cráter El Elegante (with a trail along the rim and overlooks) and Cráter Cerro Colorado (another overlook).

MAR Y SOL TRAILER PARK *(Open All Year)*

Address:	Blvd. Benito Juarez No 371, CP 83350 Puerto Peñasco, Sonora, México
Telephone and Fax:	(638) 383-3190
Email:	maresolmotel@hotmail.com

GPS Location: 31.33944 N, 113.52444 W, 100 Ft.

This trailer park adjoins the Mar y Sol Hotel on the south side. There are 24 back-in spaces suitable for rigs to 35 feet. All spaces have full hookups with 30-amp outlets, there is no shade. Restrooms have hot water showers. The hotel has a restaurant that is open for breakfast and lunch.

The campground is on the east side of the highway near Km 94 just as you arrive in Puerto Peñasco.

PUERTO PEÑASCO (PWEHR-TOE PEN-YAHS-KOE)
Population 60,000

Many Mexico travel guides ignore Puerto Peñasco as if it weren't even part of Mexico. This attitude is understandable, the town really does have a great deal of American influence. To ignore Puerto Peñasco in a camping guide to Mexico would be something of a crime, however. RVers virtually own this town, hundreds of them fill RV parks and boondock in the vicinity. On weekends and holidays Puerto Peñasco is even more popular. After all, it is only a little over an hour's driving time south of the Arizona border, it is located in a free zone requiring no governmental paperwork, and there are beaches, desert, fishing, and Mexican crafts and food. Don't forget to pick up Mexican auto insurance, however, before crossing in to Mexico.

Americans often call the town Rocky Point, you'll see why when you see the location of the old town. The road to Rocky Point was built by the American government during World War II when it was thought that it might be necessary to bring in supplies this way if the west coast was blockaded by Japanese submarines. That never happened, but the road, now paved and in good shape, makes the town easy to reach. Puerto Peñasco is also a fishing port, not everything here is tourist oriented. There are three large waterfront campgrounds here, and other smaller places too. Most of these have been here for quite some time, and now there are also large condo developments and new golf courses. Supplies of all kinds are available, big box stores include a Ley Supermarket, Bodega Aurrera (a small Walmart-owned store) and a Sam's Club.

THE JACK NICKLAUS DESIGNED VIDANTA GOLF PUERTO PEÑASCO

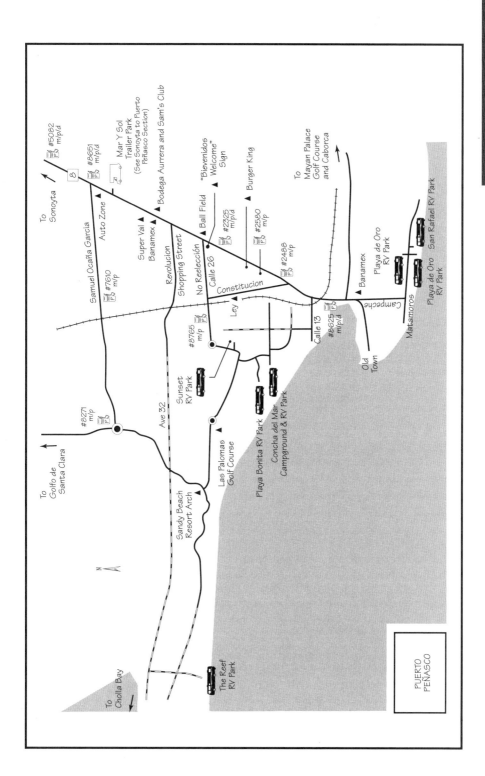

P. PEÑASCO AND GOLFO

Puerto Peñasco Campgrounds

🚐 CONCHA DEL MAR CAMPGROUND AND RV PARK
(Open All Year)

Telephone: (638) 383-4273 (Office) or (638) 113-0467 (Cell)
Email: pedgar626@hotmail.com or
conchadelmar2008@hotmail.com

GPS Location: 31.31659 N, 113.55129 W, Near Sea Level

Concha del Mar is a large flat unimproved dirt and sand area near the eastern end of Playa Bonita. It's a large area and can handle many rigs or tents. There's a good restroom building with flush toilets and cold showers. There are no hookups. Wi-Fi is useable near the office.

As you enter town from the north watch for Pemex 2488 on the left. Four-tenths of a mile (.6 km) after the Pemex is a cross road. Turn right here on Calle 13. Proceed across the railroad tracks and drive .3 mile (.5 km), turn right at the corner. Now drive north for .3 mile (.5 km) , a distance of five blocks (count the cross streets on your right). Turn left here and at the end of the road in .3 mile (.5 km) is an arch which serves as the entrance to the park. An attendant will collect your fee and you can enter.

🚐 PLAYA BONITA RV PARK *(Open All Year)*

Address: PO Box 254, Lukeville, AZ 85341-0254
Telephone: (638) 383-2596
Email: playabonitarvpark@hotmail.com or
erickaluciareyes@hotmail.com
Website: www.playabonitaresort.com

GPS Location: 31.31918 N, 113.55671 W, Near Sea Level

This is a large campground located northwest of town on Playa Bonita. The Playa Bonita RV Park is affiliated with the nice Playa Bonita Hotel next door. This campground has good access to lots of four-wheeling so it's full of off-road folks and their equipment most weekends.

There are 271 spaces in this huge campground. All are back-in slots with electricity outlets, sewer, and water. Some sites have TV hookups. Many big rigs use this campground although the sites aren't really quite long enough and maneuvering room is restricted. Restrooms are clean and have hot water. The campground has a small recreation room with a TV, a self-service laundry, a small jacuzzi-type pool and the affiliated hotel next door has a restaurant. There's free Wi-Fi. The beach out front is beautiful. One nice feature is the malecón (walkway) that fronts the entire park, a great place to walk and watch the beach action. Reservations can only be made by mail, call first for instructions.

As you enter Puerto Peñasco watch for Pemex #8651 on the left. Continue for another 1.3 miles (2.1 km) and turn right onto No Reelección (also called Calle 26). Follow No Reelección westward for .6 mile (1 km) past Pemex #8765 to a traffic circle. Drive 270 degrees around the circle and follow the road south. It will make a 90 degree bend to the right and just beyond the bend you want to turn left, the left turn is .4 mile (.6 km) from the traffic circle. In just .1 mile (.2 km) turn right, pass

P. PEÑASCO AND GOLFO

WATERFRONT CAMPING AT PLAYA BONITA RV PARK

through a gate with a guardhouse (usually manned) and continue to the campground at the end of the road.

SUNSET RV PARK *(Open All Year)*

Address:	PO Box 1338, Lukeville, AZ 85341
Location:	Plutarco Elias Calles y 25 Col Ferrocarril Playas, Puerto Peñasco
Telephone:	(638) 388-5094 (Mexico) or (480) 525-2917 (U.S.)
Email:	rvparksunset@gmail.com, reservations@rvparksunset.com, info@rvparksunset.com.
Website:	rvparksunset.com

GPS Location: 31.32446 N, 113.54883 W, Near Sea Level

The Sunset is a brand new park in Puerto Peñasco and it's built to a high standard. There are 39 large back-in sites with 50-amp power, water and sewer. Since it's not on the beach, there's a beautiful salt water pool. Restrooms are beautiful with individual rooms. There is also a barbeque palapa, a laundry room, a grass dog area, and a small restaurant.

As you enter Puerto Peñasco watch for Pemex #8651 on the left. Continue for another 1.3 miles (2.1 km) and turn right onto No Reelección (also called Calle 26). Follow No Reelección westward for .6 mile (1 km) past Pemex #8765 to a traffic circle. Drive 270 degrees around the circle and you'll see the campground entrance on the left. There's a divider in the road so you can't turn in directly. You must continue another .4 mile (.5 km) to where there is a wide intersection where you can reverse course and come back to enter the campground.

⛟ The Reef RV Park *(Open All Year)*

Address:	PO Box 742, Lukeville, AZ 85341
Telephone:	(638) 383-0650
Fax:	(638) 383-6530
Email:	reservations@thereefrvpark.com
Website:	www.thereefrvpark.com

GPS Location: 31.32722 N, 113.60333 W, Near Sea Level

This is a large RV park with 52 waterfront sites at Sandy Beach and over a hundred behind. These are all really big back-in sites with lots of room for big rigs. The parking surface is almost white crushed gravel, there isn't a bit of shade. About half the sites have full hookups with 50 and 30-amp outlets. Restrooms have flush toilets and hot showers. There is a restaurant as well as a disco bar. Construction has begun on a cruise ship dock adjacent to the campground so things may change considerably when that opens.

As you approach Puerto Peñasco watch for Pemex #8651 which is on the left. Just before you reach the Pemex turn right onto paved Samuel Ocaña Garcia. Follow this road west for 2.3 miles (3.7 km) to a traffic circle. Drive around the circle about 270 degrees and drive south. At 3.2 miles (5.2 km) you'll pass under the Sandy Beach Resort Arch and the road passes behind a large condo development. The pavement ends (for now) at 4.7 miles (7.6 km) and at 5.4 miles (8.7 km) you turn left into the entry road for the RV park.

⛟ Playa de Oro RV Park *(Open All Year)*

Address:	60 Matamoros Ave., Apdo. 76, CP 83550 Puerto Peñasco, Son., México
Reservations:	PO Box 583, Lukeville, AZ 85341
Telephone:	(638) 383-2668 or (602) 476-2242
Fax:	(638) 383-4833
Email:	playadeororv@yahoo.com
Website:	www.playadeoro-rv.com

GPS Location: 31.29734 N, 113.53461 W, Near Sea Level

This huge campground is one of the oldest ones in Puerto Peñasco. It bills itself as the only full service RV park in Rocky Point. It's now the only large park left on this side of town.

There are at least 325 spaces at the Playa de Oro. They are located south of Matamoros Ave. along and back from the beach and also extending well inland to the north of Matamoros. The sites have 30-amp (some 50-amp) electricity, sewer, and water. They have gravel surfaces, no shade, and no patios. The bathrooms are remodeled, the showers require a quarter for 4 to 5 minutes. The campground has a small, simple restaurant, a mini-mart, a self-service laundry, and a boat ramp. There is also a large long-term storage yard for those wishing to leave a trailer or boat when they go back north. Every weekend workers move many of those stored rigs onto sites for the weekend, and then move them back into storage when the owners go home. There's free Wi-Fi in the park and satellite TV.

As you approach Puerto Peñasco from the north watch for Pemex #8651 on the left. Zero your odometer here and continue straight for 2.8 mile (4.5 km). You will see that the highway is going to bend to the right ahead, you want to go straight so get in the left lane and continue straight when it's clear. Now continue another .5 mile (.8 km) to a T. Turn left and you'll see the campground gate on the right in .4 mile (.6 km).

SAN RAFAEL RV PARK *(Open All Year)*

Telephone: (638) 383-5044 or (638) 383-2681

GPS Location: 31.29733 N, 113.53331 W, Near Sea Level

The San Rafael is an older small campground with no beachfront sites even though it is south of Calle Matamoros. It's a quiet place, and it gives a 10% senior discount.

The campground has 31 slots for visitors, all have 30-amp outlets, sewer, and water. These are gravel-surfaced back-in spaces without patios or shade. They are long sites suitable for big rigs. Permanent resident rigs occupy two sides of the park. The campground has clean modern restrooms with hot showers, a TV room, a self-service laundry, and English is spoken.

As you approach Puerto Peñasco from the north watch for Pemex #8651 on the left. Zero your odometer here and continue straight for 2.8 mile (4.5 km). You will see that the highway is going to bend to the right ahead, you want to go straight so get in the left lane and continue straight when it's clear. Now continue another .5 mile (.8 km) to a T. Turn left and you'll see the campground gate on the right in .5 mile (.8 km).

SAN LUIS RÍO COLORADO, SONORA AND SAN LUIS, ARIZONA

This small town, tucked right up against the line directly south of Yuma, is the best place to cross if you are headed toward Golfo de Santa Clara. The crossing is open 24 hours and has a much better reputation with RVers than Algodones, the crossing nearest to Yuma. Besides, the route to Golfo is much shorter and quicker than if you cross in Algodones.

Yuma probably has more campgrounds than any similar sized city anywhere in the U.S. but many are filled with snowbirds for the winter season. The Cocopah Casino, described below, it a decent no-hassle place to spend the night before heading south, although it has no hookups.

Yuma Campground

COCOPAH CASINO

Address: 15318 South Avenue B, Somerton, AZ 85350
Telephone: 800 23-slots
Email: info @cocopah-casino.com
Website: www.cocopahresort.com

GPS Location: 32.60615 N, 114.65476 W, 100 Ft.

This casino is located well south of Yuma, 15 miles (24 km) north of the crossing at San

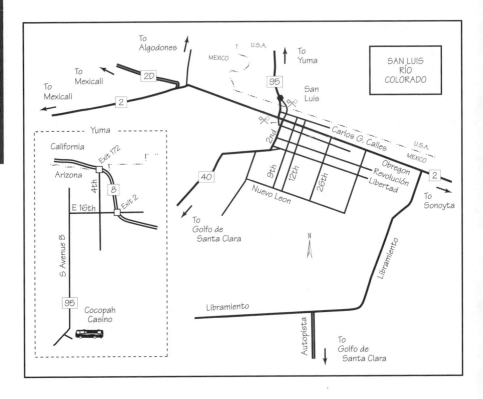

Luis. It has a parking lot dedicated to RVs with 50 slots. There are no restrooms or hookups. The casino, about 300 yards away, has restrooms (no showers), a restaurant, and of course, gambling. There is a charge, but it's only a few dollars. This is an excellent place to spend the night before heading south.

The casino is on Hwy 95 which runs from Yuma south to San Luis. The easiest route from I-8 is probably to take Exit 172 (Winterhaven Drive/4th Ave). This exit is actually in California, just west of the border. Follow 4th Avenue south for 2.2 miles (3.5 km) to E 16th Street. Turn right and drive 1.5 miles (2.4 km) west to S Avenue B. Now follow S Avenue B south for 6 miles (9.7 km) to the casino. The RV parking area is to the south of the buildings.

SAN LUIS RÍO COLORADO TO GOLFO DE SANTA CLARA
73 Miles (118 Km), 2.0 Hours

There is a new reasonably priced toll road that runs south from the southern outskirts of San Luis Río Colorado toward Golfo. It's 35 easy miles (57 km) on the toll road and then another 25 easy miles (40 km) on the upgraded Highway 3 to Golfo. Just as you're about to enter Golfo you'll spot another beautiful new road headed east. This is the new paved road to Puerto Peñasco, a distance of 82 miles (133 km) from this point.

When you cross the border in San Luis Río Colorado immediately head east on Mex 2 for 6 miles (10 km) to a new ring road, also called a Libramiento. Turn south and follow it for 7.5 miles (12 km) to the beginning of the toll road.

GOLFO DE SANTA CLARA (GOLF-OH DAY SAHN-TAW CLAW-RAH)
Population 1,500

If you are looking for a piece of the real outback Mexico with no tourist glitz Golfo de Santa Clara is the place for you. This is a small fishing village surrounded by miles and miles of sand. Most tourist guides don't even mention the town but it is becoming something of a popular camping destination. A camping club operates the best RV campground in town, however, so your choices of places to stay are limited if you are not a member. See *Other Camping Possibilities* below for more about this club campground. Non-member choices are largely beachfront restaurants with shade ramadas or huge sandy parking areas to the south. During holidays this town really fills with Mexicali residents seeking a little beach time. The beach south of town stretches for miles and ATVs are welcome.

The busiest day of the year for Golfo is June 1, Día de la Marina, lots of people come down from Mexicali and San Luis for the party.

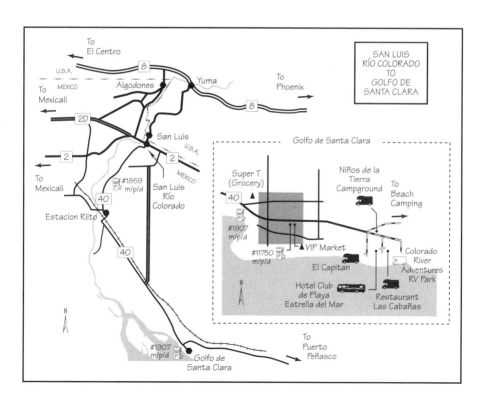

TENT CAMPING UNDER THE RAMADAS AT EL CAPITAN

Golfo de Santa Clara Campgrounds

EL CAPITAN *(Open All Year)* $$

GPS Location: 31.67861 N, 114.49028 W, Near Sea Level

The El Capitan is a palapa-style restaurant and bar near the beach. It advertises that it has the best shrimp in town – cheap. The restaurant also has a row of ramadas for tent campers out front, you can park an RV here too if you want. There are bathrooms with flush toilets and cold showers. Expect this place to be pretty busy during any holidays and watch for soft spots in the sand.

To find the El Capitan watch for Pemex #1907 as you come in to town. Zero your odometer and keep going straight. Continue to the end of the pavement at 1.1 mile (1.8 km) and you'll see the entrance to the El Capitan on the right.

HOTEL CLUB DE PLAYA ESTRELLA DEL MAR $$$ $$$$
    (Open All Year)

Telephone: (653) 112-1276, (653) 515-7311,
         (653) 515-7108
Email: raulagraz2012@hotmail.es

GPS Location: 31.67746 N, 114.48979 W, Near Sea Level

This modest little hotel and RV park near the beach has 12 back-in full-hook RV sites. These are large sites that will take any rig and there's lots of maneuvering room. The hookups are in poor shape. Restrooms are old but have flush toilets and cold showers. There are five rooms for rent.

Since members at the nearby club campground can't stay there without leaving occasionally, they sometimes use this place. They can divide their time between the two campgrounds.

Follow the directions to the El Capitan given above. Then continue one more block, turn right, and you'll see the campground on the right in two blocks.

RESTAURANT LAS CABAÑAS
    (AKA EL GOLFO QUADS RENTAL) *(Open All Year)*

GPS Location: 31.67698 N, 114.49020 W, Near Sea Level

This is another palapa-style beach campground which also has motel rooms. It sits right next to the club campground. It, like the El Capitan, has connected ramadas for tent camping and will allow RVs to park on the grounds. There are flush toilets and showers. To find this campground just follow the El Capitan directions above. You'll find the Las Cabañas about a block beyond the El Capitan.

NIÑOS DE LA TIERRA CAMPGROUND *(Open All Year)*
    Telephone: (653) 103-6700

GPS Location: 31.67881 N, 114.48822 W, Near Sea Level

This is a very small campground a few block back from the beach. There are 9 metal roofed ramadas that are suitable only for tenters and short RVs, there's little room to maneuver or park. There are electrical outlets and restrooms have flush toilets and cold showers.

If you zero your odometer at the Pemex you'll come to a fork in the road at 1.1 miles (1.8 km). The campground occupies the middle of the fork.

Other Camping Possibilities

There is an RV park about a mile south of town on the beach. We stayed there several years ago, it had a great location but terrible facilities. The new operator has improved the facilities so this is the best RV park in Golfo. Now called **El Golfo Beach Resort** it is operated by Colorado River Adventures, a camping club with several campgrounds along the lower Colorado River. You must be a member to stay there. They are affiliated with Coast to Coast so members of that organization may also find a spot. Call (760) 663-4941 to check.

The El Capitan and the las Cabañas are just two of the places out near the Colorado River Adventures campground. Many more offer ramadas along the beach, you could probably arrange to stay at many of them. Be aware of security, however, it's best to be at a place that offers an on-site manager and night watchman.

There are large areas for parking at the end of the road, that's about .6 miles (1 km) beyond Niños de la Tierra Campground and the other places in that group. You'll probably be charged a fee of $5 for parking overnight in the areas with solid sand, four-wheel drive is definitely recommended. Facilities include palapas at some locations and sometimes outhouses.

APPENDIX - BAJA ROAD SIGNS

Speed Bump
(Tope)

CAMINO SINUOSO PROXIMOS 38 km

Winding Road
Next 38 Kilometers

DESVIACION A 500 MTS

Detour
In 500 Meters

GRACIAS POR USAR EL CINTURON DE SEGURIDAD

Thanks For Using
Your Seat Belt

DISMINUYA SU VELOCIDAD

Reduce Your Speed

 HASSLE FREE VEHICLE ZONE

No Vehicle Permit
Required

Stay Right

CON NIEBLA ENCIENDA SUS LUCES

In Fog Turn On Lights

DISMINUYA SU VELOCIDAD CURVA PELIGROSA

Reduce Your Speed
Dangerous Curve

MANEJE CON PRECAUCION

Drive With Caution

CEDA EL PASO

Yield

CONCEDA CAMBIO DE LUCES

Dim Your Lights
For Oncoming Traffic

EN B.C.S. ES OBLIGATORIO EL CINTURON DE SEGURIDAD

In Baja California South
Seat Belts Are
Mandatory

MAS VALE TARDE QUE NUNCA

Better Late
Than Never

Falling Rocks
(Derumbe)

CURVA PELIGROSA A 400 m

Dangerous Curve
In 400 Meters

ENTRADA Y SALIDA DE CAMIONES

Truck Entrance
And Exit

MIRADOR DE MOLINERO

Roadside Viewpoint

No Passing

DESPACIO

Slow

ESTA CARRETERA NO ES DE ALTA VELOCIDAD

This Is Not A High
Speed Road

NO MALTRATE LAS SEÑALES

Do Not Mistreat
The Signs

No Right
Turn

Livestock On
The Road

Stop

Speed Bump
(Tope)

NO FRENE CON MOTOR

No Braking With Engine

PRECAUCION ZONA DE GANADO

Precaution Livestock Zone

TOPES A 100m

Speed Bumps In 100 Meters

NO DEJE PIEDRAS SOBRE EL PAVIMENTO

Do Not Leave Rocks On The Road

PRINCIPIA TRAMO EN REPARACION A 500 m

Main Highway Under Repair in 500 Meters

TRANSITO LENTO CARRIL DERECHO

Slow Traffic Right Lane

NO REBASE CON RAYA C O N T I N U A

No Passing When Continuous Line

PROHIBIDO GRAFFITEAR

Graffiti Prohibited

TROPICO DE CANCER

Tropic Of Cancer

OBEDEZCA LAS SEÑALES

Obey The Signs

PROHIBIDO TIRAR BASURA

Throwing Garbage Prohibited

VADO A 300 m

Gully (Ford) In 300 Meters

PRECAUCION CRUCE DE PEATONES

Caution Pedestrian Crossing

 **REDUCTOR DE VELOCIDAD A 400 m**

Speed Bump (Tope) In 400 Meters

ZONA DE VADOS

Gully (Ford) Zone

ZONA URBANA MODERE VELOCIDAD

Urban Zone Slow Down

PRECAUCION CURVA PELIGROSA A 300MTS

Caution Dangerous Curve In 300 Meters

RESPETE LIMITE DE VELOCIDAD

Respect the Speed Limit

PRECAUCION ENTRADA Y SALIDA DE MAQUINARIA

Precaution Entrance And Exit of Machinery

SI TOMA NO MANEJE

If You Drink Don't Drive

Water Over Road (Vado)

TERMINA B.C. PRINCIPIA B.C.S.

Leaving Baja California Entering Baja California South

Kilometer Marker

Level Of Water Over Road

Index

268

ABOUT THE AUTHORS

For the last twenty five years Terri and Mike Church have traveled in the western U.S., Alaska, Canada, Mexico, and Europe. Most of this travel has been in RVs, a form of travel they love. It's affordable and comfortable; the perfect way to see interesting places.

Over the years they discovered that few guidebooks were available with the essential day-to-day information that camping travelers need when they are in unfamiliar surroundings. *Traveler's Guide to Camping Mexico's Baja, Traveler's Guide to Mexican Camping, Southwest Camping Destinations, Pacific Northwest Camping Destinations, Traveler's Guide To Alaskan Camping, Traveler's Guide to European Camping,* and *RV* and *Car Camping Vacations in Europe,* are designed to be the guidebooks that the authors tried to find when they first traveled to these places.

Terri and Mike live full-time in an RV – traveling, writing new books, and working to keep these guidebooks as up to date as possible. The books are written and prepared for printing using laptop computers while on the road.

270

Traveler's Guide To Mexican Camping
6" x 9" Paperback, 576 Pages, Over 250 Maps
ISBN 978-0982310106

Fourth Edition - Copyright 2009

Mexico, one of the world's most interesting travel destinations, is just across the southern U.S. border. It offers warm sunny weather all winter long, beautiful beaches, colonial cities, and excellent food. Best of all, you can easily and economically visit Mexico in your own car or RV.

The fourth edition of *Traveler's Guide To Mexican Camping* is now even better! It has become the bible for Mexican campers. With this book you will cross the border and travel Mexico like a veteran. It is designed to make your trip as simple and trouble-free as possible. Maps show the exact location of campgrounds and the text gives written driving instructions as well as information regarding the size of RV suitable for each campground. In addition to camping and campground information the guide also includes information about cities, roads and driving, trip preparation, border crossing, vehicle care, shopping, and entertainment.

Pacific Northwest Camping Destinations
6" x 9" Paperback, 720 Pages, Over 180 Maps
ISBN 978-0982310120

Third Edition - Copyright 2012

Seashores, snow-capped mountains and visitor friendly cities have made the Pacific Northwest one of the most popular RV and tent camping destinations in North America, and this guide takes you to more than 140 destinations and 1,300 campgrounds throughout Oregon, Washington, and British Columbia.

Combining the functions of a campground directory and a sightseeing guide, each entry describes a vacation spot and its attractions and recommends good camping locations in the area, including privately owned, federal, state, and county campgrounds. Each campground is described in detail including a recommendation for the maximum size RV suitable for the campground. Written driving instructions as well as a map are provided showing the exact location. Tourist destinations are described and several itineraries are provided for driving on scenic routes throughout the region.

RV and Car Camping Vacations in Europe
6" x 9" Paperback, 320 Pages, Over 140 Maps
ISBN 978-0965296892

First Edition - Copyright 2004

People from North America love to visit Europe on their vacations. One great way to travel in Europe is by RV or car, spending the night in convenient and inexpensive campgrounds. It's a way to travel economically and get off the beaten tourist trail. It's also a great way to meet Europeans. Many of them travel the same way!

Most of us lead busy lives with little time to spend on planning an unusual vacation trip. With this book a camping vacation in Europe is easy. It tells how to arrange a rental RV or car from home, when to go and what to take with you. It explains the process of picking up the rental vehicle and turning it back in when you're ready to head for home. There's also information about shopping, driving, roads, and other things that you should know before you arrive. Then it describes a series of tours, each taking from a week to two weeks. The ten tours cover much of Western Europe and even the capitals of the Central European countries. The book has details about the routes and roads, the campgrounds to use, and what to do and see while you are there.

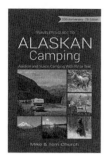

Traveler's Guide To Alaskan Camping
6" x 9" Paperback, 486 Pages, Over 100 Maps
ISBN 978-0982310168
Seventh Edition - Copyright 2017

Alaska, the dream trip of a lifetime! Be prepared for something spectacular. Alaska is one fifth the size of the entire United States, it has 17 of the 20 highest peaks in the U.S., 33,904 miles of shoreline, and has more active glaciers and ice fields than the rest of the inhabited world. In addition to some of the most magnificent scenery the world has to offer, Alaska is chock full of an amazing variety of wildlife. Fishing, hiking, kayaking, rafting, hunting, and wildlife viewing are only a few of the many activities which will keep you outside during the long summer days.

Traveler's Guide To Alaskan Camping makes this dream trip to Alaska as easy as camping in the "Lower 48". It includes almost 500 campgrounds throughout Alaska and on the roads north in Canada with full campground descriptions, appropriate RV size for each campground, and maps showing exact locations. It also is filled with suggested things to do and see including fishing holes, hiking trails, canoe trips, wildlife viewing opportunities, and much more.

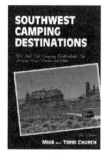

Southwest Camping Destinations
6" x 9" Paperback, 544 Pages, Over 100 Maps
ISBN 978-0974947198
Second Edition - Copyright 2008

Bryce Canyon, Carlsbad Caverns, the Grand Canyon, and Mesa Verde are among the 100 destinations covered in this travel guide for RVers and car campers. Native American sites and desert habitats are also of interest in this region, making it a great vacation destination for families with children. Maps are provided for each destination along with descriptions of tourist attractions and listings for more than 500 traveler campgrounds.

For those who want to escape to a warm climate in the winter there is a special "snowbird" chapter which gives details on top snowbird destinations in the southwest. Over 350 campgrounds are compared in destination like Palm Springs, Las Vegas, Lake Havasu and Parker, Needles and Laughlin, Yuma, Quartzsite, Phoenix, Mesa, Apache Junction, Casa Grande, and Tucson. This analysis is accompanied by maps showing the exact locations of campgrounds in these favorite destinations.

Traveler's Guide To European Camping
6" x 9" Paperback, 640 Pages, Over 400 Maps
ISBN 978-0965296885
Third Edition - Copyright 2004

Over 350 campgrounds including the best choice in every important European city are described in detail and directions are given for finding them. In many cases information about convenient shopping, entertainment and sports opportunities is included.

This guide will tell you how to rent, lease, or buy a rig in Europe or ship your own from home. It contains the answers to questions about the myriad details of living, driving, and camping in Europe. In addition to camping and campground information *Traveler's Guide To European Camping* gives you invaluable details about the history and sights you will encounter. This information will help you plan your itinerary and enjoy yourself more when you are on the road. Use the information in this book to travel Europe like a native. Enjoy the food, sights, and people of Europe. Go for a week, a month, a year. Europe can fill your RV or camping vacation seasons for many years to come!

HOW TO BUY BOOKS
PUBLISHED BY ROLLING HOMES PRESS

Rolling Homes Press is a specialty publisher. Our books can be found in many large bookstores and almost all travel bookstores. Even if such a bookstore is not convenient to your location you can buy our books easily from Internet bookstores or even directly from us. Also, most bookstores will order our books for you, just supply them with the ISBN number shown on the previous pages or on the back cover of this book.

We maintain a Website – **www.rollinghomes.com**. If you go to our Website and click on the tab labeled *How To Buy* you will find instructions for buying our book from a variety of Web and storefront retailers as well as directly from us. The instructions on the Website change periodically, they reflect the fact that we are sometime out of the country for long stretches of time. When we are not available we make arrangements to be sure that you can obtain our books quickly and easily in our absence.

Retailers and individuals can always obtain our books from our distributor:

Independent Publisher's Group
814 North Franklin Street
Chicago, Illinois 60610

(800) 888-4741 or (312) 337-0747

www.ipgbook.com